THE EARTH IS BUT ONE COUNTRY

THE EARTH IS BUT ONE COUNTRY

by

JOHN HUDDLESTON

©1976 The National Spiritual Assembly of
The Bahá'ís of The United Kingdom

3rd Edition 1988

British Library Cataloguing in Publication Data

Huddleston, John
  The Earth Is But One Country

  ɪ Bahá'ísm
  I Title   BP 365

ISBN 0-900125-90-X Cloth
ISBN 0-900125-91-8 Paper

Printed by Richard Clay Ltd, Bungay, Suffolk.

Contents

NOTE: Book references marked (UK) indicate Published by Bahá'í Publishing Trust, 27 Rutland Gate, London SW7 1PD, and those marked (USA) indicate Published by the Bahá'í Publishing Trust, 415 Linden Avenue, Wilmette, Illinois, 60091.

To: All my brothers and sisters of the human race past, present and future.

Acknowledgements

This book has come about with the help of many friends who gave both encouragement and much useful advice. Particular mention should be made of Lois Hainsworth, Hugh McKinley, Rustom Sabit, Sue Cannon and Frank Stewart. To all of these friends who contributed so much I wish to express my deepest gratitude.

I should also like to thank the various publishers, referred to in the body of the text, who gave permission for reproduction of quotations from their books and periodicals.

Preface to the Third Edition

This edition is essentially the same as the two earlier editions. However, the opportunity has been taken to update some statistics in the first chapter, and, most important, to add, in chapter eight, several paragraphs on the persecution of the Bahá'ís in Iran since 1979 and on the increasing prominence given to the Bahá'í community by the world's media and its involvement in the fields of Peace and Social and economic development. In addition, some other amendments have been made to take account of some earlier errors and points needing clarification which were kindly brought to my attention by several friends.

McLEAN, VIRGINIA

Introduction

The purpose of this book is to show how the Bahá'í Faith meets the needs of mankind today, and how it is building up what is believed will be a new world-wide civilization in which all peoples can live together in justice, harmony, and peace. The emphasis is on the practical means to this end as well as on the dream.

Many, concerned about the condition of society and about the sense of unfulfilment in their personal lives, automatically assume that they will not find an answer in religion. Past experience has left a negative impression of superstition and escapism. This book is primarily addressed to those who have this point of view.

What is asked of such readers is that they have an open mind. It is healthy to approach new ideas with scepticism. However, there is a need to guard against scepticism being confused with prejudice, and against it degenerating into an anti-life cynicism.

CHAPTER I

THERE IS A NEW WIND BLOWING

A — *The Challenges of the Day*

THERE can be little doubt that the challenges which mankind faces today are immense. They are those which come with the attainment of adulthood. If we meet them successfully there is the prospect of a golden age of a beauty and depth unimaginably greater than at any other period in man's history. If we fail the future is likely to be one of increasing bestiality and, quite probably, of the most horrifying destruction. There seems little chance of a middle way. We grow to meet our destiny or we sink to the lowest depths.

The first challenge is how to establish a universal and lasting peace. In the past, war has been seen too often as an inevitable aspect of the human condition and has been even justified by armchair philosophers as necessary for the progress of man because, they argued, it tends to eliminate the weak and encourage the strong. The traumatic events of the twentieth century seem at last to have shaken men out of this apathetic view and forced them to see war for what it really is: the most sickening and degrading experience of the human race.

But the issue runs deeper than that. The issue now is one of sheer survival. Since 1945 the human race has had the power to destroy itself. This threat is no less certain because in our everyday life most of us prefer to push the matter to the back of our consciousness until such time as the next international crisis forces us back to a nightmarish reality.

Comfort cannot be taken from the apparent recognition of the consequenes of full-scale war by at least some of the world's leaders, as is indicated by their words and some of their actions. For it is evident that, for a wide range of reasons of state, most governments are, in fact, prepared to risk war, including war in which weapons of mass destruc-

1

tion will be used. We know that political leaders, as Herman Kahn has said, do think the unthinkable. Nuclear bombs were dropped on Japan twice in 1945 and we know of at least some occasions since then when their use has been seriously considered — 1951, 1955, 1962, 1968 — to cite the dates of the more well known instances. Every nation which possesses such weapons has contingency plans for their use, otherwise they would not have acquired them in the first place. Perhaps even worse than the danger of cold calculation is the possibility of government's misunderstanding a situation and striking out in fear to cause an accidental holocaust.

It is part of the conventional wisdom of the age that war will be avoided only if nations make it clear they will use their nuclear weapons to "defend" themselves. This is what Winston Churchill called the peace of mutual terror. The terrible, inherent dangers of such a policy are only too apparent. In short, we have survived since the end of the Second World War far more by good fortune than by good management. To continue to rely on good fortune to get the human race through, say, the next twenty-five years, would seem to be somewhat unreasonable.

The second major challenge of our time might be described broadly as how best to use the limited resources available on our planet. There are at least three interlocking facets to this problem.

The first is the maldistribution of wealth amongst the world's four-and-a-half-billion people. Even in the richest countries there are many who live in abject poverty. For instance, in the United States there are at least thirty million, or fourteen per cent of the population, who are defined by the government as poor. More serious is the existence of whole nations crushed by poverty where hunger, malnutrition, disease and an early death is the lot of millions. In 1982 there were over fifty countries in the world where the average annual income per person was less than seventeen hundred dollars and nearly thirty where it was less than three hundred dollars. Furthermore, it was estimated that the poorest forty per cent in these countries had an average income which was less than half the national average. By contrast the average income per person in the United States at that time, including allowance for the thirty million poor, was about thirteen thousand two hundred dollars, and in Western Europe it was about nine thousand dollars.[1] Another indication of the gross inequality of wealth between nations is the fact that the United States which only has about six per cent of the world's population uses forty per cent of the world's total annual product.[2]

Since the beginning of history there have been great extremes of wealth. Most have lived in poverty, and even if society had devised a more just distribution of resources it probably would not have made a great deal of difference to the material circumstances of the poor. What is different today is that modern science has made it possible for all men to escape from the crushing burden of poverty and attain a basic degree of material comfort — but only if this objective is treated as a high priority. The poor are becoming conscious of this possibility and they no longer accept their poverty as an inevitable fact of life. Whilst such inequalities exist there cannot be a lasting world peace. The elimination of such inequalities requires massive assistance by the rich countries and a great effort on the part of the poor countries not only to increase their material resources but also to see that this is of particular benefit to their poorest citizens.

The second factor which has considerable impact on the use of resources is the size and growth of world population. As many, including officials of the World Bank, have pointed out, population growth is one of the main obstacles to raising the standard of living in developing countries. Shortage of capital and the fact that a fast growing population has a high proportion of dependent children means that the growth of wealth in a poor country is created

[1] 1985 World Bank Atlas, a publication of the World Bank Group, Washington D.C.
[2] Speech of Robert McNamara, President of the World Bank at the 1970 Annual Meeting of the World Bank (published by World Bank, 1970).

by a minority of the population; additional population only means that the limited wealth available has to be shared amongst a larger number. Thus, if a developing country should increase its total wealth by five per cent and its population is growing at the rate of three per cent, then the average increase in the standard of living of its people is going to be two per cent instead of the five per cent, which would have been achieved if the population size had been stable.

Even more serious is the long-term effect of population growth on all countries rich and poor alike. Until modern times the world's population has been small in relation to the size of the earth and its resources, and the growth rate has been low because natural forces such as disease and famine have kept deaths almost in balance with births. Modern science has upset that balance by reducing the impact of such natural forces, thus lowering the death rate without having a parallel effect in reducing the birth rate. The resulting increase in numbers has been at an accelerating rate because growth is cumulative. Thus, the world population took one hundred years to rise from one to two billion, and just thirty years more to rise from two billion to three billion. During the nineteen seventies, the population increased fifty per cent, from three billion to four-and-a-half billion. It is true that the rate of growth is now showing signs of slowing down, but if present trends continue it will not slow down to replacement level — in effect, an average of two children per family — until the year 2020. On that basis, the world's population might finally stabilize at about ten billion sometime towards the end of the twenty-first century.

If such an increase in population should take place there is much evidence that there will be an increasing shortage of basic resources. There are many who maintain that the shortages could be so severe as to be disastrous. The most obvious resources which would fall into short supply are fertile and otherwise usable land, fresh water and fossil fuels. Some argue that past history shows that shortages always induce man to find substitutes. Most will find the immensity of risk involved in such an optimistic laissez-faire attitude too great to be acceptable.

The third facet of the problem of distribution of wealth is the effect on the environment of present methods of making use of resources. Until the industrial revolution it might be said that man was merely scratching on the face of the earth and, with perhaps the major exception of deforestation, what he did had little noticeable effect on the process of nature. That is no longer so. Crude, greedy, short-sighted exploitation of resources and extravagant social habits are now recognized as causing massive pollution of the air, land and sea. If this tendency were allowed to continue to grow, and it should be remembered that most of the pollution is caused by the rich minority whom the poor majority wish to emulate, then our planet might become difficult to inhabit. Once the problem is recognized there are technical ways of alleviating the worst side effects of industrial and social processes. However, these new methods will be costly and could therefore slow down economic growth. The poor countries being in the greatest need of economic growth would probably suffer the most. It is therefore all the more important that the rich countries give them every assistance as well as practising a new environmental consciousness at home.

The third major challenge which mankind faces, and probably the one that is least recognized as such, is how to cure the deep spiritual malaise which has spread to all levels of society in very nearly every country of the world. This malaise or deep sense of loss of direction has been growing for several decades and, as is to be expected, was first recognized by the artistic community. Since the mid-nineteenth century there has been a noticeable change of direction in the general tone of what has been said by writers and artists from one of optimism, or at least acceptance of the ways of the world, to one of increasing pessimism and anguish. Much has been written on this subject and it would seem sufficient here to refer to a few examples to make the point desired. Possibly one of the most dramatic and moving descriptions of what is happening in society was made by Nietzsche, the significance of whose famous dictum, "God is dead", has been summarized as follows:

"That is, it is not primarily a theological utterance, but amounts to saying that nineteenth century civilization had lost its faith. But this remark was more to Nietzsche than the commonplace it has become, because Nietzsche insisted that the death of God counted — not merely was God dead but there was no other principle of order to be believed in either; men were adrift and rootless in the universe, and at heart they knew it."[1]

As Jung observed, scepticism can be a burden rather than a remover of tensions. A similar sense of despair and alienation can be detected in the ideas of Dadaists, the Existentialists, the Theatre of the Absurd, the cult of the anti-hero, and the cult of the ugly. Albert Camus epitomized this feeling when he said that the only philosophical question of importance is why not commit suicide?

For a long time the rest of the world chose not to listen. Many intellectuals thought that the problem would pass away as men became used to living without religion and that they would come to accept humanistic and political ideals as substitutes. However, in recent years it has become increasingly clear that the spiritual malaise described by writers and artists has deepened and spread rapidly. There are now too many manifestations at all levels of society and in a wide range of differing situations for the issue to be any longer ignored.

Thus the majority of the poor in all countries feel they have no stake in society and that there is no hope for the future. At one time there were brave attempts to unite to improve the lot of the poor but too often the hoped for changes were never really achieved. Now there is a prevailing attitude of listlessness which periodically erupts into violent expressions of bitterness and frustration in which the poor themselves suffer the most.

Those whom they envy and whom they see as their oppressors barely seem more satisfied. Many of the middle

[1] *New Society,* September 17, 1970. Article on Nietzsche by Alan Ryan.

class find their only satisfaction in their job and the rest of their life is a desert. Even with regard to their occupation there is a growing disenchantment with the wearing, tearing, rat race. The boredom and frustration of private life produce reliance on sedatives and, in the case of the more prosperous, the psychiatrist's couch. The more adventurous try to escape from their frustrations in an ever-speeding round of frantic sex, descending to every conceivable permutation, or into frequent use of alcohol and drugs.

The children of both rich and poor alike are increasingly disgusted by the empty materialism, hypocrisy, and above all, loveless life of their elders, and feel completely alienated from established society. Left to themselves with little to admire or strive for in society, all too often they also sink into spiritual inertia, all the more horrifying because of the contrast with that spiritual growth which the young can achieve when properly motivated.

The lowering of morale at all levels of society is expressed in the growing interest in drugs. There are those who argue that most drugs do no physical harm and can often widen man's appreciation of his senses. Whether or not this is true, the habit does make more grave an already existent sense of alienation and discourages interest or concern for others and society in general. Hard drugs, of course, have very evident and direct consequences — damaged personal health and, because of their high cost and the effect they have on the willingness or ability to work to support the habit, a tremendous increase in the incidence of violent crime.

The tendency for the use of drugs to aggravate the growth of crime does not mean, of course, that crime would not otherwise be increasing. On the contrary, even allowing for the possibility of inaccurate statistics, it is apparent that crime is growing at a great rate throughout the world, certainly much faster than the growth in population. Official crime, however, is only the tip of the iceberg. For crime as such is only the most obvious side of a general decline in social morality which is also shown in such things as the prevalence of petty dishonesty in day-to-day transactions, deception with regard to service, price, and quality of goods, and the constant bombardment of half-truths and straightforward lies in commercial advertisements and in the political arena.

This leads on to the next facet of the social malaise of our time, which is the crumbling away of respect for all forms of authority. Respect for governments, whether democratic or authoritarian, right or left wing, has declined precipitously in recent years. Policemen the world over are seen as oppressors, particularly of the underprivileged, instead of the protectors of society, and, as observed earlier, the young increasingly despise and ignore their parents and their teachers.

All these manifestations of an all-pervading spiritual sickness come together in horrific profusion in the big cities. In these great sprawling inhuman-sized growths, people who in previous times would have welcomed social contact with other human beings, now see them under the pressure and frustrations of their environment, as threats and rivals, at best to be avoided, at worst to be pushed aside, and metaphorically trampled upon. As always it is the poor, the defenceless, who are the most ferociously treated. A sense of social responsibility seems to wither in such a state. In New York a girl could be murdered in full view and with the knowledge of many neighbours without a single person getting up to come to her aid. At this rate of development, the city, hub of our society, will soon become, if it is not already in some instances, a hell on earth. How sad the contrast with the ancient dream of the city as the centre of refinement and culture, the pride of civilization.

All three challenges to man which have been discussed, war and peace, the rational distribution of world resources, and the all-pervading spiritual malaise, are about man in conflict with himself, with his fellow-men, with his environment. They are world-wide in scope and require world-wide answers. All three are closely linked and might be said to be three aspects of one challenge. The question is what sort of response can man now make to resolve these conflicts and so grasp the glorious opportunities which lie ahead if only the challenges are successfully met?

B — *There is no Hiding Place*

Though it becomes more evident each day that we will have to respond to these challenges, it is still probably true that the most prevalent attitude is to try to ignore them; to forget them and hope that they will evaporate or at least not come to boiling point in our time. Natural inclination is reinforced by ignorance and by a sense of powerlessness: "What can I do anyway?" Meanwhile we have our own lives to live and all we can do is make the best of it.

Life in the average middle class suburb in the western world is typical of this point of view. In the past the cocoon of unreality which has surrounded life in suburbia has sometimes been remarkably effective. For example, in some towns in the United States it has been possible for people to live for seventy years without having been affected by the two world wars in which the United States was involved, except for a few minor and temporary inconveniences. The cocoon is now no longer quite so strong. The breakdown of law and order, of public morality, the alienation of the young, and the possibility of their being sucked into the drug world are threats which hang over every suburb. So, too, in a more subtle way is the growing consciousness of the futility of the life that so many lead, which cannot be put right with a new cocktail dress or a renewal of a prescription for sedatives.

Another variation on the escapist theme in the West, where there is sufficient wealth to allow such luxury, is the growing practice for young people to drop out of conventional society, to terminate their education, which they see as being irrelevant to their aspirations and the true needs of society, and to live with the minimum of work. They are able to do this because they have, to their credit, reduced their material needs, and less worthily because they have been able to live off others. Communes of all sizes and variations are formed and for a time they embody some of the more attractive characteristics of the young: a greater display of love and tolerance for others, and less emphasis on material possessions than is found in the society of their elders. Soon, however, troubles begin to occur. As was the experience of previous utopian experiments, living in a community without self-discipline and deep training leads to quarrels, the emergence of exploiters and a decline in self-respect. All too often drugs, sporadic violence, and slovenliness, the latter an over-reaction against the emphasis on physical as distinct from spiritual cleanliness in middle class suburbia, turn idealistic communes into slums of physical disease and emotional unreality. Even sympathetic journalists have described Haight Ashbury, one of the first centres of the commune movement as "looking like a disaster area". Generally, those in a commune have little thought for the future — what it will be like to live in the same commune in ten years or fifty years.

"It is the hippie problem and the hippie resolution: all youth growing to maturity must change: very few can change for what they believe to be the better; so in hippie art the resolution is death."[1]

This approach is just as much an "Alice in Wonderland" way of living as is that of the middle class professional living in the rich suburb. Even if all did go well with such communities they are not an answer for the majority, and the bitterness and injustice in the rest of the world would still be there. Sooner or later things will come to a breaking point, and when they do, revolution, war, the bomb, will not respect the commune any more than the suburb. There is no hiding place. It is both selfish and short-sighted to believe that there is.

C — *A Political Solution?*

For those who accept that the challenges of the day must be met, probably the first approach would be to turn to political institutions. The way to change the course of

[1] *New Society,* August 20, 1970. Article on Shelley by Anne Jellicoe.

events is to influence or actually control the machinery of government. Throughout history, and particularly during the secular age which has come into its own since the revolutions of the late eighteenth century, this has been the most predominant view of those who have been concerned about the condition of society. There is no doubt that those who have chosen the political road have achieved much that is to their credit in such fields as improvements in the living conditions of the poor and deprived, and other areas of social justice; in the establishment of national independence and national self-respect, and in the defence of freedom of thought and expression.

However, having said that, it should be recognized also that there have been very grave disappointments. Somehow the hoped-for results are never quite achieved. At some stage in its development the process always seems to go sour. The most obvious case, of course, is the cycle of revolution. Less dramatic but nevertheless significant examples can be found in experience with liberal and social reforms. For instance, few would deny that in many ways the welfare state has not been as successful as originally hoped.

It is not surprising therefore that there is a growing sense of dissatisfaction with the effectiveness of politics. An increasing number of people seem to feel that the political process is just not producing the answers any more. This view is remarkably widespread and can be seen not only in the rich Western countries, but also in the socialist world and in the developing countries too.

In the Western countries democratic politics are regarded by many as a meaningless game between similar party groups, a game which is irrelevant to the real issues at stake.

"The future of the human race hangs in the balance: yet we cast our votes on the balance of payments. We despise ourselves for doing so and our politicians for not raising the level of debate. This accounts in part for the disrepute into which politics and politicians have fallen, particularly among the young. There never was a generation that could say with more justice 'we are they on whom the ends of the

earth are come'. It is a generation born and brought up in the consciousness of mankind's power of total self-destruction or limitless self-improvement . . . beneath the surface the roots still live, the desperate yearning in times of trouble for a perfect world in which all things are made new after the conquest of the last enemy. Obviously we have to get the bread and butter matters right. But beyond them looms what I call the meta-political question: to what end? We ignore this question at our peril."[1]

Confidence in the political system is no stronger in the socialist countries. Hopes that the system would evolve to give more freedom of thought and expression have been gravely disappointed. Yearnings for national freedom and self-respect in Eastern Europe have been brutally crushed by military force in just the same way as they were by the imperialist powers in the nineteenth century. This happened although it was Karl Marx who said that a people which oppresses others cannot be free.

In the third world of the developing countries which at long last achieved liberation from the indignity and exploitation of colonial rule in the years after the Second World War, disappointment has been frequently just as great. Respected leaders in many countries, instead of bending every effort to helping their peoples escape from poverty and illiteracy, have spent desperately precious resources on useless prestige projects; palaces, super-highways, independent and uneconomic airlines, and, of course, outsized armouries.

. . . There's nothing but a fancy-dress parade and the blare of the trumpets. There's nothing save a minimum of readaptation, a few reforms at the top, a flag waving: and down there at the bottom an undivided mass, still living in the middle ages, endlessly marking time." Franz Fanon.[2]

Though some political systems are more civilized and responsive to man's needs than others, the very fact that discontent is so widespread suggests that all systems have in common some major defects when it comes to dealing

---

[1] London *Observer,* December 20, 1970. Article by Maurice Latey.
[2] *The Wretched of the Earth,* p. 147, Grove Press, 1968.

with the problems of the age. The important question is whether or not these defects are of a temporary nature. To try to answer that question some of the more obvious defects are discussed in the following paragraphs.

First, the political system relies far too much for success on individual leaders. This is just as true of nominally collectivist systems as those which make no such claim. The burden and the temptation of individual leadership is ultimately more than men can bear. Even the best motivated of men become confused, in the heat of the political battle, between their own personal interest and that of those whom they supposedly serve. Men in politics come to believe in their own indispensability because, as they believe, only they know what must be done and how to do it, and almost inevitably personal power and its retention becomes the overriding objective of their career. Perhaps this is what Lord Acton had in mind when he said,

"Power tends to corrupt, and absolute power corrupts absolutely. Great men are almost always bad men."[1]

Those who should be united in a common cause quarrel over who will lead. History is littered with the corpses of socially concerned groups weakened or destroyed by struggles for power between those who wanted to be the leaders.

The second inherent defect in the political system is, it is suggested, the inevitability of factionalism. In politics the main goal is to influence or seize the reins of government as soon as possible. To do this a political party will build up a coalition out of the most powerful existing or potential social groups in the political arena — the aristocracy, industrialists, the middle class, regional interests, trade unions, tribes and so on — to lever itself into power. It will certainly not try to weld all the people into a united force for justice. This would take far too long and would require far more emphasis on total integrity and moral education than is thought practical. On the contrary, the way to obtain power is to play on differences in society: nothing unites a political party like common hatred for an enemy.

[1] *The Penguin Dictionary of Quotations,* 1960.

How often have we witnessed politicians inflaming grievances in a community to serve their own ends. Political unity within the state is normally only achieved at times of extreme national crisis, as occurred in England in 1940. When politicians talk of unity at other times it is usually a cover up for a "do-nothing" policy.

When power is obtained, the political leader will then have to pay the necessary price to those groups who helped him to power and on whose support he will have to rely to stay in power. Top positions in the government will be given out on this basis far more frequently than on the basis of ability, integrity or dedication to the interests of all the people. Perhaps worse, such factors will decide government policies affecting the lives of all the people who live under the authority of that government. In democratic countries what matters is whether or not a policy can be packaged and sold to the electorate. The objective merit of a question will only be taken seriously if the issue is minor, or if the alternatives are too obviously against the general interest and this fact cannot be covered over with some sort of fancy packaging, or diversion. The result as one would expect is that it is those needing the assistance of the state more than anyone, the poor and defenceless, who suffer most at its hands. The price of political factionalism is high indeed.

Politicians, particularly those in authoritarian countries, will strongly deny this analysis. More sophisticated apologists in democratic countries often admit that much of what is said above is so, and then either maintain that nevertheless the end result is usually in the public interest or that it is a waste of time to moralize — this is the way life is and the only rational thing to do is to turn the system to one's own advantage.

Many who are repelled by the corruption and ineffectiveness of conventional politics believe the answer lies in violent revolution. History has shown that they follow an illusion. The old basic defects of the system remain, though ironically with the added twist that revolutionaries tend to be more élitist, and consequently even more arrogant than conventional politicians. However noble the original inspiration, a revolutionary is almost inevitably tainted by his own violence or the violence of the toughs who join his cause for their own ends. Che Guevara is reported to have said that revolutionaries are cold, calculating killing-machines to be turned against the enemy. It is not to be wondered at that when they do seize power such attitudes and methods usually continue, and that in history revolutionaries have often become as great oppressors as the tyrants they have overthrown. Bitter experience made George Orwell write 'Animal Farm'. Political revolutionaries are not radical enough and violent revolution is not the stuff out of which a brave new world will arise.

There are others, perhaps less revolutionary in their views, who recognize the faults of conventional politics and who believe that perhaps the world could be put right if only governments were placed in the hands of experts — maybe philosophers or economists or scientists or business-men. However, experts are every bit as prone to the vices of the political process as anyone else and, if there is any distinction to be made, experience shows that experts tend to be even more extreme in their quarrelsomeness and self-righteousness.

So far our discussion has dealt with two major flaws in the political system — the over-emphasis on the leader figure and the tendency to create division in society. A third and most critical flaw — which is not unconnected with the other two — is that the political system is based on the national sovereign state. As pointed out earlier the major problems which we now have to face are world-wide in their scope, and they require world-wide answers. The fractional interest of political parties which are so damaging within an individual nation become even more so when placed in the context of a world society.

As the nation is the basis for the power of a political party, its leaders tend to believe that it cannot afford to see any surrender of the state's sovereignty for the good of all mankind, for then the party's ability to influence policies would be seriously weakened. It is true, of course, that in times of overwhelming fear or strong public feeling concessions are made — as was the case in the formation of the League of Nations in 1919 and the United Nations in 1945, at the close of the two most devastating wars in the history of mankind. In recent years, in face of the possibility of a third world war the governments of some of the more powerful nations have, after much argument and heart-searching, signed some nuclear arms treaties which do place some restraints on their nation's sovereignty. However, praiseworthy as these institutions and treaties are, it would be foolish to ignore their flimsiness and their essentially peripheral nature in relation to the enormity of the danger.

It is very noticeable, too, that as soon as the immediate cause of fear recedes there is a tendency for nations to try to undermine or curtail such international agreements as have been made. For instance, the offhand way in which the United Nations is ignored or spurned by all its members, including the western democracies, when it seems to suit their immediate selfish purpose, is one of the most discouraging, hypocritical, and reactionary features of our time.

The same disregard for the long-term general interest is the unwillingness of the rich nations to make any significant sacrifice to help the poor countries raise the standard of living of their peoples. For example, when the United Nations declared a Development Decade in the nineteen-sixties the rich countries were asked to raise their contributions for international aid to one per cent of their national income. This modest target was never achieved. In recent years there has even been some falling off in the proportions of wealth in the rich countries devoted to international aid, with the result that the gap in the standard of living between rich and poor countries has widened rather than narrowed. To give some idea of the scale of priorities which the political system produces, it should be observed that the nations of the world spend annually 5.3 per cent of the world's production on military affairs (two hundred billion dollars in 1979).[1]

The whole situation was summarized by former Secretary General, U Thant, in a speech to the Youth of the World in 1970:

"In the world today, appeals for peace often are but a prelude to the stepped-up use of force. Calls for disarmament are followed by increased expenditures for ever more horrible weapons. Solemn assurances about human rights are contradicted by growing complacency and apathy concerning the plight of millions of our fellow human beings. Realistic recognition of the immense needs of the greater part of mankind is rarely matched by generous and farsighted action."[2]

There have been few, a very few, occasions when highly motivated politicians have tried to break through the shackles of the national sovereign state to form bonds of unity across international frontiers. Unfortunately such brave ideals have always proved very weak when put to the ultimate test. Progressive politics has never been the same since that dark day in August 1914 when the German Social Democrats decided to throw in their lot with the German Empire rather than stand united with their brother workers in Russia, France, and England, against a nonsensical imperialist war.

Nation states, and the political groups which govern them, are not only a negative influence preventing rational solutions to world problems, they positively add to those problems in a most dangerous fashion. Fear and narrow-spirited ambition lead governments to see their interests primarily in terms of military, economic and political influence. Nations seem compelled to extend their power as much as possible. Thus the United States spreads across the world; the Soviet Union forces its way into Eastern Europe, the Mediterranean, the Indian Ocean, and the Pacific; China seeks footholds in Southeast Asia, Africa and Latin America. It is the same with lesser powers though the

[1] *World Military Expenditures and Arms Transfers, 1970-79*, a report of the United States Arms Control and Disarmament Agency.

[2] *The Secretary General's Message to Youth*, UN Day School Leaflet, 1970.

pattern is usually not quite so obvious. One great power can seriously toy with the idea that it would be to its advantage to see the other two engage in nuclear war. To what end? Such games are of absolutely no benefit to ordinary people. On the contrary, they entail needless poverty, a constant threat of violence, and the stunting of intellectual and spiritual freedoms.

The welfare of mankind and the self-defined interests of the national power system not only do not coincide, they are diametrically opposed to one another. Undoubtedly, the nation state has played a useful part in the evolution of man, by, for example, developing a sense of community and cultural heritage, but there is now overwhelming evidence that history has passed it by and that it has become an ineffective and dangerous anachronism.

With such characteristics it is not surprising that national governments are becoming alienated from those they seek to rule. Conditioned by their own values and ambitions, they become bewildered by the antagonism of their peoples, and in an effort to maintain their authority resort to violence and every sort of deviousness ranging from widespread spying on their own subjects (not to speak of spying on other governments!), manipulation of the news and, as was noted earlier, widespread use of falsehood. Often the forces of law and order seem to be more concerned with crushing ideas or people which question the activities of the government than with their proper function. Numerous incompetent governments in all parts of the world divert opposition from themselves by encouraging persecution of defenceless minority groups within their power. As Bertold Brecht once remarked the political system often seems to work on the principle that if the government is no good, change the people!

All this seems to suggest that the defects of the political system are really fundamental. They are so deeply imbedded in the system that there seems little possibility of it ever being able to respond effectively to the major problems of our time. If politics continue to be the main means of organizing our affairs then man will not reach his full potential. On the contrary, however optimistic one may be about the immediate future, it cannot be doubted that in the long run politics will almost certainly continue to cause deep unrest and will involve a high risk of war and the destruction of civilization.

D — A Religious Solution?

The challenges which we face clearly demand a profound and continued change in attitudes, a willingness to see life in a much wider frame of reference than the satisfaction of our own immediate needs; in short, a moral or spiritual rebirth.* If politics cannot provide the answers to today's needs then maybe religion can. After all, spiritual guidance is traditionally one of the main concerns of religion.

To many this approach may seem like a waste of time. The influence and support enjoyed by religion has declined drastically in recent decades, and that process shows no sign of ending. The authoritative World Christian Encyclopaedia estimates that between 1900 and 1980 the proportion of the world's population which was nonreligious or atheistic increased from 0.2 per cent to nearly 21 per cent.[1] This trend is particularly true of the Christian churches in the West. Polls of church attendance have shown a persistent pattern of falling numbers throughout Europe and North America. A study in England by Rowntree and Laver showed that in York, Easter church attendance had been 35.5 per cent of the adult population in 1901, 17.7 per cent in 1935 and 13 per cent in 1948.[2] An American survey in France in 1953 concluded that only six million out of forty million baptized Roman Catholics were at all active in the church.[3] A 1970 survey showed that only about 40 per cent of English people believe there is a God.[4] The 1982 Yearbook of American and Canadian

* A point stressed at the UN Conference on the Human Environment which was held in Stockholm in 1972.
[1] World Christian Encyclopaedia, a comparative survey of churches and Religions in the Modern World, AD 1900-2000, Oxford University Press, 1982.
[2] Religion and the Rise of Scepticism by Franklin L. Baumer, p. 6, Harbinger Books, N.Y., 1960.
[3] Religion and the Rise of Scepticism p. 5.
[4] New Society, August 20, 1970.

Churches reported that in the 1970's the United States population grew by 11.5 per cent but religious institutions grew by only 4.1 per cent.[1] Scepticism concerning the established churches is now so prevalent, especially among the educated and the young, that it is no longer accurate to describe many Western countries as Christian.

However, before dismissing religion out of hand as a possible answer to our needs, it might be worthwhile to examine the causes of this development to see what is its long-term significance. In making such a review it is perhaps useful to focus primarily on Western experience where the severest challenges to organized religion have occurred.

From the fifth century, after the fall of Rome, the Christian Church was a centre of learning in a barbaric world. However, it had already, for various and often very human reasons, added a great deal to the original teachings of Jesus, and as time passed these additions gradually solidified into dogma and ritual. Such beliefs became so deeply embedded in the proceedings of the churches that they could only react with a stubborn, closed-mind hostility when scholars advancing the bounds of human knowledge made discoveries which cast doubt on the validity of many of these encrusted beliefs. The history of the churches' rearguard action against, for instance, Galileo in the sixteenth century and Darwin's theories in the nineteenth century is well known. Over a period of time the churches squandered their intellectual prestige until the point came when the majority of the well-educated could not take them seriously. This development was partly hidden in some countries because many continued to pay lip service to formal religion as it was deemed useful for social advancement.

Though the fires of battle between science and religion have now largely died down, and though some of the more farseeing clergy have tried hard to heal the wounds, it seems that matters have gone too far for real reconciliation.

Perhaps as important a reason for the alienation of the educated and certainly of the young, has been the general

[1] *Washington Post*, October 3, 1982.

failure of the churches to provide that spiritual inspiration and moral leadership which is their ultimate justification. In the glorious days of its early history the Christian Church, besides being a centre of learning, was also undoubtedly responsible for the raising of standards of civilization at all levels of society. Unfortunately its very success became the source of its undoing. The Church became a power in its own right, it became involved in politics and closely thereafter corruption followed. Such activities as the Crusades, the sale of indulgences, the Inquisition, to say nothing of the low personal moral standards of many churchmen, caused doubt as to the Church's loyalty to the teachings of Jesus, and its claim to be the spiritual guide for mankind.

In modern times the divided Christian churches, with reduced independent political power, have all too often allied themselves with political rulers, no matter how bloody and uncharitable their regimes. In the eighteenth century intellectuals openly began to accuse the churches of being barriers to progress. Voltaire candidly talked about "crushing the infamous thing." With a few honourable exceptions the churches were disgracefully indifferent to slavery and racial discrimination, which was indeed widely practised within the churches themselves, and to the misery of the poor in the mushrooming slums of the new cities of the industrial revolution.* The bishops built beautiful churches and lived in luxury, and sent their priests out to tell the poor to accept their lot. The taunt of Marx that religion was the opium of the people had some justification. It is little wonder that the churches were savagely treated in the French and Russian revolutions.

Many churches have been equally insensitive in providing guidance with regard to the conduct of personal life. Laws on birth-control, inter-faith marriages, divorce, medical care, burials, and other personal matters, have been harshly enforced without regard to the circumstances of peoples'

* In noting this generally sad record it should not be forgotten that the black churches, with a little support from a few white churches actually trying to follow Christ's teachings, played a most important role in keeping alive the spirit and the will to live of the black people of America during the long, cruel years of slavery.

lives or to the ultimate purpose of religion. In consequence, instead of being a means for raising up the human spirit, religious laws have frequently become instruments of oppression. With emphasis on the letter of church law, rather than the spirit, it is not surprising that this should be reflected in the churchgoing public. The hypocrisy of churchgoing has become a by-word. Many of those who go to church do so without enthusiasm, only to preserve a respectable social image, or at best as a gesture of conscience to be indulged in on Sunday, but to be forgotten for the rest of the week. A 1970 survey[1] of attitudes and habits of churchgoers in the United States carried out by the University of Michigan showed that for the most part the teachings of the church had little or no bearing on the way most American Roman Catholics conducted their lives. It also showed that there was a clear correlation between the intensity of devoutness of Protestant churchgoers and the bigotry of their social attitudes.

Another matter which undoubtedly turns many away from present-day Christianity is its division into a multitude of sects which have arisen since it became institutionalized and ritualistic. The quarrels between these sects have caused some of the most bloody and un-Christian behaviour in the whole of recorded history, a fact which is indeed difficult to forget. This feeling is reinforced when the differences between the sects are now examined and it is found that for the most part they involve obscure theological doctrines of little relevance to the positive teachings of Jesus or the needs of society. All sects, no matter how just their original stand may have seemed, have been tainted in this fratricidal struggle.

With regard to the challenges which we face today it is not unreasonable for anyone to ask how can the Christian churches provide the necessary moral leadership when they cannot even agree amongst themselves. To their credit many churchmen have recognized the validity of this question and have made noble efforts to bring some of the churches together in the ecumenical movement. The

[1] *The Washington Post*, August 15, 1970.

process is painfully slow and it is clear from the continuing debate that the spirit dominating the proceedings is often very weak. Sectional interest plays as significant a part as it does when politicians toy with the idea of an international organization. Laudable as the ecumenical movement is, it has to be recognized that, even if successful, the unity which it would bring about would only cover one third of the world's population — that is, the part of the world which is nominally Christian. As the Christian churches do not recognize the station of the Founders of the other great religions, it could not embrace Islám, Buddhism, Hinduism and Judaism.

The history of Islám has many parallels with that of Christianity. It, too, in its early years, inspired a great spiritual advance in the society of the time. The inhabitants of the Arabian Peninsula, previously one of the most backward social groups in the world, for whom murder and theft were a way of life, achieved moral standards and a social integrity as high as any existing at that time, by following the person and teachings of Muhammad. Within a few decades of Muhammad's ministry, a peace and prosperity was achieved in the Middle East and along the coast of North Africa far more complete and deeply implanted than perhaps even the Roman Empire enforced at the peak of its power. That civilization, which was tolerant of Christians and Jews, showed more concern for the poor than any other up to that time, not excluding the Greeks, the Romans and Medieval Christian Europe, and raised up the position of women from that which previously had been lower than a domestic animal. Islamic civilization built up the greatest universities and libraries of the time and made very significant contributions to the development of many fields of science, for instance, chemistry, metallurgy, medicine, algebra, geometry, astronomy and agriculture. The balanced appreciation of that great civilization for nature and the material things of life can be seen in the beauty of all its arts.

However, there can be little doubt that Islám has long since fallen from these great heights. Its spirit has been weighed down and weakened by dogmatism, superstition, division and the most fierce reactionary social attitudes. Certainly, the followers of the prophet Muhammad in recent centuries have been associated with acts as cruel and bloody as any in the history of Christendom. Not surprisingly their moral influence has greatly declined. It is true that in some countries belief in Islám is still strong throughout society, but this is usually when it is used as a cultural defence against Western influence. It is true also that in recent years black people in the West, trying to re-establish their cultural heritage and to find political allies against the dominant white middle class, have been to some extent attracted to Islám. Furthermore, Islám has had some success in parts of Africa because it is easy to understand in contrast with the conflicting theological positions of the Christian missionaries. Nevertheless, the overall picture is one of gradual disintegration, with the young and the educated breaking away from the embrace of their Faith at an ever increasing rate.

Though the details vary, the story is similar with regard to Judaism, Hinduism and Buddhism. In its day each of these religions was a tremendous power for progress; now each is but a pale shadow of its former greatness. That some Westerners are attracted to certain schools of Buddhism and Hinduism because they give more emphasis to detachment from material things and to spiritual disciplines than is normal in Western society, does not significantly affect the tide of history.

What is significant about the history of the old established religions is that their decline has not demonstrated that religion as such is a false guide to reality and the best welfare of mankind. On the contrary, there is much evidence that when religion has been pure and vigorous it has led man to his greatest moral, spiritual and intellectual achievements. Having experienced civilization essentially without religion, many leading thinkers are coming to realize that there is not a substitute, and that there will have to be a religious renaissance if man is to meet successfully the challenges of the day. For example, a few years ago an article in Partisan Review said:

"At present many thinkers sound an insistent note of warning that Western civilization cannot hope to survive without the reanimation of religious values."[1]

Arnold Toynbee has expressed a similar theme in the *"Study of History"*:

"Discord is inveterate in human life because Man is the most awkward of all things in the World that Man is compelled to encounter; he is at one and the same time a social animal and an animal endowed with free will. The combination of these two elements means that, in a society consisting exclusively of human members, there will be a perpetual conflict of wills, and this conflict will be carried to suicidal extremity unless Man experiences the miracle of conversion ... The unity of Mankind ... can be achieved only as an incidental result of acting on a belief in the unity of God and by seeing this unitary terrestrial society as a province of God's Commonwealth ..."[2]

However, the faults which have developed in the old-established religions are clearly very serious and it is not realistic to expect a religious renaissance if the price is continued acceptance of these faults.

"Faith will not be restored in the West because people believe it to be useful. It will return only when they find that it is true."[3]

There can be little doubt that the most basic requirement is the reconciliation of science and religion.

"To recapture the imagination and character of man, religion must first make terms with science; not by surrendering to science one jot of truth or principle but by restating spiritual truth in terms compatible with the known and accepted truths of science."[4]

Furthermore, a religion which is to help man deal with worldwide issues must have an appeal to men of all cultural and religious backgrounds, and it must provide specific

---

[1] *"Scepticism and the Decline of Religion"* p. 10.

[2] Volume 2 of abridged version by D. C. Somervell of the *"Study in History"* by Arnold Toynbee, pp. 121-122, Dell Publishing Co. N.Y., 1965.

[3] *Faith and Freedom*, by Barbara Ward: p. 265, W. W. Norton, N.Y., 1954.

[4] *Tomorrow and Tomorrow*, by Stanwood Cobb, p. 56, Bahá'í Publishing Trust, Wilmette, Illinois, 1951.

guidance on social organization as well as on matters at the individual level.

Many of the most forward-looking have to come to realize that a renewal of religion along these lines implies a new religion which will embrace all other religions within its fold. In *"Religion and the Rise of Scepticism"*, Franklin Baumer describes the thoughts of Arthur Koestler, himself a chronicler of the ideas and hopes of mid-twentieth century man, as follows:

"Although Koestler's 'guess' is not a prediction, he is convinced of one thing: if there is to be a spiritual reawakening, it will be like nothing that we have ever seen before ... There can be no question of a swingback to the traditional churches which are "venerable anachronisms" which ask us to split our brains into halves and speak the language of a past epoch. What will be required — at least for most thinking people — is the birth of new gods, the emergence of a 'new religion' a 'new type of faith' which, as DeLattre remarks to Hydie in the 'Age of Longing', will demand a cosmic loyalty with a doctrine acceptable to twentieth century man.' 'Is it really too much to ask and hope,' Koestler says again in "The Trail of the Dinosaur", for a religion whose content is perennial but not archaic, which provides ethical guidance, teaches the lost art of contemplation and restores contact with the supernatural without requiring reason to abdicate?"[1]

It is the theme of this book that such a religion does exist. The religion is the Bahá'í Faith. Its principal tenets are intellectual integrity, the complementary roles of science and religion, the essential unity of all religions, and the brotherhood of all mankind. It provides for a new highly democratic system of participatory government crowned by a world assembly, and for the application of spiritual principles to social as well as individual conduct. Special attention is paid to the avoidance of the disunity and corruption of principles which have affected other religions. It is a religion which speaks specifically to the challenges of this age and one which is spreading rapidly amongst all

[1] Religion and the Rise of Scepticism, p. 231.

peoples and all classes around the world. It has a special attraction to the idealistic young and the oppressed. Already its followers have establised the embryo of a world government with supporting bodies in very nearly every country of the world. It holds the promise of a golden age. It was of Bahá'u'lláh, the Founder of the Bahá'í Faith, that Leo Tolstoy wrote:

"We spend our lives trying to unlock the mystery of the universe, but there was a Turkish prisoner, (Bahá'u'lláh in 'Akká, Palestine,) who had the key."[1]

---

[1] Star of the West, Volume XXIII, p. 233 (USA).

CHAPTER II

THE TIME FOR WORLD UNITY

A — *The Unifier*

BAHÁ'U'LLÁH was born in Persia in 1817. His father was a minister of the Sháh. As a youth Bahá'u'lláh was known for His intelligence and sensitivity and it was expected that one day He also would be a minister of the crown. Instead, at an early age, He chose to lead a life of meditation and of giving assistance to the poor and He took no part in the activities of high society.

In 1844 another young man, named the Báb, publicly declared in Shíráz, Persia, that a great World Educator was about to appear to reform religion and society. Without a moment's hesitation Bahá'u'lláh became one of His staunchest supporters. Thousands followed the Báb, and a frightened and reactionary priesthood and government, seeing a threat to their own position, organized a most ferocious persecution in the course of which the Báb was publicly executed (1850), and thousands of His followers were murdered, tortured, imprisoned, or driven into exile. Bahá'u'lláh was stripped of His property and rights, and He and His family were rendered destitute. He was beaten, imprisoned, tortured, imprisoned again and then exiled to Baghdád, in the Ottoman Empire.

During the period of imprisonment Bahá'u'lláh came to understand that it was His destiny to be that World-Educator foretold by the Báb. After several years of preparation for this immense task He announced His mission, first to His companions (1863) and then to the world at large (1867-68). After several years in Baghdád, the Ottoman Government ordered Him first to Constantinople, then to Adrianople and finally to 'Akká, Palestine, where he spent the last 24 years of His life until His death in 1892.

The Writings which Bahá'u'lláh left behind fill one hundred volumes. In this and the next six chapters an attempt will be made to outline some of the themes which run through these volumes and to say how they are related to the needs of mankind today. The discussion will first touch on the Bahá'í view of the nature of the universe and man's place in it, then with man as a spiritual and intellectual being, and finally with man and society.

In addition to the words of Bahá'u'lláh, reference will be made to those of 'Abdu'l-Bahá (1844-1921) Who was Bahá'u'lláh's eldest son and from youth onwards, His Father's closest companion throughout His life and Whom He appointed to lead the nascent Bahá'í Community after His death. There will be many quotations too from the writings of 'Abdu'l-Bahá's grandson, Shoghi Effendi Rabbani, who, from 1921 until his death in 1957, guided the Faith in the establishment of its institutional framework.

After discussing these themes, there will be in Chapter 8 a short history of the Bahá'í Faith, including brief accounts of the lives of the Báb, Bahá'u'lláh, 'Abdu'l-Bahá and Shoghi Effendi.

B — *The Unknowable Essence*

Bahá'í Writings describe the physical universe as consisting of units of energy which are continually forming and reforming into larger units of matter according to a universal law of attraction, repulsion, composition and decomposition.

"Love is the most great law that ruleth this mighty and heavenly Cycle, the unique power that bindeth together the divers elements of this material world, the supreme magnetic force that directs the movements of the spheres in the celestial realms." 'Abdu'l-Bahá.[1]

The power of attraction or love, organizes matters at several differing levels of complexity of which the most primitive is the mineral. At a more sophisticated level it forms the vegetable which has the power of growth and self-reproduction. At a still higher level is the animal, which

[1] Divine Art of Living, p. 108 (USA).

has the power of sensory perception. The highest and most complex form of matter is that which has not only the power of growth, reproduction, and sensory perception but also the ability to conceive ideas beyond itself — transcendental power. This is man.

"Just as the animal is more noble than the vegetable and mineral, so man is superior to the animal. The animal is bereft of ideality; that is to say, it is a captive of the world of nature and not in touch with that which lies within and beyond nature; it is without spiritual susceptibilities, deprived of the attractions of consciousness, unconscious of the the world of God and incapable of deviating from the law of nature. It is different with man. Man is possessed of the emanations of consciousness; he has perception, ideality and is capable of discovering the mysteries of the universe. All the industries, inventions and facilities surrounding our daily life were at one time hidden secrets of nature ... According to nature's laws they should have remained latent and hidden, but man having transcended those laws, discovered these mysteries and brought them out of the plane of the invisible into the realms of the known and visible." 'Abdu'l-Bahá.[1]

All levels of matter are forever changing and developing in relation to themselves and to the environment. Man himself has developed over an immense period of time from the most primitive beginnings and in the process of evolution has passed through many different forms. However, he has always had the potential to be ultimately what he has become, just as the acorn, though humble in size and appearance, has the potential of becoming a mighty oak tree. From this perspective evolution not only results from ancestry and environment but involves the fulfillment of inherent potential.

The scale of the universe is incredibly vast in both space and time. The various levels of material development appear all over the universe, and there is life on the planets of other stars besides on those of our own sun. Though individual planets and stars form and break up at different

[1] Promulgation of Universal Peace pp. 235-236 (USA).

times, the basic units of existence have no beginning in time:

"... *It is certain that this world of existence, this endless universe, has neither beginning nor end. Yes, it may be that one of the parts of the universe, one of the globes, for example, may come into existence, or may be disintegrated, but the other endless globes are still existing; the universe would not be disordered nor destroyed; on the contrary, existence is eternal and perpetual. As each globe has a beginning, necessarily it has an end, because every composition, collective or particular, must of necessity be decomposed; the only difference is that some are quickly decomposed and others more slowly, but it is impossible that a composed thing should not eventually be decomposed.*" 'Abdu'l-Bahá.[1]

The Bahá'í view is that the universe is not an accident but the creation of some force outside itself. 'Abdu'l-Bahá made the following statement on this point in a letter to Dr. Auguste Forel, a Swiss scientist:

"*Now, formation is of three kinds and of three kinds only: accidental, necessary and voluntary. The coming together of the various constituent elements of beings cannot be accidental, for unto every effect there must be a cause. It cannot be compulsory, for then the formation must be an inherent property of the constituent parts and the inherent property of a thing can in no wise be dissociated from it, such as light that is the revealer of things, heat that causeth the expansion of elements and the (solar) rays which are the essential property of the sun. Thus under such circumstances the decomposition of any formation is impossible, for the inherent properties of a thing cannot be separated from it. The third formation remaineth and that is the voluntary one, that is, an unseen force described as the Ancient Power, causeth these elements to come together, every formation giving rise to a distinct being.*"[2]

That unseen force is God. Bahá'u'lláh said that the evidence of the existence of God is all around for us to see, in nature, in man himself, in history:

[1] Some Answered Questions pp. 209-210 (USA).
[2] Bahá'í Revelation, pp. 225-226 (UK).

"Every created thing in the whole universe is but a door leading into His knowledge, a sign of His sovereignty, a revelation of His names, a symbol of His majesty, a token of His power, a means of admittance into His straight Path."[1] and added that:

"He hath endowed every soul with capacity to recognize the signs of God. How could He, otherwise, have fulfilled His testimony unto men, if ye be of them that ponder His Cause in their hearts. He will never deal unjustly with any one, neither will He task a soul beyond its power."[2]

The evidence may be seen in the order and breathtaking beauty of the universe from the smallest molecule to the pattern of the stars at night, in the evolutionary process of nature toward higher forms of life, in the inner-most feelings of the human heart.

In teaching the meaning of life, the churches have tried in the past to make their message more vivid by portraying God in anthropomorphic terms, a very human development but unfortunate, because in modern times these simple minded portrayals have become so much a part of the idea of God that the educated have tended to find the whole concept unacceptable. In speaking of God, Bahá'u'lláh swept away these old images:

"So perfect and comprehensive is His creation that no mind nor heart, however keen or pure, can ever grasp the nature of the most insignificant of His creatures; much less fathom the mystery of Him Who is the Day Star of Truth, Who is the invisible and unknowable Essence. The conceptions of the devoutest of mystics, the attainments of the most accomplished amongst men, the highest praise which human tongue or pen can render are all the product of man's finite mind and are conditioned by its limitations. . . . From time immemorial He hath been veiled in the ineffable sanctity of His exalted Self, and will everlastingly continue to be wrapt in the impenetrable mystery of His unknowable Essence. Every attempt to attain to an understanding of His inaccessible Reality hath ended in complete bewilderment,

[1] Gleanings, p. 160 (UK).
[2] Ibid., pp. 105-106 (UK).

and every effort to approach His exalted Self and envisage His Essence hath resulted in hopelessness and failure.'[1]

'Abdu'l-Bahá explained that it was unreasonable of man to think that he could know the essence of God:

"It is a self-evident fact that phenomenal existence can never grasp nor comprehend the ancient and essential reality. Utter weakness cannot understand absolute strength. When we view the world of creation we discover differences in degree which make it impossible for the lower to comprehend the higher. For example, the mineral kingdom, no matter how much it may advance can never comprehend the phenomena of the vegetable kingdom. Whatever development the vegetable may attain, it can have no message from nor come in touch with the kingdom of the animal. However perfect may be the growth of a tree it cannot realize the sensation of sight, hearing, smell, taste and touch; these are beyond its limitation. Although it is the possessor of existence in the world of creation, a tree nevertheless has no knowledge of the superior degree of the animal kingdom. Likewise no matter how great the advancement of the animal it can have no idea of the human plane; no knowledge of intellect and spirit. Difference in degree is an obstacle to this comprehension. A lower degree cannot comprehend a higher although all are in the same world of creation, whether mineral, vegetable or animal. Degree is the barrier and limitation. In the human plane of existence we can say we have knowledge of a vegetable, its qualities and product, but the vegetable has no knowledge or comprehension whatever of us. No matter how near perfection this rose may advance in its own sphere it can never possess hearing and sight. Inasmuch as in the creational world which is phenomenal, difference of degree is an obstacle or hindrance to comprehension, how can the human being which is a created exigency, comprehend the ancient divine reality which is essential? This is impossible because the reality of divinity is santified beyond the comprehension of the created being man."[2]

---

[1] Gleanings, p.62 (UK).
[2] The Reality of Man, pp. 53-54 (USA).

Many readers undoubtedly find it difficult to accept belief in God, as indeed did the writer before becoming a Bahá'í. For those readers it is suggested that to form an objective judgment it is important to grasp how much of our whole way of thinking is influenced, not to say prejudiced, by the passing fashion of our intellectual environment. The word "fashion" is used deliberately, and it is believed justly, in view of the innumerable ideas which have been taken up in the last fifty years or so and accepted as the answer, only to be discarded soon afterwards.

Clearly much of the present scepticism is a reaction against the established churches whose creeds could not bear the searching light of science and reason and whose teachings seemed often irrelevant to our time. An example of this bias is the commonly accepted assumption that God was invented by man because he felt a need for an explanation of the workings of nature and for a father-figure. That this universal need for something beyond man might be in itself evidence of the reality of God rarely seems to be considered.

The prevalent empirical method of enquiry, though extremely useful in many areas of intellectual endeavour, does have certain limitations:

"... *European philosophers,* ... *say that the principal method of gaining knowledge is through the senses; they consider it supreme, although it is imperfect, for it commits errors. For example, the greatest of the senses is the power of sight. The sight sees the mirage as water, and it sees images reflected in mirrors as real and existent; large bodies which are distant appear to be small, and a whirling point appears as a circle* .... *Therefore we cannot trust it.*

" ... *ancient philosophers* ... *proved things by reason, and held firmly to logical proofs, all their arguments are arguments of reason. Notwithstanding this, they differed greatly, and their opinions were contradictory. They even changed their views; that is to say, during twenty years they would prove the existence of a thing by logical agruments, and afterwards they would deny it by logical arguments. So much so, that Plato at first logically proved the immobility of*

the earth and the movement of the sun; later by logical
arguments he proved that the sun was the stationary centre,
and that the earth was moving.

"... *Therefore it is evident that the method of reasoning is*
not perfect; ..." 'Abdu'l-Bahá.[1]

It may well be that other methods of including intuition,
which after all, as Arthur Koestler and others have pointed
out, is very much used in science, may be more effective
when investigating spiritual or transcendental phenomena.

Although provable by rational argument (see page 30), in
the last resort having a sense of the existence of God is very
much a personal experience and each person must resolve
his own questions.

Nevertheless it is sometimes useful to hear of the
experiences of others because they may sound a note of
recognition. Acceptance of the idea of God came to the
writer, for instance, not so much from rational argument
nor even from meditation on nature, though these
approaches had provoked much reflection and self-
questioning, as from straightforward study of Bahá'í
Writings. In those parts of the Writings where he felt
competent to make a independent judgment as a normal
thinking human being, it became clear that their
profundity and breadth exceeded anything previously
thought possible and he could not but take on trust from
such an Author what was written on subjects of a nature
which were outside our normal understanding. The
evidence seemed to be overwhelming that the first steps
toward a truly just civilization can be taken only after man
humbles himself before God. It is suggested to the reader
who has difficulties with the idea of God that he keep his
patience awhile and discover more of what the Bahá'í Faith
means in practical terms before making any judgment.

C — *The Nature of Man*

The teachings of most of the Christian churches portray
man as innately sinful. In secular thinking there are many

[1] Some Answered Questions, pp, 341-342 (USA).

variations on this point of view of which perhaps one of the more well known is the idea apparently supported by Konrad Lorenz that man is basically an aggressive creature. On the other hand, there are those who advocate Rousseau's theory that man, the noble savage, is essentially good and is only corrupted by institutions. Probably the majority today find both these extreme positions unrealistic and contrary to experience.

The Bahá'í view is that man has potential for both good and evil. Man has two sides to his nature: the lower self which is associated with his physical "animal" needs, and the higher self, the distinguishing characteristic of man, which is the ability to think and feel independently of his own immediate desire. When his higher self is cultivated and grows then man is extending himself and he is on the way to fulfilment. If his lower self acquires a position of dominance then he sinks into himself, down to a level far below his potential, indeed below that of the animal, for an animal has powerful instinct against excess to protect itself.

"In man there are two natures; his spiritual or higher nature and his material or lower nature. In one he approaches God, in the other he lives for the world alone. Signs of both these natures are to be found in man. In his material aspect he expresses untruth, cruelty and injustice; all these are the outcome of his lower nature. The attributes of his divine nature are shown forth in love, mercy, kindness, truth and justice, one and all being expressions of his higher nature. Every good habit, every noble quality belongs to man's spiritual nature, whereas all his imperfections and sinful actions are born of his material nature." 'Abdu'l-Bahá.[1]

As with all forces in nature, the pull between the two sides of man creates constant motion. Within limits man has the free choice of following the pull of either self:

"Some things are subject to the free will of man, such as justice, equity, tyranny, and injustice, as well as all the good and evil actions; it is evident and clear that these actions are, for the most part, left to the will of man. But there are certain

[1] *Paris Talks, p.60 (UK).*

things to which man is forced and compelled: such as sleep, death, sickness, decline of power, injuries, and misfortunes; these are not subject to the will of man, and he is not responsible for them, for he is compelled to endure them. But in the choice of good and bad actions he is free, and he commits them according to his own will." 'Abdu'l-Bahá.[1]

This means responsibility for one's own actions. However, Bahá'í Writings make it clear that the circumstances of men's lives vary greatly, some having much greater difficulties to contend with than others, and that what is important is not so much absolute standards as how far a man has progressed toward the highest standards from his point of departure. The Writings also show that as man responds to his higher nature it becomes easier to do so again. Nobility can be a habit just as easily as meanness. It is the function of religion, indeed of all true eduction, to cultivate the habit of nobility. When man stretches himself and begins to fulfil his potential then indeed he is the glory of creation!

"If there were no man, the perfections of the spirit would not appear, and the light of the mind would not be resplendent in this world. This world would be like a body without a soul.

"This world is also in the condition of a fruit-tree, and man is like the fruit; without fruit the tree would be useless.
'Abdu'l-Bahá.[2]

D — *The Spiritual Evolution of Man*

There have been numerous theories to explain the meaning of the history of man. One of the most accepted today is that of dialectical materialism as described by Marx. Another is that of man responding to the challenge of his physical environment, a theory laid out in detail by Arnold Toynbee. The Bahá'í view of history is that, though such theories may shed some light on man's development, what is significant is spiritual history: man's growth as a

[1] Some Answered Questions, p.287 (USA).
[2] Ibid, p. 234 (USA).

moral being, his understanding of the true nature of the universe, and his purpose in it. History in reality is about the growth of the higher nature of man. Evolution did not stop at the creation of physical man but continues with the growth of his spiritual awareness:

"When the body of man is perfected, physical evolution comes to an end, since nature does not seek to build a higher form than that of man. But the evolution of the spirit continues until reason, the mental powers, and the emotional capacities are evolved in it." 'Abdu'l-Bahá.[1]

Like movement in the physical universe, such a development is not a straight line but a series of cycles each with its seasons: a spring of awakening, a summer of achievement, an autumn of decline, and a winter of despondency. As a tree grows from year to year, so, too, the end of each spiritual cycle sees man at a higher level of development than in the preceding one.

Bahá'ís believe that though man is free to choose between the pull of the two parts of his nature, there are limits beyond which he cannot develop his higher potential without external assistance, for it takes inspiration and imagination beyond that of a man to show him his own unsuspected potentiality. The normal sources of knowledge, empirical investigation and rational deduction and induction are inadequate. The required inspiration and imagination comes at certain critical points in the cycles of history from great "Educators", or "Manifestations of God", Who have perspective and extraordinary insight into the meaning of life.

" . . . He hath ordained that in every age and dispensation a pure and stainless Soul be made manifest in the kingdom of earth and heaven . . . Through the Teachings of this Day Star of Truth every man will advance and develop until he attaineth the station at which he can manifest all the potential forces with which his inmost true self hath been endowed." Bahá'u'lláh.[2]

Seen in perspective, there is nothing unnatural about the

---

[1] The Renewal of Civilization by David Hofman, p. 90, George Ronald, London, 1945.

[2] Gleanings, pp. 66-67 (UK)Some Answered Questions, p.287 (USA).

appearance of these Educators. They come forward as part of what might be called a spiritual law, in response to the needs of society, at times of great moral confusion and despair which occur with the decline of established beliefs or because new circumstances have arisen for which traditional answers are no longer suitable. Phrased in another way, these flashes of light occur when society reaches a point of explosion, just as in nature, at critical points, a solid will turn into liquid, a liquid into gas, a seed will burst into a plant, a chrysalis into a butterfly.

The Educators are the Founders of the great religions. Many lived before recorded history; others have come to societies who have lost much of their record of the past. Those Whom we do have some knowledge of are Abraham, Moses, Krishna, Buddha, Zoroaster, Jesus, Muhammad, and now the Báb and Bahá'u'lláh.

Bahá'í Writings distinguish two aspects to the teachings of these Educators. First, they all have in common the same universal themes which must govern man's attitude toward God, his fellowmen and the universe at large: love, justice, detachment from personal desire, honesty, selflessness, faithfulness, humility, forgiveness, charity, obedience, mercy, trustworthiness, sincerity, truthfulness, moderation. These truths are not just words. When society forgets them, the resulting pain is sharp and deep. Secondly, each includes social teachings appropriate to the level of development of the society existing at the time. These social teachings are the practical guidelines for the application of the general themes in day-to-day life:

"*Each divine Revelation is divided into two parts. The first part is essential and belongs to the eternal world. It is the exposition of divine truths and essential principles. It is the expression of the love of God. This is one in all the religions, unchangeable and immutable. The second part is not eternal; it deals with practical life, transactions and business, and changes according to the evolution of man and the requirements of the time of each Prophet . . .*

"*According to the exigencies of the time. His Holiness Moses revealed ten laws for capital punishment. It was*

39

impossible at that time to protect the community and to preserve social security without these severe measures, for the children of Israel lived in the wilderness of Tah, where there were no established courts of justice and no penitentiaries. But this code of conduct was not needed in the time of Christ." 'Abdu'l-Bahá.[1]

As a pupil progresses through a school, each teacher in turn builds on what the pupil was taught in his previous class. So, too, with the great Educators; Each has the greatest love and respect for His Predecessors, speaks of Them as His equals and far from destroying Their work, strengthens and adds to it.

"Beware, O believers in the Unity of God, lest ye be tempted to make any distinction between any of the Manifestations of His Cause, or to discriminate against the signs that have accompanied and proclaimed their Revelation. This indeed is the true meaning of Divine Unity, if ye be of them that apprehend and believe this truth. Be ye assured, moreover, that the works and acts of each and every one of these Manifestations of God, nay whatever pertaineth unto them, and whatsoever they may manifest in the future are all ordained by God, and are a reflection of His Will and Purpose. Whoso maketh the slightest possible difference between their persons, their words, their messages, their acts and manners, hath indeed disbelieved in God, hath repudiated His signs, and betrayed the Cause of His Messengers." Bahá'u'lláh.[2]

Not only did the Educators recognise Their Predecessors but They have also had the vision to see that the need would continue. In Their teachings They would refer to Their own return, not as a bodily reincarnation as some have mistakenly believed, but in the spirit. Sometimes the reference would be to periodic returns, sometimes to one specific return when mankind would make a particularly significant advance in the standard of civilization, for instance, what is referred to in the Bible as: "the Time of the End". The promise of the coming of a Messiah in

---

[1] Bahá'u'lláh and the New Era, by J. E. Esselmont, pp. 117-118 (UK).
[2] Gleanings, p. 59 (UK).

Judaism, of the return of Christ in Christianity, the coming of the Qá'im, expected by Shí'ih Muslims, or the Mihdí, awaited by Sunní Muslims, are well known. Perhaps less well known in the West are the promises of Hinduism, Budhism and Zoroastranism. In the *Bhagavad Gita* (Fourth Discourse) verses 7 and 8, Krishna is recorded as having said:

"Whenever there is a decay of righteousness. O Bharata, and there is exaltation of unrighteousness, then I Myself come forth for the protection of good, for the destruction of the evil-doers, for the sake of firmly establishing righteousness, I am born from age to age."

A similar statement is reported of Buddha:

"I am not the first Buddha who came upon earth, nor shall I be the last, In due time another Buddha will arise in the world, a Holy One, a supremely enlightened One, endowed with wisdom in conduct, auspicious, knowing the universe, an incomparable leader of men, a master of angels and mortals. He will reveal to you the same eternal truths which I have taught you. He will preach his religion, glorious at the goal, in the spirit and in the letter. He will proclaim a religious life wholly perfect and pure such as I now proclaim."[1]

Zoroaster made the remarkable prophecy in the *Dinkird* that:

"When a thousand two hundred and some years have past from the inception of the religion of the Arabian and the overthrow of the Kingdom of Iran and the degradation of the followers of My Religion, a descendent of the Iranian Kings will be raised up as a Prophet."*

Bahá'u'lláh Himself said that as new problems arose in the distant future then new guidance would be needed and a new Educator would arise to provide it. He said that such an Educator would not come for at least one thousand years.

In short, all the great religions have been as one for the worship of one God and for the advancement of mankind.

---

[1] *Gospel of Buddha* by P. Carcus, p.245, Open Court Publishing Co., Chicago & London, 1915.

*The Bahá'í Faith began in the year 1260 of the Muslim calendar and Bahá'u'lláh was descended from the Sásáníyan kings of Persia.

"There can be no doubt whatever that the peoples of the world, of whatever race or religion, derive their inspiration from one heavenly Source, and are the subject of one God. The difference between the ordinances under which they abide should be attributed to the varying requirements and exigencies of the age in which they were revealed."
Bahá'u'lláh.[1]

This theme is of the utmost importance in providing a basis for the unity of mankind. It means that men of all religions may have a common belief concerning the most significant aspects of existence, without having to deny the essence of their previous belief. If men were to remain divided on questions concerning their deepest feelings and beliefs then there could be no true brotherhood, at best a fragile tolerance based on indifference. The theme is also of considerable significance for those who have in the past turned against religion, because it shows that when religion is truly practised it is not exclusive, narrow, and a source of incessant quarrelling but the instrument for establishing mutual understanding and appreciation between all men.

One distinguishing feature of the great Educators is the beauty of Their teachings which, if examined at their source with scrupulous absence of prejudice, are clearly for the good of all mankind. Another is the example of Their lives which fire love and respect in all men of sensibility. Like mirrors reflecting the light of the sun, the great Educators reflect the qualities of God in the manner of Their lives. The depth of feeling They inspire is quite different from what may be felt about other men. The love that men may have for a great artist or national hero is as nothing compared with what is felt, for instance, for Jesus or Muhammad.

Governments and established churches seeing the influence of these Teachers as a threat to their own position may try to repress Them but once They have made Their claim to be the Educator for that age They will never retract even unto death. Their followers, too, will risk all to break

[1] Gleanings, p. 216 (UK).

with the shackles of the past to put into practice the new teachings, stumbling often, of course, but nevertheless gloriously pressing forward to the highest attainments of life. This is the ultimate answer to the question of how we distinguish true from false prophets. Jesus said:

"Even so every good tree bringeth forth good fruit; but a corrupt tree bringeth forth evil fruit. A good tree cannot bring forth evil fruit, neither can a corrupt tree bring forth good fruit. Every tree that bringeth not forth good fruit is hewn down, and cast into the fire. Wherefore by their fruits ye shall know them."[1]

The summer time of the new teachings is the phoenix-like rise of a new and more advanced civilization out of a previously moribund society. Whatever may have been the weakness of early Christian society, no objective assessent could fail to remark on its progressiveness in terms of its humanity and its understanding of life as compared with the circus culture of Rome at the time of Tiberius and Caligula. The same thrust forward in the quality of society is noticeable in the Persia of Cyrus after Zoroaster, India after Buddha, the Kingdom of David after Moses, and the great Islamic civilization which followed Muhammad. It should be added that Bahá'u'lláh said that the rise of Greek civilization was in response to the teachings of the Prophets of Israel.

Then comes the autumn. Over a period of time men gradually lose touch with the real nature of their Educator. They start to elaborate on His teachings, adding many interpretations which soon have the force of law. Parables used by the Educators to make a spiritual or moral point easier to understand and remember are later read literally and the original point is lost. Different views appear and quarrels break out, superstition becomes widespread and the true religious spirit begins to die. Men become hollow, they continue for a time to pay lip service to religion but their actions have less and less connection with their words. Thereafter the fabric of society itself begins to weaken and tear. New conditions and problems arise for which there

[1] *Matthew* 7: 17-20.

43

seems no answer. Winter has come. 'Abdu'l-Bahá was very direct about religions which have deteriorated to this extent:

"*Religion should unite all hearts and cause wars and disputes to vanish from the face of the earth, give birth to spirituality, and bring life and light to each heart. If religion becomes a cause of dislike, hatred and division, it were better to be without it, and to withdraw from such a religion would be a truly religious act. For it is clear that the purpose of a remedy is to cure; but if the remedy should only aggravate the complaint it had better be left alone. Any religion which is not a cause of love and unity is no religion.*"[1]

Then men begin to feel instinctively that something must happen to help society find its direction. It is time for the cycle of life to begin again and for a new Educator to bring new teachings. These teachings will be, of course, ahead of the thinking of contemporary society but not so far ahead that all men cannot understand them. They will be so much in tune with the needs of the time that should there be excessive resistance by government or a prejudiced people, the agony which society is then undergoing will become all that much greater.

E — *A New Age*

If, as Carlyle suggested, the eighteenth century was one of the most sterile periods of history, there is little doubt that the nineteenth century was one of the most exhilarating.* Something in the temper of the time and in the actions of men suggested that one of the critical points of history was at hand — that civilization was poised for a great leap forward.

Quite suddenly the material wealth and scientific knowledge which had been accumulated since the late Middle Ages, especially since the Renaissance, began to bear fruit. New means of harnessing the power of water and steam laid the basis for an industrial economy. First applied

[1] Bahá'í Revelation, pp. 289-290 (UK).

*Actually the main characteristics of the 19th century were beginning to emerge in the last twenty years of the 18th century.

in England in such industries as cotton, pottery, iron, coal, and engineering the new methods soon spread to Western Europe, the United States and thence around the world. In their wake grew large industrial towns which brought much misery for many millions, especially in terms of wretched working and living conditions. Another unpleasant side-effect of industrialization was that it made possible an increasing array of more and more destructive weapons of war. Nevertheless, the industrial revolution signified for the majority the possibility of a break from the age-long struggle to stay at or just above a subsistence level of life. For the first time in history it was not unreasonable to dream of a time when men could live free from want of the necessities of life.

The industrial revolution also played a significant part in broadening man's horizons in another sense. Though the globe had been long since circumnavigated by pioneer sailors and explorers, it was not until the nineteenth century that regular, cheap and speedy communication between all parts of the world became possible as a result of the construction of the first fast sailing ship, the railway engine, the steamship, the telegraph and the telephone. The last great isolated areas were brought into the main circles of civilization: Africa, Australia, the Poles, the American West. With the growth of a world economy which followed from industrialization and the adoption of free trade policies by most of the rich and powerful countries men became conscious of a growing interdependence between all parts of the world. For the first time men were beginning to understand though dimly, that no country is an island unto itself, but as Bahá'u'lláh said:

"The earth is but one country, and mankind its citizens."[1]

Such changes in the very expectations and assumptions of society added to the discontent already voiced with traditional institutions and codes of behaviour. The churches in the West, whose influence had been in decline since the Reformation, saw their influence shrink even

---

[1] Gleanings, p. 249 (UK).

more because they were unable to provide leadership in the new environment.

Without a strong guiding moral philosophy men struggled on as best they could to respond to the new needs of the world. It was accepted that the times called for a more just and dignified station for a much wider spectrum of society. In France during the Revolution, and later in other countries, legal and parliamentary equality was won by the middle class whose power and significance had grown so much. Then came the struggle for more influence by the lower middle class and downtrodden minority cultural groups, the latter awakening to a new-found identity and self-respect. There followed the bitter fight of the agricultural workers and the factory workers in the new industrial towns to obtain social justice. At last society grudgingly recognized how unbearably unjust and demoralizing for all concerned was the institution of slavery. By the end of the century the more enlightened were calling attention to society's oppression of women. Such strugglers were often bloody and caused great strains to the social fabric. The results were spasmodic and fell short of the high hopes held by those oppressed and those who dreamed of a just society.

It was at such a time that Bahá'u'lláh recognized that He was to be the Educator for this age. His theme was the significance of this day in the history of man. This is the "promised day of all ages", the time of fulfilment of religious prophecies, when swords would be beaten into ploughshares and the lion would lie down in peace with the lamb, the golden age when peace and justice would begin.

"Great indeed is this day! The allusions made to it in all the sacred Scriptures as the Day of God attest its greatness. The soul of every Prophet of God, of every Divine Messenger, hath thirsted for this wondrous Day. All the divers kindreds of the earth have, likewise, yearned to attain it." Bahá'u'lláh.[1]

Now is the time when man can and must unite in one world society in order to move on to higher planes of

[1] Bahá'í World Faith, p. 11 (USA).

civilization. Growing social and economic interdependence and the danger of sovereign powers using weapons of mass destruction against one another* can only confirm this analysis for all thinking people. The development of modern means of communication has made it a practical possibility for the first time in history.

"At one time it was passing through its stage of childhood, at another its period of youth, but now it has entered its long-predicted phase of maturity, the evidences of which are everywhere apparent. . . . Man must now become inbued with new virtues and powers, new moral standards, new capacities. . . . The gifts and blessings of the period of youth, although timely and sufficient during the adolescence of mankind, are now incapable of meeting the requirements of its maturity." 'Abdu'l-Bahá.[1]

And yet all around men are in conflict, lost in a materialistic wilderness, without direction or purpose. Bahá'u'lláh said that society can be given direction only by a new Faith which would breathe new life into and unite within its fold all existing religions. Morality, ethics, systems of values which are the cement of civilization cannot be separated from the concept of the highest authority, God:

"That which the Lord hath ordained as the sovereign remedy and mightiest instrument for the healing of all the world is the union of all its peoples in one universal Cause, one common Faith. This can in no wise be achieved except through the power of a skilled, an all-powerful and inspired Physician. This, verily, is the truth, and all else naught but error." Bahá'u'lláh.[2]

Often religion is thought of as being essentially otherwordly, or as the old saying goes, concerned with "pie in the sky". This was never the case with true religion as originally expounded by the great Educators. It is true that

[1] Bahá'í World Faith, p. 11 (USA).

[2] World Order of Bahá'u'lláh, p. 164 (USA).

*At a meeting in Paris 'Abdu'l-Bahá told the Japanese Ambassador that "There is in existence a stupendous force, as yet, happily, undiscovered by man. Let us supplicate God, the Beloved, that this force be not discovered by science until spiritual civilization shall dominate the human mind. In the hands of men of lower material nature, this power would be able to destroy the whole earth." Quoted on p. 184 of 'The Chosen Highway' by Lady Blomfield.

They would provide information on the wider aspects of existence but this was basically to give perspective to the everyday life of man. The major emphasis was always on how to develop life on earth individually and collectively. This is also true of Bahá'u'lláh. His Writings are a practical guide to the achievement of self-fulfilment and the establishment of the true brotherhood of man on a global scale. They contain nothing that is arbitrary or irrational. Each law or ordinance is consistent with the other and all add up to a comprehensive plan for the establishment of a new civilization.

CHAPTER III

A NEW RACE OF MEN

A — *Independent Investigation of the Truth*

BAHÁ'Í teachings for a new civilization begin with the individual. Each individual who partakes in the building of a just society will be most effective when he comes to terms with himself, when he knows who he is and what is his purpose in life. Then a man has humility, but values himself for what he can give; he has dignity and an inner peace. By contrast the egocentric, the self-indulgent man is not dignified; he gives little, and ironically receives little and consequently his potential for growth is severely limited. The man of self-pity, riddled with guilt, full of self-doubt and sometimes hatred, is equally crippled. He can give little love to others and does not value what he is given because he has no vision of what he might be. Often in present-day society the egocentric and the guilt-ridden are the same man, at differing levels of consciousness, victim of institutions and a system of values which mix encouragement of selfishness and greed, with a sense of guilt for pleasure in material things.

Self-realization can only come as we develop our capacity to think independently and objectively. This is the way to reality, to self-confidence, and self-reliance.

"God has given man the eye of investigation by which he may see and recognize truth. He has endowed man with ears that he may hear the message of reality and conferred upon him the gift of reason by which he may discover things for himself. This is his endowment and equipment for the investigation of reality. Man is not intended to see through the eyes of another, hear through another's ears nor comprehend with another's brain. Each human creature has individual endowment, power and responsibility in the creative plan of God. Therefore depend upon your own reason and judgment and adhere to the outcome of your own

investigation; otherwise you will be utterly submerged in the sea of ignorance and deprived of all the bounties of God." 'Abdu'l-Bahá.[1]

It is not enough to be independent of others. A man must free himself from the influence to which he is subject by the very nature of his environment.

"In order to find truth we must give up our prejudices, our own small, trivial notions,; an open receptive mind is essential. If our chalice is full of self, there is no room in it for the water of life. The fact that we imagine ourselves to be right and everybody else wrong is the greatest of all obstacles in the path toward unity, and unity is necessary if we would reach truth, for truth is one. . . .

"It means, also, that we must be willing to clear away all that we have previously learned, all that would clog our steps on the way to truth; we must not shrink if necessary from beginning our education all over again. We must not allow our love for any one religion or any one personality to so blind our eyes that we become fettered by superstition. When we are freed from all these bonds, seeking with liberated minds, then shall we be able to arrive at our goal." 'Abdu'l-Bahá.[2]

Bahá'í teachings stress that in his search for knowledge man should look to both science and religion. Science deals with the discovery of facts, religion with their meaning; science helps with the material needs of man, religion with his moral and spiritual requirements. Both are highly rational. When religion is feeble, science may be changed from a source of enlightenment to one of narrowness of concepts, arrogance and destruction. For instance, scientists have discovered the secret of the atom and are on the verge of understanding genetic engineering. Unless these advances are used within the bounds of a strong and comprehensive ethical code, which in the Bahá'í view can be only provided by true religion, they may prove a disaster for man instead of a boon. On the other hand, when science is undeveloped religion is strangled with useless ritual and superstition.

[1] Promulgation of Universal Peace, p. 287 (USA).
[2] Paris Talks, pp. 136-137 (UK).

"Religion and science are the two wings upon which man's intelligence can soar into the heights, with which the human soul can progress. It is not possible to fly with one wing alone! Should a man try to fly with the wing of religion alone he would quickly fall into the quagmire of superstition, whilst on the other hand, with the wing of science alone he would also make no progress, but fall into the despairing slough of materialism." 'Abdu'l-Bahá.[1]

If a religion clashes with science and is irrational then there is something very wrong with that religion.

"Any religious belief which is not comfortable with scientific proof and investigation is superstition, for true science is reason and reality, and religion is essentially reality and pure reason; therefore the two must correspond. Religious teaching which is at variance with science and reason is human invention and imagination unworthy of acceptance, for the antithesis and opposite of knowledge is superstition born of the ignorance of man. If we say religion is opposed to science we either lack knowledge of true science or true religion, for both are founded upon the premises and conclusions of reason and both must bear its test." 'Abdu'l-Bahá.[2]

It should be recognized that scientific knowledge is constantly expanding and what is thought to be the truth today may be modified or reversed tomorrow. Sometimes a religious teaching will be ahead of what can be proved or disproved by science at a given point in time. There are, however, many superstitions connected with religions which obviously contradict known physical laws of the universe and it is these which should be recognized for what they are.

The scientific methods of acquiring knowledge by empirical investigation and rational deduction and induction are well known. Religious methods are perhaps less well appreciated now because they have been so abused in the past. Attitude of mind is of fundamental importance in evaluating information and it is here that religious

[1] Paris Talks, p. 143 (UK).
[2] Promulgation of Universal Peace, p. 103 (USA).

methods play a significant role. One religious method of search is meditation which frees a man from his environment, frees his mind from conscious direction and allows it to contemplate the essence of being:

"... In that state man withdraws himself from all outside objects; in that subjective mood he is immersed in the ocean of spiritual life and can unfold the secrets of things-in-themselves. To illustrate this, think of man as endowed with two kinds of sight; when the power of insight is being used the outward power of vision does not see. This faculty of meditation frees man from the animal nature, discerns the reality of things, puts man in touch with God."
'Abdu'l-Bahá.[1]

Another religious method of investigation is prayer, the very act of which induces a feeling of humility, detachment and thought on the things which really matter in life.

"While man prays he sees himself in the presence of God."
'Abdu'l-Bahá.[2]

In doing so it gives a new strength

"Prayer and fasting is the cause of awakening and mindfulness and is conducive to protection and preservation from tests." 'Abdu'l-Bahá.[3]

This is particularly true of those prayers given by the Educators which always deal with the loftiest sentiments of man.

"O my God! O my God! Unite the hearts of Thy servants, and reveal to them Thy great purpose. May they follow Thy commandments and abide in Thy law. Help them, O God, in their endeavour, and grant them strength to serve Thee, O God, leave them not to themselves, but guide their steps by the light of knowledge, and cheer their hearts by Thy love. Verily, Thou art their Helper and their Lord." Bahá'u'lláh.[4]

For a Bahá'í, prayer is like going outside the house to receive the warmth of the sun. The sun is there all day, but cannot reach us unless we go out into the open.

"O Son of Being! Love Me that I may love thee. If thou

[1] Paris Talks, p. 175 (UK).
[2] The Pattern of Bahá'í Life, p. 55 (UK).
[3] Divine Art of Living, p.27 (USA).
[4] Bahá'í Prayers, No. 59 (UK).

*lovest Me not, My love can in no wise reach thee. Know this,
O servant."* Bahá'u'lláh.[1]

Bahá'ís place great importance on the prayer as a vehicle
of education. To keep a continuing sense of proportion
Bahá'ís have a moral obligation to pray at least once a day
in private. They should do this at a time when they are alert
and are truly conscious of what they are doing. When a
group of Bahá'ís wishes to pray, the procedure is for
individual members of the group to pray aloud on behalf of
all. Except for the special circumstances of a funeral,
Bahá'ís do not have congregational prayer because as is
evident from past experience this can so easily become an
empty ritual.

Prayers may be said at any place conducive to reverence and
dignity:

*"Blessed is the spot, and the house, and the place, and the
city, and the heart, and the mountain, and the refuge, and the
cave, and the valley, and the land, and the sea, and the
island, and the meadow where mention of God hath been
made, and His praise glorified."* Bahá'u'lláh.[2]

They may also be said at any time, though there is a
special significance given to dawn prayers, perhaps because
of the sacrifice involved in being up at that time, the
spiritual symbolism of the birth of a new day, and the peace
before daily activities begin.

For Bahá'ís who come from a non-religious background,
praying is sometimes a difficult thing to do at first. Over a
period of time, however, inhibition gradually melts away
and one begins to feel the mind-cleansing effect which so
increases one's alertness and consciouness of what life
signifies.

*"O God, refresh and gladden my spirit. Purify my heart.
Illume my mind. I lay all my affairs in Thy hand. Thou are
my Guide and my Refuge. I will no longer be sorrowful and
grieved, I will be a happy and joyful being. O God, I will no
longer be full of anxiety, nor will I let trouble harass me. I*

[1] Hidden Words (Arabic), No. 5 (UK).
[2] Bahá'í Prayers, frontispiece (USA).
[3] Bahá'í Prayers, No. 69 (UK).

art kinder to me than I am to myself. I dedicate myself to Thee, O Lord.". 'Abdu'l-Bahá.[1]

B — *Perspective and Purpose*

The search for knowledge will bring perspective and understanding of man's purpose in life. The Bahá'í view is that such understanding starts with God. Though the essence of God is unknowable to man there is the assurance in the words and in the personalities of His Educators of His goodness, love and justice. These qualities extend into creation itself. Nature is seen as wholly good; and evil only arises when nature is misused. Evil is the absence of good, a negative state, just as darkness is the absence of light.

"In creation there is no evil; all is good. Certain qualities and natures innate in some men and apparently blameworthy are not so in reality. For example, from the beginning of his life you may see in a nursing child the signs of desire, of anger, and of temper. Then, it may be said, good and evil are innate in the reality of man, and this is contrary to the pure goodness of nature and creation. The answer to this is that desire, which is to ask for something more, is a praiseworthy quality provided that it is used suitably. So, if a man has the desire to acquire science and knowledge, or to become compassionate, generous, and just, it is most praiseworthy. If he exercises his anger and wrath against the bloodthirsty tyrants who are like ferocious beasts, it is very praiseworthy; but if he does not use these qualities in a right way, they are blameworthy. . . . It is the same with all the natural qualities of man, which constitute the capital of life; if they be used and displayed in an unlawful way, they become blameworthy. Therefore it is clear that creation is purely good." 'Abdu'l-Bahá.[2]

The beauty and pleasure offered by nature are there for man's benefit and enjoyment. Clearly, this is not in anyway an ascetic view.

"Should a man wish to adorn himself with the ornaments

[1] Bahá'í Prayers, No. 69 (UK).
[2] Some Answered Questions, p. 250 (USA).

of the earth, to wear its apparels, or partake of the benefits it can bestow, no harm can befall him, if he alloweth nothing whatever to intervene between him and God, for God hath ordained every good thing, whether created in the heavens or in the earth, for such of His servants as truly believe in Him. Eat ye, O people, of the good things which God hath allowed you, and deprive not yourselves from His wondrous bounties. Render thanks and praise unto Him and be of them that are truly thankful.'' Bahá'u'lláh.[1]

The fullest enjoyment of the fruits of nature is obtained, however, if they are taken in moderation or according to the golden rule. The same idea is expressed in economics in the principle of marginal value. When moderation gives way to excess and the demands of the animal self begin to dominate, then there can be no happiness for such demands can never be satisfied.

"If carried to excess, civilization will prove as prolific a source of evil as it had been of goodness when kept within the restraints of moderation. . . .

"All other things are subject to this same principle of moderation." Bahá'u'lláh.[2]

It is important to keep a sense of proportion with material things. They should be enjoyed when the opportunity is there; but it is unwise and unhealthy to become attached to them. Their possession can be at best only ephmeral.

". . . Rejoice not in the things ye possess; tonight they are yours, tomorrow others will possess them." Bahá'u'lláh.[3]

Most important of all is the appreciation that the most profound sources of happiness are not to be found in material things but in the growth of the higher nature of man.

"Man is, in reality, a spiritual being, and only when he lives in the spirit is he truly happy." 'Abdu'l-Bahá.[4]

A question often asked by sceptics in the eighteenth century and after was how to reconcile a good God with all the pain and misery in the world. The Bahá'í view is that

[1] Advent of Divine Justice, p. 28 (USA).
[2] Gleanings, p. 342 (UK).
[3] Gleanings, p. 137 (UK).
[4] Paris Talks, p. 72 (UK).

pain is an instrument of education, the cause by which man can become detached and grow spiritually:

"The mind and spirit of man advance when he is tried by suffering. The more the ground is ploughed, the better the seed will grow, the better the harvest will be. Just as the plough furrows the earth deeply, purifying it of weeds and thistles, so suffering and tribulation free man from the petty affairs of this worldly life until he arrives at a state of complete detachment. His attitude in this world will be that of divine happiness. Man is, so to speak, unripe: the heat of the fire of suffering will mature him. Look back to the times past and you will find that the greatest men have suffered the most." 'Abdu'l-Bahá.[1]

As C. S. Lewis pointed out in *"The Problem of Pain"* most of the suffering of man is caused by man himself (he estimated some eighty per cent of the total). Negligence, ignorance, pride, selfishness, attract pain for those who are responsible and those around them almost as a self-correcting spiritual law. If there is free will there must be pain if there is to be justice.

The Bahá'í response to pain is quite different from the passive acceptance of the "will of God" so prevalent in the East, and from the frustrated bitterness often expressed in the non-religious West. It is understood that pain has a purpose and that it is a test for growth which calls for a vigorous response by the individual or by the community. The pain inflicted on men by the injustice of society is perhaps the greatest challenge of all and the whole direction of the Bahá'í community is to meet this challenge — to establish a truly just society. The Bahá'í view has been described as follows:

"Happiness for a Bahá'í is having tests and knowing how to summon the courage to pass them in such a way that his knowing and loving capacities are further developed in service to humanity."[2]

This approach acquires deeper perspective when physical existence is viewed as the embryonic preparation for a

[1] Paris Talks, p. 178 (UK).
[2] *"Becoming Your True Self"*, by Daniel Jordan, p. 16.

lasting spiritual life after death. Bahá'u'lláh said that in his physical existence man experiences a time of growth when all his effort should be toward the development of spiritual characteristics which he will require as a non-physical being. In the same way a child in the womb develops limbs, eyes and ears for the time when he is born into the world. The nature and joy of the future spiritual life is quite beyond anything man can experience as a physical being and the consequent lack of comprehension of man limits what he can learn about it from the Educators.

"The nature of the soul after death can never be described, nor is it meet and permissible to reveal its whole character to the eyes of men. The Prophets and Messengers of God have been sent down for the sole purpose of guiding mankind to the straight Path of Truth. The purpose underlying their revelation hath been to educate all men that they may, at the hour of death, ascend, in the utmost purity and sanctity and with absolute detachment, to the throne of the Most High. . . . The world beyond is as different from this world as this world is different from that of the child while still in the womb of its mother." Bahá'u'lláh.[1]

'Abdu'l-Bahá said that the soul, like the mind, is abstract in the sense that it does not have a physical existence and it is reflected in the human body rather than forming part of it. As it is not physical it is not composed and therefore it does not disintegrate.

"This composition of atoms, which constitutes the body or mortal element of any created being, is temporary. When the power of attraction, which holds these atoms together, is withdrawn, the body, as such ceases to exist.

"With the soul it is different. The soul is not a combination of elements, it is not composed of many atoms, it is of one indivisible substance, and therefore eternal. It is entirely out of the order of the physical creation; it is immortal." 'Abdu'l-Bahá.[2]

'Abdu'l-Bahá pointed to the experience of dreams, when the spirit moves about without reference to the physical

[1] Gleanings, pp. 156-157 (UK).
[2] Paris Talks, pp. 90-91 (UK).

body, and to the man who is mutilated physically but whose spirit remains the same, as examples of how the soul is independent of the physical body.

Bahá'í Writings say that all survive death but at different levels of spirituality. The higher the level, the greater the understanding and joy in the creation of God. All are aware of their level and those who have only achieved a low level because of their lack of growth when in the physical existence can only regret what they have failed to achieve. This is the state which religions have called hell. Hell, too, is the state of mind of the man still existing in the physical world who has allowed his spiritual qualities to wither away.

The knowledge of growth to a spiritual life after death puts not only pain but death itself into perspective. 'Abdu'l-Bahá said man should see death as the end of a journey and greet it:

"with hope and with expectation. It is even so with the end of this earthly journey. In the next world, man will find himself freed from many of the disabilities under which he now suffers."[1]

Thus in a Bahá'í community a funeral is not an occasion for sadness.

"I have made death a messenger of joy to thee. Wherefore doest thou grieve? I made the light to shed on thee its splendour. Why dost thou veil thyself therefrom?"
Bahá'u'lláh.[2]

Bahá'í teachings emphasize, however, that man should not spend his life in contemplation of what is to come. His duty is to look to his life and actions during his physical existence. If he does this, the future spiritual life, which in any case for the most part can be only a subject of idle conjecture, will look after itself when the time comes. It cannot be repeated too often that the aim of the Bahá'í Faith is to improve the quality of life on earth, not to divert men with dreams of a later existence.

In present-day society so many are afflicted by anxiety

[1] Divine Art of Living, p. 24 (USA).
[2] Hidden Words (Arabic), No. 32 (UK).

that most of their energy is devoted to self-protection. The positive attitude to both the known and the unknown shown in the Bahá'í Writings releases man from anxiety so that he can devote all of his power to the fulfilment of his purpose in life.

Bahá'u'lláh described that purpose as twofold. First, it is the development of the power of the spirit, to cultivate man's higher nature, to acquire virtues, to know and love God and to grow toward Him:

"The purpose of God in creating man hath been, and will ever be, enable him to know his Creator and to attain His Presence. To this most excellent aim, this supreme objective, all the heavenly Books and the divinely-revealed and weighty Scriptures unequivocally bear witness." Bahá'u'lláh.[1]

""Love Me, that I may love thee. If thou lovest Me not, My love can in no wise reach thee." Bahá'u'lláh.[2]

Secondly, and as part of that process, it is to assist one's fellow human beings, one's children, the family, the whole of humanity, in the development of their higher nature — in short to help build a new Jerusalem.

"All men have been created to carry forward an ever-advancing civilization." Bahá'u'lláh.[3]

With such goals and with such a perspective of life every man, no matter how insignificant he might seem in the material weighing of the conventional world, can find self-respect.

"Noble have I created thee, yet thou hast abased thyself. Rise then unto that for which thou wast created." Bahá'u'lláh.[4]

On the other hand man is very much aware of his humble position in relation to God.

"Every man of discernment, while walking upon the earth, feeleth indeed abashed, inasmuch as he is fully aware that the thing which is the source of his prosperity, his wealth, his might, his exaltation, his advancement and power is, as ordained by God, the very earth which is trodden beneath the

---

[1] Gleanings, p. 70 (UK).
[2] Hidden Words (Arabic), No. 5 (UK).
[3] Gleanings, p. 214 (UK).
[4] Hidden Words (Arabic), No. 22 (UK).

feet of all men. There can be no doubt that whoever is cognizant of this truth, is cleansed and sanctified from all pride, arrogance and vainglory." Bahá'u'lláh.[1]

He can never be self-righteous because always he knows there is scope for more learning and achievement on his part and he is conscious that he can at any time right up to the end of his life slip backwards and deny his whole achievement.

"He should forgive the sinful, and never despise his low estate, for none knoweth what his own end shall be." Bahá'u'lláh.[2]

Such a man cannot have that overweening pride of which the Greeks wrote so passionately as the bane of man and society. He can and does know shame not as a negative, debilitating emotion but as one which spurs on to attainment of the highest spiritual qualities.

C — *The Human Body*

The view of life expressed in the foregoing section clearly has much bearing on a man's attitude to his physical self. A man of self-respect will not neglect his body. He will appreciate it and respect it as the creation of God. It is the temple of the human spirit, the highest creation of God. This is true whether the body is whole or blemished in some way. A blemised body has its own special beauty in that it often has a compensating physical attribute and, of more importance, the trials it imposes will strengthen the associated spiritual qualities. The man of self-respect will understand that the more healthy is his body the more energy he can devote to the purpose of his life. It is not surprising therefore that the Bahá'í Faith, like all the great religions, has a special concern for the strength and well being of the human body.

Clearly a good diet is essential for bodily health. Accordingly, in their teachings Moses and Muhammad laid emphasis on the avoidance of foods which, in the conditions

---

[1] Epistle to the Son of the Wolf, p. 44 (USA).
[2] Kitáb-i-Íqán (Book of Certitude), P. 194.

then prevailing, might have been dangerous. In Bahá'í Writings, we are advised to look to a balanced natural diet, without excess, and adapted to the climate and the type of work in which the body is engaged. For the present, meat is considered necessary for many people in many areas, but in the future it is said that man will be able to live on a vegetarian diet:

"The food of the future will be fruit and grains. The time will come when meat will no longer be eaten. Medical science is only in its infancy, yet it has shown that our natural food is that which grows out of the ground." 'Abdu'l-Bahá.[1]

When this happens there will be no necessity for the mass killing of animals which now blunts the spiritual qualities of the whole race of man so much.

In March of each year for a period of nineteen days* Bahá'ís are enjoined to observe a fast from food and drink between sunrise and sunset. The fast permits a periodic cleansing of the body which can be a healthy practice when not enforced too harshly as has been the practice with some religions. It is worth noting in this connection that the Bahá'í Fast is held during the nineteen days preceding the spring equinox which happens to be a time of most moderate climate in all parts of the world. In the northern hemisphere it is the time of spring and in the south, of autumn. Thus extremes of cold, when food might be more necessary during the day, and of heat when drink might be needed, are avoided. It is also the period when the time between dawn and dusk is about twelve hours in most parts of the world. It should be observed, too, that Bahá'ís who are physically weak, such as children under the age of fifteen, the old, the sick, women who are pregnant or are breast feeding, and those who are travelling, do not need to observe the Fast.

More important are the spiritual aspects of the Fast. Abstinence for a short period gives a man practice in self-discipline and makes him appreciate all the more those things which he has during the rest of the year and which

[1] Bahá'u'lláh and the New Era, p. 98 (UK).

* A Bahá'í Month. See chapter six for information on the Bahá'í calendar.

he might otherwise take for granted. The knowledge that all over the world Bahá'ís are observing the Fast with him adds very much to the real feeling of belonging to one great worldwide family. Most important of all, the Fast is symbolic of man's detachment from the physical world:

"Fasting is a symbol. Fasting signifies abstinence from lust. Physical fasting is a symbol of abstinence, and is a reminder; that is, just as a person abstains from physical appetites, he is to abstain from self-appetites and self-desires. But mere abstention from food has no effect on the spirit. It is only a symbol, a reminder. Otherwise it is of no importance. Fasting for this purpose does not mean entire abstinence from food. The golden rule as to food is, do not take too much or too little. Moderation is necessary. There is a sect in India who practice extreme abstinence, and gradually reduce their food until they exist on almost nothing. But their intelligence suffers. A man is not fit to do service for God with brain or body if he is weakened by lack of food. He cannot see clearly." 'Abdu'l-Bahá.[1]

Bahá'í teachings stress that the chief means for maintaining a healthy body is to use proper foods. However, if the body should be sick then medical treatment must be used to restore health.

"Do not neglect medical treatment when it is necesary, but leave it off when health has been restored. Treat disease through diet, by preference, refraining from the use of drugs; and if you find what is required in a single herb, do not resort to a compounded medicament.

". . . Abstain from drugs when the health is good but administer them when necessary." 'Abdu'l-Bahá.[2]

In the future, 'Abdu'l-Bahá said that medical science would turn more and more to the great curative powers of herbs and other agents of nature. Such cures will prove more gentle and balanced in their effects than the crude attack of surgery and high-powered drugs which are now necessary.

"The science of medicine is still in a condition of infancy:

[1] Bahá'u'lláh and the New Era, p. 171 (UK).
[2] Bahá'u'lláh and the New Era, p. 102 (UK).

it has not reached maturity; but when it has reached this point, cures will be preferred by things which are not repulsive to the smell and taste of man; that is to say by aliments, fruits and vegetables which are agreeable to the taste and have an agreeable smell. For the provoking cause of disease — that is to say, the cause of the entrance of the disease into the human body — is either a physical one or is the effect of the excitement of the nerves.

"But the principal causes of disease are physical; for the human body is composed of numerous elements, but in the measure of an especial equilibrium. As long as the equilibrium is maintained, man is preserved from disease; but if this essential balance, which is the pivot of the constitution, is disturbed, the constitution is disordered, and disease will supervene.

"For instance, there is a decrease in one of the constituent ingredients of the body of man, and in another there is an increase; so the proportion of the equilibrium is disturbed, and disease occurs. . . . When by remedies and treatments the equilibrium is re-established, the disease is banished. . . . All the elements that are combined in man, exist also in vegetables; therefore if one of the constituents which compose the body of man diminishes, and he partakes of foods in which there is much of that diminished constituent, then the equilibrium will be established, and a cure will be obtained. So long as the aim is the readjustment of the constituents of the body, it can be effected either by medicine or by food. . . . When the science of medicine reaches perfection, treatment will be given by foods, aliments, fragrant fruits and vegetables, and by various waters, hot and cold in temperature." 'Abdu'l-Bahá.[1]

Bahá'í teachings warn, however, that sickness has emotional as well as physical causes.

"Yield not to grief and sorrow: they cause the greatest misery. Jealousy consumeth the body and anger doth burn the liver: avoid these two as you would a lion."
Bahá'u'lláh[2]

[1] Some Answered Questions, pp. 296-298 (USA).
[2] Bahá'u'lláh and the New Era, p. 103 (UK).

Other illnesses of the body can be symptoms of a sickness in the mind and then only a spiritual regeneration will provide the cure. This might come from a doctor. It might come from contact with another person who has grown to a high level of love and spirituality. It might come when the sick person begins to understand his purpose in life through, for instance, prayer and meditation. It might come from the attention of a loving family or community.

Bahá'í Writings seek to protect man from the most harmful habits of consumption and warnings are made against those habits which damage the body. Smoking, for instance, is discouraged as a dirty and useless habit and as man grows more adult in his behaviour it is foreseen that he will gradually abandon this practice.

"There are other forbidden things which do not cause an immediate evil and of which the pernicious effect is only gradually produced. They are also abhorred, blamed and rejected by God, but their prohibition is not recorded in an absolute way. . . .

"One of these last prohibitions is the smoking of tobacco, which is unclean, malodorous, disagreeable and vulgar and of which the gradual harmfulness is universally recognized. All clever physicians have judged, and have also shown by experiment, that one of the constituents of tobacco is a mortal poison and that smokers are exposed to different indispositions and maladies." 'Abdu'l-Bahá.[1]

Those things which, in addition, damage the mind, which lower the station of man and degrade him are strictly forbidden except when required for medical purposes:

"The drinking of wine is . . . forbidden; for it is the cause of chronic diseases, weakeneth the nerves and consumeth the mind." 'Abdu'l-Bahá.[2]

There are some who are otherwise attracted to the Bahá'í Faith who find its stand on alcohol a major difficulty. This difficulty should take on its true dimensions if the issue is examined in perspective. First, it is worth asking why alcohol is considered so desirable. The truth is that it is not

---

[1] Bahá'í World Faith, p. 334 (USA).
[2] Advent of Divine Justice, p. 27 (USA).

to quench thirst or to savour the finest tastes, popular salesmanship notwithstanding; rather, it is to create an artificial euphoria and to allow some escape from the realities of life. It is a real indication of the state of our society that at social functions people can only face one another after they have blurred their senses with cocktails and hard liquor. The Bahá'í view is that instead of retreating from the society we have created we should be bending all our faculties to its improvement. Secondly, alcohol to a lesser or greater degree makes man act in an unnatural manner, often absurdly and without dignity — contrary to the whole purpose of the Bahá'í Faith. Thirdly, medical science is now showing, as 'Abdu'l-Bahá said many years ago, that even small amounts of alcohol regularly taken damage the brain cells, and therefore not just temporarily, but permanently reduces a man's capacity as a human being. The United States Food and Drug Administration warned in 1979 that even mild drinking by the mother may cause birth defects in the unborn child.*

But the issue goes much deeper than all this. When seen in a world context, the abuse of alcohol is revealed as one of the most terrible of man-made afflictions. For millions around the world alcohol has spelt poverty, degradation, and early death. In some areas, whole societies, such as the Indian nations of North America, or some tribes of Africa, have virtually disintegrated under the influence of alcohol. In these cases the heavy use of alcohol is a symptom of a deeper affliction, the loss of self-confidence in face of the white man's power and contempt, but the point is that alcohol (brought, in many cases, by the white man) has compounded the problem. In Western society, though the proportion of people damaged may be less, nevertheless there is a sizable minority whose lives have been wrecked by alcohol. If we are all not familiar with Skid Row which exists in nearly every big city, most know of a family deprived or broken up by an alcoholic parent, or of an

---

* For a more detailed Bahá'í view see "In Search of Nirvana" and "Alcohol and Alcoholism: An Overview" by Bahia Deloomy Mitchell, World Order Magazine, Spring 1974.

acquaintance needlessly killed on the roads by a drunken driver.**

Many ask what harm is there in taking an occasional drink. One answer is that all who use alcohol even occasionally are making its consumption socially respectable, not to say necessary, and thereby increasing the probability that others will become prisoners of this most cruel compulsion. Further, all users of alcohol are, in effect, supporting a worldwide system of wastage of resources which might otherwise have been used for the better wellbeing of millions of people. It is not enough to pass the responsibility elsewhere. Surely it is ignoble to count a frivolous fashion more important than the elimination of these terrible burdens on society.

The Bahá'í position on drugs, unlike that of most of society, is consistent with its position on alcohol. Drugs, like alcohol, are forbidden.

"Alcohol consumeth the mind and causeth man to commit acts of absurdity, but . . . this wicked hashish extinguisheth the mind, freezeth the spirit, petrifieth the soul, wasteth the body and leaveth man frustrated and lost." 'Abdu'l-Bahá.[1]

Bahá'ís deeply sympathize with the young in their search for greater spiritual awareness but are certain that it cannot be acquired through drugs. Drug-taking is the cheap, speedy, supermarket approach to life, and not only does not work but diverts energy and attention from the true search. Drugs like alcohol, induce flight from reality — an act which is likely to make reality worse, not better. Many countries, including the one where Bahá'u'lláh was born, have witnessed the debilitating effect of drugs for centuries and they feel no need to engage in intellectual debate about the issue; their hard experience is enough. They know drugs are anti-life. At best, drugs are useless and escapist; at worst they are also highly dangerous. Social acceptance and use of the less dangerous makes it more

** In a report on alcoholism issued in February 1972 by the U.S. Department of Health, Education and Welfare, it was estimated that some twenty eight thousand people are killed each year in the U.S.A. by drunken drivers. The report added that regular use of alcohol reduced average life expectancy by about ten to twelve years.

[1] National Bahá'í Review, March 1968 (USA).

likely that ultimately the dangerous will be used too. There can be no room for compromise when laying down basic principles for the preservation of the health of future generations of man around the world.

Not unconnected with the subject of alcohol and drugs is that of personal cleanliness. As noted earlier, many youth today cultivate slovenliness to demonstrate their break with the values of bourgeois suburbia. To Bahá'ís the break with materialistic values is noble, but this gesture is empty. In the long run cleanliness is a socially desirable habit from the point of view of health and self-respect as is demonstrated by even the most cursory study of the social history of any country. Personal and social cleanliness is important also because it symbolizes something much deeper:

"External cleanliness, although it is but a physical thing, hath a great influence upon spirituality." 'Abdu'l-Bahá.[1]

"When man in all conditions is pure and immaculate, he will become the centre of the reflection of the manifest Light. In all his actions and conduct there must first be purity, then beauty and independence. The channel must be cleansed before it is filled with sweet water. The pure eye comprehendeth the sight and the meeting of God; the pure nostril inhaleth the perfumes of the rose garden of bounty; the pure heart becometh the mirror of the beauty of truth. This is why, in the heavenly Books, the divine counsels and commands have been compared to water. . . . cleanliness and sanctity, purity and delicacy exalt humanity and make the contingent beings progress. Even when applied to physical things, delicacy causeth the attainment of spirituality, as it is established in the Holy Scriptures." 'Abdu'l-Bahá.[2]

Finally, 'Abdu'l-Bahá gave the following advice concerning those two other necessities for a healthy body and a clear mind, sleep and exercise:

"If a man sleep, it should not be for pleasure, but to rest the body in order to do better, to speak better, to explain more

---

[1] Bahá'í World Faith, p. 334 (USA).
[2] Bahá'í World Faith, p. 333 (USA).

beautifully, to serve the servants of God and to prove the truths."[1]

"... *some games are innocent, and if pursued for pastime cause no harm; but there is danger that pastime may degenerate into waste of time. Waste of time is not acceptable in the Cause of God, but recreation which may improve the bodily powers, as exercise, is desirable.*"[2]

[1] Tablets of 'Abdu'l-Bahá, p. 460 (USA).
[2] Bahá'u'lláh and the New Era, p.99 (UK).

CHAPTER IV

THE WAVES OF ONE SEA

A — *Love, Not Prejudice*

IN the last chapter the discussion dealt with the individual finding his relationship with God, with the universe and with himself. This chapter is concerned with the individual coming to terms with his fellow creatures of the human race. Perhaps a useful way for an individual to look at his relationship with others is for him to see it from two points of view: how he should think of others, and how others may think of him.

Bahá'u'lláh said that mankind is one family. For a Bahá'í this is the guiding thought in relating to others.

"Do not be satisfied until each one with whom you are concerned is to you as a member of your family. Regard each one either as a father, or as a brother, or a sister, or as a mother, or as a child. If you can attain to this, your difficulties will vanish; you will know what to do." 'Abdu'l-Bahá.[1]

This guiding thought is given additional meaning when all men and women are thought of as spiritual beings:

"Each sees in the other the Beauty of God reflected in the soul, and finding this point of similarity, they are attracted to one another in love. This love will make all men the waves of one sea." 'Abdu'l-Bahá.[2]

In some the spiritual qualities are more developed than in others:

"The only difference between members of the human family is that of degree. Some are like children who are ignorant and must be educated until they arrive at maturity. Some are like the sick and must be treated with tenderness and care. None are bad or evil! We must not be repelled by these poor children. We must treat them with great kindness, teaching

---

[1] The Pattern of Bahá'í Life, p. 24 (UK).
[2] Paris Talks, pp. 180-181 (UK).

the ignorant and tenderly nursing the sick." 'Abdu'l-Bahá.[1]

To help develop the best in people, Bahá'ís are enjoined to make a point of emphasizing the positive qualities in others and to pass over those characteristics which are negative. Clearly this approach also has a very beneficial effect on the character development of those who put it into practice.

"To be silent concerning the faults of others, to pray for them, and to help them, through kindness, to correct their faults.

"To look always at the good and not at the bad. If a man has ten good qualities and one bad one, to look at the ten and forget the one; and if a man has ten bad qualities and one good one, to look at the one and forget the ten." Abdu'l-Bahá.[2]

In following this principle Bahá'ís will strive to avoid engagement in useless argument. Modelling themselves after the example of 'Abdu'l-Bahá, they will try to do more listening than talking and to bring out in others those ideas which are constructive.

"O Son of Dust! Verily, I say unto thee: Of all men the most negligent is he that disputeth idly and seeketh to advance himself over his brother!" Bahá'u'lláh.[3]

The positive approach if sincerely followed will always have its effect.

"If you desire with all your heart, friendship with every race on earth, your thought, spiritual and positive, will spread; it will become the desire of others, growing stronger and stronger, until it reaches the minds of all men." 'Abdu'l-Bahá.[4]

Bahá'ís are devoted to the unity of mankind but the unity sought is not one of uniformity, but one of diversity. Far from wanting all people to be the same, Bahá'ís glory in the diversity of the human race because they see in that diversity an enrichment of the culture and experience of world society as a whole.

"Consider the flowers of a garden, though differing in

[1] Paris Talks, p. 138 (UK).
[2] Bahá'u'lláh and the New Era, p. 80 (UK).
[3] Hidden Words (Persian), No. 5 (UK).
[4] Paris Talks, pp. 29-30 (UK).

kind, colour, form and shape, yet, inasmuch as they are refreshed by the waters of one spring, revived by the breath of one wind, invigorated by the rays of one sun, this diversity increaseth their charm and addeth unto their beauty. How unpleasing to the eye if all the flowers and plants, the leaves and blossoms, the fruits, the branches and the trees of that garden were all of the same shape and colour! Diversity of hues, form and shape, enricheth and adorneth the garden, and heighteneth the effect thereof. In like manner, when divers shades of thought, temperament and character, are brought together under the power and influence of one central agency, the beauty and glory of human perfection will be revealed and made manifest. Naught but the celestial potency of the Word of God, which ruleth and transcendeth the realities of all things, is capable of harmonizing the divergent thoughts, sentiments, ideas, and convictions of the children of men." 'Abdu'l-Bahá.[1]

All over the world the Bahá'í community is striving to have this principle put into practice. One example is in the Americas, where Bahá'ís are helping Indians rediscover the Indian achievements of the past. In doing so, they encourage the Indians to take a pride in their culture and not to be overwhelmed by the white man with his bustle and technical know-how.

The sufferings which many of the oppressed peoples of the world have undergone have deepened their potential spiritual qualities more than might be the case with others, and Bahá'í Writings indicate they will have a special contribution to make to the spiritual development of the future world society.

"Bahá'u'lláh once compared the coloured people to the black pupil of the eye surrounded by the white. In this black pupil is seen the reflection of that which is before it, and through it the light of the spirit shineth forth." 'Abdu'l-Bahá.[2]

When writing to the American Bahá'í community during the First World War 'Abdu'l-Bahá said:

---

[1] The Advent of Divine Justice, pp. 45-46 (USA).
[2] The Advent of Divine Justice, p. 31 (USA).

"You must attach great importance to the Indians, the original inhabitants of America. For these souls may be likened unto the ancient inhabitants of the Arabian Peninsula, who, prior to the Revelation of Muhammad, were like savages. When the Muhammadan Light shone forth in their midst, they became so enkindled that they shed illumination upon the world. Likewise, should these Indians be educated and properly guided, there can be no doubt that through the Divine teachings they will become so enlightened that the whole earth will be illumined."[1]

Though more and more people the world over, especially amongst the young, are coming to think of mankind as one family there are still many more who are strongly opposed to such ideas. Bahá'ís attribute the absence of a general feeling of brotherhood to widespread prejudice: ignorance and fear of those who are different. 'Abdu'l-Bahá wrote to the Central Organization for a Durable Peace which met at the Hague in 1919 as follows:

". . . As long as these prejudices prevail, the world of humanity will not have rest. For a period of six thousand years history informs us about the world of humanity. During these six thousand years the world of humanity has not been free from war, strife, murder and bloodthirstiness. In every period war has been waged in one country or another and that war was due to either religious prejudice, racial prejudice, political prejudice or patriotic prejudice. It has therefore been ascertained and proved that all prejudices are destructive of the human edifice. As long as these prejudices persist, the struggle for existence must remain dominant, and bloodthirstiness and rapacity continue. Therefore, even as was the case in the past, the world of humanity cannot be saved from the darkness of nature and cannot attain illumination except through the abandonment of prejudices and the acquisition of the morals of the Kingdom."[2]

One of the main tasks of Bahá'ís is to eliminate all such prejudice. This is partly done by the dissemination of

---

[1] The Advent of Divine Justice, p. 46 (USA).

[2] Bahá'í Revelation, p. 210 (UK).

factual information. One example of Bahá'í action in the field of religious prejudice is the strong defence of Islám in the West where, despite the decline of the Christian churches, there is still a strong bias against anything pertaining to Islám — except perhaps for some appreciation of its art. This is of particular interest because among the Muslim clergy are to be found the most persistent, fierce, and unreasoning persecutors of Bahá'ís. Another interesting aspect of Bahá'í action to eliminate religious prejudice is that many Jews have learned to love the figure of Jesus through Bahá'í teachings, a love which they have never acquired from Christians, who have persecuted and vilified the Jewish people for nearly two thousand years.

A second area where the Bahá'ís have been very active in countering prejudice with information is that of race relations. The American Bahá'ís have been conscious for many years that the elimination of racial prejudice is the "most challenging issue" both for the United States and ultimately for the world at large. An example of their efforts to counter racial prejudice with information is a pamphlet* which deals with the common white fears and assumptions concerning the "negroid race". It points out how unscientific is the "average" when dealing with racial groups, especially when specific facts concerning environment are not taken into account. Another point made is that if racists wish to prove that whites are innately more intelligent than blacks because the average white cranial capacity in one survey proved to be fourteen hundred and fifty cubic centimetres as compared with fourteen hundred cubic centimetres for the black, then they would have to concede that whites are inferior in intelligence to the Kaffirs and Amoxosa of Africa, to the Eskimos, Japanese and the Polynesians, all of whom have higher average capacities than the Caucasian. Elsewhere it shows that, other things being equal, an interracial marriage usually produces offspring which are more than normally healthy and vigorous.

The main method of eliminating prejudice, however, is

* 'What is Race' by Glenford E. Mitchell and Daniel C. Jordan (USA).

action not words. Bahá'ís believe that the most effective way of removing fears about people you do not know is to go out and mix with them.

"Wherefore, O my loving friends! Consort with all the peoples, kindreds and religions of the world, with the utmost truthfulness, uprightness, faithfulness, kindliness, goodwill and friendliness; that all the world of being may be filled with the holy ecstasy of the grace of Bahá, that ignorance, enmity, hate and rancour may vanish from the world and the darkness of estrangement amidst the peoples and kindreds of the world may give way to the Light of Unity."
'Abdu'l-Bahá.[1]

In conventional society the majority only mix on a voluntary basis with their peers: one has for instance only to look at housing patterns in any city to see that the rich live with the rich, the poor with the poor, the white with the white and so on. In their social lives it is the same, as is shown in membership of societies and clubs, the playing of games and in other social activities. How often do white middle-class Americans socialize on a regular and voluntary basis with their fellow citizens from the poor black areas? Can one imagine the upper middle-class British family from the "best" part of Surrey mixing happily with working class people from Lancashire! "But we have nothing in common to discuss," goes up the familiar defence!

In the Bahá'í world it is very different. Bahá'ís of every conceivable background meet together regularly in a loving and constructive atmosphere at local, regional, national and international conferences. The feeling of security and love, the sense of belonging to a great family working in unity toward the most magnificent goals, helps those who at first may be wary, coming as they do from conventional old world society, sometimes dragging in with them for a time some of their old fears and misconceptions, to withstand the initial shock of a different culture, for that is usually the problem, to find it is not quite as bad as expected, to see it has some merit, to understand that it has great beauty which has perhaps universal relevance, to be glad that

[1] Bahá'í Revelation. p. 313 (UK).

74

mankind has so much diversity and colour. One of the greatest pleasures the writer has experienced occurred soon after he became a Bahá'í, when he attended a Bahá'í regional conference and saw not only blacks and whites mixing together like true brothers and sisters — for this he had seen at local meetings earlier — not only the most educated in earnest discussion with those with little or no formal education, but some frail looking old ladies in feathered hats quite at home in consultation and fun with a group of the most formidable-looking long-haired and bearded students one could hope to meet. So much for the gap between generations! A variation on this theme is not only the coming together of people of different cultures, who find they have a much greater common culture, but the loving acceptance of many who in outside society are rejected as misfits or eccentrics. It is one of the glories of the Bahá'í Faith that the otherwise lost and lonely can find in it a home and a shelter. The Bahá'í Faith is for all peoples, every man, woman and child.

"Know ye not why We created you all from the same dust? That no one should exalt himself over the other. Ponder at all times in your hearts how ye were created. Since We have created you all from one same substance it is incumbent on you to be even as one soul, to walk with the same feet, eat with the same mouth and dwell in the same land, that from your inmost being, by your deeds and actions, the signs of oneness and the essence of detachment may be made manifest." Bahá'u'lláh.[1]

The experience of being members of one great diverse family is strengthened by other aspects of the Bahá'í way of life. Telling others about the Bahá'í Faith, having one's home an open house (see next chapter) visiting other homes are all actions which advance one's spiritual education. Typical is the work now being done by Bahá'ís amongst poor black people of the rural South of the United States. The give and take in the cultural coming together has been truly life-giving. Bahá'ís of all backgrounds have been regularly in homes which are little more than wooden

[1] Hidden Words (Arabic), No. 68 (UK).

shacks, sometimes containing barely enough fuel to last the winter. As a result they have understood in a deeper way than ever before Bahá'u'lláh's teaching on detachment from material possessions: how could they ever again be concerned about fancy new cars or houses after having seen such grinding poverty in their own family — and to have witnessed nevertheless such a cheerful spirit. Nor will they ever forget that such cruel poverty is allowed to exist side by side with the most blatant opulence in this, the richest and "most democratic" country in the world. If this is the best that such a country can do then it is confirmed as never before that the world is indeed in desperate need of a radical change in its values and methods.

The sense of world community is further strengthened when Bahá'ís travel all over the world, as they are encouraged to do, serving and meeting with other communities, bringing and receiving experiences and ideas. When Bahá'ís travel they know that in just about every country they can expect to be greeted as old friends by persons they may never have met before. The community spirit is also nurtured by newsletters and other communications which are designed to let every Bahá'í know is happening in all parts of the Bahá'í world.

Though more precise with reference to particular issues of this age such as racial and religious bigotry, these principles and practices are clearly in keeping with the teachings of Jesus and the other great Educators of the past. What is significant is the fact that a worldwide community is making a serious attempt to live up to such standards.

B — *The Qualities of Attraction*

It was suggested at the beginning of this chapter that the second way of thinking of our relationship with others, is to imagine how they might see us. The Bahá'í view is that it is not sufficient to have a sense of love and respect for our fellow human beings. This love must be reflected in our own character as well as in our views. If we wish to be loved by others we should not make it difficult for them. It is our responsibility to make ourselves worthy of that love.

"... *Let him, before all else, teach his own self, that his speech may attract the hearts of them that hear him. Unless he teacheth his own self, the words of his mouth will not influence the heart of the seeker.*" Bahá'u'lláh.[1]

The basis for a sound relationship between two parties is trust. It should be the ambition therefore of every man who wants a new just society to make himself worthy of others' trust.

"... *Show ye an endeavour that all the nations and communities of the world, even the enemies, put their trust, assurance and hope in you; that if a person falls into errors for a hundred-thousand times he may yet turn his face to you, hopeful that you will forgive his sins; for he must not become hopeless, neither grieved nor despondent.*" 'Abdu'l-Bahá.[2]

The first requirement in obtaining the trust of others is truthfulness.

"*Truthfulness is the foundation of all the virtues of the world of humanity. Without truthfulness, progress and success in all the worlds of God are impossible for a soul. When this holy attribute is established in man, all the divine qualities will also become realized.*" 'Abdu'l-Bahá.[3]

Today the lie pervades all aspects of society. Many governments deceive those whom they rule and are accordingly mistrusted. In many parts of the world the public is incessantly bombarded with commercial advertisements, the claims of which are at best half-true, and frequently completely false or nonsequitur. When deceit is on such a vast scale society begins to lose its grasp of reality — even the deceivers themselves become confused by their own words, and life itself begins to wither. Progress cannot be made because there is no foundation on which to build.

Another prerequisite of trust is honesty.

"... *enjoineth on you honesty and piety. Blessed the city that shineth by their light. Through them man is exalted,*

---

[1] Gleanings, p. 276 (UK).
[2] Tablets of 'Abdu'l Bahá, Vol. II, P. 436 (USA).
[3] Bahá'í World Faith, p. 384 (USA).

and the door of security is unlocked before the face of all creation." Bahá'u'lláh.[1]

As noted in the first chapter, present-day standards of honesty are indeed low. This is not just a simple matter of crime rates, but of bribery and corruption in public administration, shoddy goods, poor service, and exorbitant prices in commerce, and the dishonest activity of much of private life. Whilst there is so much dishonesty there can be no genuine trust between men. If there is no trust there is little chance of a just society.

Trust can be readily given only to a person who is upright, faithful, reliable, sincere. How frequent in present-day society are the hollow words of friendship, which are not supported by acts of friendship, or the easily made promises which are never kept.

"The essence of faith is fewness of words and abundance of deeds; he whose words exceed his deeds, know verily that his death is better than his life." Bahá'u'lláh.[2]

"Take heed, O people, lest ye be of them that give good counsel to others but forget to follow it themselves." Bahá'u'lláh.[3]

A strong and fruitful relationship between two parties requires more than trust, important as this is. Needed in addition are the qualities of warmth such as kindliness, compassion, courtesy and generosity — in short, concern for the welfare and feelings of others.

"O Son of Spirit! My first counsel is this: Possess a pure, kindly and radiant heart, that thine may be a sovereignty ancient, imperishable and everlasting." Bahá'u'lláh.[4]

Kindliness and gentleness are amongst the most rewarding of qualities for they bring an immediate sense of well-being and warmth to both giver and receiver.

"A kindly tongue is the lodestone of the hearts of men. It is the bread of the spirit, it clotheth the words with meaning, it

---

[1] Epistle to the Son of the Wolf, p. 23 (USA).
[2] The Reality of Man, p. 4 (USA).
[3] Gleanings, p. 276 (UK).
[4] Hidden Words (Arabic), No. 1 (UK).

is the fountain of the light of wisdom and understanding."
Bahá'u'lláh.[1]

Closely related to kindliness is compassion, the particular concern for those who have had misfortune.

"Happiness is a great healer to those who are ill. In the east it is the custom to call upon the patient often and meet him individually. The people in the east show the utmost kindness and compassion to the sick and the suffering. This has greater effect than the remedy itself. You must always have this thought of love and affection when you are visiting the ailing and afflicted." 'Abdu'l-Bahá.[2]

Compassion should be felt not only for those who have had misfortune but also for those who may have done wrong. 'Abdu'l-Bahá pointed out that:

"Among the teachings of Bahá'u'lláh is one requiring man, under all conditions and circumstances, to be forgiving, to love his enemy and to consider an ill-wisher as a well-wisher. Not that one should consider another as an enemy and then put up with him ... and be forbearing toward him. This is hypocrisy and not real love. Nay, rather you must see your enemies as friends, your ill-wishers as well-wishers and treat them accordingly. Your love and kindness must be real ... not merely forbearance, for forbearance, if not of the heart, is hypocrisy."[3]

Bahá'ís are forbidden gossip or backbiting because this is considered one of the most unkind, indeed savage, acts that one human being can inflict on another.

". . . For the tongue is a smouldering fire, and excess of speech a deadly poison. Material fire consumeth the body, whereas the fire of the tongue devoureth both heart and soul. The force of the former lasteth but for a time, whilst the effects of the latter endure a century.

"Backbiting quencheth the light of the heart, and extinguisheth the life of the soul." Bahá'u'lláh.[4]

"Remember above all the teaching of Bahá'u'lláh concerning gossip and unseemly talk about others. Stories

---

[1] Gleanings, p. 288 (UK).
[2] Promulgation of Universal Peace, p. 199 (USA).
[3] Bahá'u'lláh and the New Era, p. 79 (UK).
[4] Book of Certitude, p. 193 (USA).

repeated about others are seldom good. A silent tongue is safest. Even good may be harmful if spoken at the wrong time or to the wrong person." 'Abdu'l-Bahá.[1]

Gossip can only thrive where there is an audience. It is therefore incumbent on a Bahá'í not to listen to gossip as well as not to speak it.

The strain and frustration of living in modern society has caused a decline in the regard for courtesy as a virtue. Some maintain that courtesies are old fashioned, suffocating mannerisms which must be swept away as being of no relevance. Yet courtesy is really an aspect of kindliness: small every day acts of refinement which show a concern for the feelings of others.

"O people of God! I exhort you to courtesy. Courtesy is in the primary station, the lord of all virtues. Blessed is he who is illumined with the light of courtesy, and is adorned with the mantle of uprightness! He who is endowed with courtesy is endowed with a great station." Bahá'u'lláh.[2]

One of the most unpleasant and common manifestations of discourtesy is the habit of looking down on the views of others: the middle-aged snorting at the "nonsense" of the young, the young contemptuously dismissing the archaic sermons of their elders, the social snob, and now, everywhere, the intellectual snob — the expert who believes he knows it all and is required to speak civilly only to his peers. How much unkindness is implied by that euphemism — he did not suffer fools gladly — a characteristic which it seems we half admire.

Beware! Beware! Lest ye hurt any soul!

Beware! Beware! Lest ye deal unkindly toward any person!

Beware! Beware! Lest ye be the cause of hoplessness to any creature!

Should one become the cause of grief to any one heart, or of despondency to any one soul, it were better to hide oneself in the lowest depths of the earth than to walk upon the earth." 'Abdu'l-Bahá.[3]

---

[1] The Pattern of Bahá'í Life, p. 31 (UK).

[2] Bahá'í World Faith, p. 175 (USA).

[3] Bahá'u'lláh and the New Era, p. 78 (UK).

Another common example of discourtesy is bad language and abuse. In recent years foul language has been the fashion with pseudo-progressive intellectuals to show how liberated they are from bourgeois cant. Such gestures are not edifying and bring down rather than raise up the spirit of man.

"Defile not the tongue with cursing or execrating anyone and guard your eyes against that which is not worthy." Bahá'u'lláh.[1]

The warm-hearted person, the man of kindliness and of concern for others, will show it in generosity and charity. A sign of spiritual maturity is the degree to which we are attached to the well being of others rather than to our own material possessions.

"Blessed is he who prefers his brother before himself: such a one is of the people of Bahá." Bahá'u'lláh.[2]

"The poor in your midst are My trust; guard ye My trust, and be not intent only on your own ease." Bahá'u'lláh.[3]

"They who are possessed of riches, however, must have the utmost regard for the poor, for great is the honour destined by God for those poor who are steadfast in patience . . . and well is it with the rich who bestow their riches on the needy and prefer them before themselves." Bahá'u'lláh.[4]

It should be added that our concern should not stop at our fellow human beings. As the most intelligent and powerful creatures on earth we have grave responsibilities to protect all living things. Animals may only be killed in self-protection or to meet our genuine needs for food and clothing, and even then there must be no cruelty.

"Ye must not only have kind and merciful feelings for mankind, but ye should also exercise the utmost kindness toward every living creature. The physical sensibilities and instincts are common to animal and man. Man is, however, negligent of this reality and imagines that sensibility is peculiar to mankind, therefore he practises cruelty to the animal. In reality what difference is there in physical

---

[1] Bahá'í World Faith, p. 196 (USA).
[2] Bahá'í World Faith, p. 185 (USA).
[3] Hidden Words (Arabic), No. 54 (UK).
[4] Gleanings, p. 201 (UK).

sensations! Sensibility is the same whether you harm man or animal: there is no difference. Nay, rather, cruelty to the animal is more painful because man has a tongue and he sighs, complains and groans when he receives an injury and complains to the government and the government protects him from cruelty; but the poor animal cannot speak, it can neither show its suffering nor is it able to appeal to the government. If it is harmed a thousand times by man it is not able to defend itself in words nor can it seek justice or retaliate. Therefore one must be very considerate toward animals and show greater kindness to them than to man. Educate the children in their infancy in such a way that they may become exceedingly kind and merciful to the animals. If an animal is sick they should endeavour to cure it; if it is hungry, they should feed it; if it is thirsty, they should satisfy its thirst; if it is tired, they should give it rest." 'Abdu'l-Bahá.[1]

Not many societies today live up to these standards. For instance Western countries spend millions on pampering domestic animals but find it amusing to hunt and cruelly kill innocent wild animals for no other reason than the pleasure of the chase, and the "colour of it all". They ruthlessly kill millions of other animals to provide luxurious clothing for those with too much money and too little sensibility.

C — Service to Others

The teachings of the Bahá'í Faith concerning man's relationship with God, himself, and his fellowmen come to ultimate fruition, not in words or attitudes, but in action. A man fulfils himself in his work, which is an act of creation. Bahá'ís view an act of creation as prayer, a means of expressing appreciation of our existence. It follows that we should take the greatest pride and care in every piece of work we do, no matter how humble. Cleaning a street is just as much an act of creation when done with care and pride, as the administration of a giant industrial complex, or the designing of a beautiful building, or the writing of a poem.

Work becomes a burden when no pride is taken in it and it is seen only as a way of earning our living or of acquiring property and power.

"Ye are the trees of My garden; ye must give forth goodly and wondrous fruits, that ye yourselves and others may profit therefrom. Thus it is incumbent on every one to engage in crafts and professions, for therein lies the secret of wealth, O men of understanding." Bahá'u'lláh.[1]

"It is made incumbent on every one of you to engage in some occupation such as arts, trades, and the like. We have made this — your occupation — identical with the worship of God, the True One. . . .

"Waste not your time in idleness and indolence, and occupy yourselves with that which will profit yourselves and others beside yourself. . . . The most despised of men before God is he who sits and begs." Bahá'u'lláh.[2]

But Bahá'í teachings go further. What gives work real meaning is when it is done in the service of others. The highest station which man can achieve is when he is serving humanity.

". . . The people of God must . . . be busied in whatever may be conducive to the betterment of the world and the education of its peoples . . .

"They who are the people of God have no ambition except to revive the world, to ennoble its life and regenerate its peoples." Bahá'u'lláh.[3]

'Abdu'l-Bahá said:

"In the Bahá'í Cause arts, sciences and all crafts are counted as worship. The man who makes a piece of notepaper to the best of his ability, conscientiously, concentrating all his forces on perfecting it, is giving praise to God. Briefly, all effort and exertion put forth by man from the fulness of his heart is worship, if it is prompted by the highest motives and the will to do service to humanity. This is worship: to serve mankind and to minister to the needs of the people. Service is prayer. A physician ministering to the sick, gently, tenderly,

---

[1] Bahá'u'lláh and the New Era, p. 76 (UK).
[2] Bahá'í World Faith, p. 195 (USA).
[3] Gleanings, p. 269 (UK).
[4] Bahá'u'lláh and the New Era, p. 77 (UK).

free from prejudice, and believing in the solidarity of the human race, is giving praise."[1]

It is one of the more encouraging signs of our times that young people in the rich countries have turned against those values of their elders which place so much emphasis on personal acquisition of material riches. They are looking for ways of contributing to the public good; of serving their fellowmen. It is interesting to note in this context the views attributed to Viktor Frankl, one of the many outstanding psychiatrists to come from Vienna:

"Human beings hunger for meaning, especially Americans whose supply is already dangerously low. A few years ago, catchy experiences like "self-realization" or "self-encounter" were big, until some busy selves saw how little interiority they had to realize or encounter. Going inside oneself for the answers to life is perhaps the hollowest answer of all, since often only hollowness is run into. Instead, meaninglessness, according to Frankl, is best cured by going outside, extending the self rather than contracting it, in service to others, in upholding a value, in embracing suffering positively rather than negatively. The decisions of attitude that a person makes are often more crucial to mental health than the conditions he makes them in, whether Germany 1941 or anywhere 1971."[2]

Like many other young people, but probably with a greater consciousness of what they are doing, and certainly with more clearly defined goals, Bahá'í youth are more and more entering such necessary fields of service to humanity as medicine, agriculture, education and social work and those professions concerned with the preservation and improvement of our environment.

Such service can be made more effective the more skills a person has, and it is one of the basic principles of the Bahá'í Faith to encourage education as much as possible in those sciences which will increase the capacity for service, as well as in the moral teachings provided by religion.

"To acquire knowledge is incumbent on all, but of those

[1] Bahá'u'lláh and the New Era, p. 77 (UK).

[2] Colman McCarthy; *Viktor Frankl, the Value of Meaning,* No. XII in series Thinkers & Their Thoughts, *Washington Post* 1971.

sciences which may profit the people of the earth, and not such sciences as begin in mere words, and end in mere words. The possessors of sciences and arts have a great right among the people of the world." Bahá'u'lláh.[1]

Service to mankind is particularly meritorious when it involves sacrifice. In Bahá'í Writings sacrifice is shown as a beneficial act, contributing to the spiritual growth and detachment of both giver and receiver. Sacrifice is the real test of sincerity. It is the test of whether one is willing to put conscious standards, hopes and ideals before personal comfort. Too often those who talk of a brave new world are those who want others to make the sacrifices. The man who sacrifices for others is a man indeed! This is morality.

D — *The Standard*

The most appropriate way to summarize this chapter is to quote a passage each from Bahá'u'lláh and 'Abdu'l-Bahá in which They describe those qualities which will make a new race of men who in turn will build a new world society.

"*Be generous in prosperity, and thankful in adversity. Be worthy of the trust of thy neighbour, and look upon him with a bright and friendly face. Be a treasure to the poor, an admonisher to the rich, an answerer of the cry of the needy, a preserver of the sanctity of thy pledge. Be fair in thy judgment, and guarded in thy speech. Be unjust to no man, and show all meekness to all men. Be as a lamp unto them that walk in darkness, a joy to the sorrowful, a sea for the thirsty, a haven for the distressed, an upholder and defender of the victim of oppression. Let integrity and uprightness distinguish all thine acts. Be a home for the stranger, a balm to the suffering, a tower of strength for the fugitive. Be eyes to the blind, and a guiding light unto the feet of the erring. Be an ornament to the countenance of truth, a crown to the brow of fidelity, a pillar of the temple of righteousness, a breath of life to the body of mankind, an ensign of the hosts of justice, a luminary above the horizon of virtue, a dew to the soil of the human heart, an ark on the ocean of knowledge,*

[1] Bahá'í World Faith, p. 189 (USA).

a sun in the heaven of bounty, a gem on the diadem of wisdom, a shining light in the firmament of thy generation, a fruit upon the tree of humility." Bahá'u'lláh.[1]

"*For you I desire spiritual distinction; that is, you must become eminent and distinguished in morals. In the love of God you must become distinguished from all else. You must become distinguished for loving humanity; for unity and accord; for love and justice. In brief, you must become distinguished in all the virtues of the human world; for faithfulness and sincerity; for justice and fidelity; for firmness and steadfastness; for philanthropic deeds and service to the human world; for love toward every human being; for unity and accord with all people; for removing prejudices and promoting international peace. Finally, you must become distinguished for heavenly illumination and acquiring the bestowals of God. I desire this distinction for you. This must be the point of distinction among you.*" 'Abdu'l-Bahá.[2]

---

[1] Gleanings, p. 284 (UK).
[2] Promulgation of Universal Peace, p. 185 (USA).

CHAPTER V

A NEW FAMILY LIFE

A — *The Equality of Men and Women*

THE Bahá'í view is that there are two essential requirements for the establishment of a just society where all will have the opportunity to find a fruitful and meaningful life. The first is a commitment by the individual to think and live according to the highest moral principles, that is, the creation of a new race of men. The second is a completely new system of institutions which will give expression to, shape and strengthen the aspirations of such a race of men.

So far the discussion has dealt with the qualities in individual men and women which will make for a more just society. It is now time to say something of institutions which are also required. The oldest, strongest and most basic of all social relationships is the family. In recent years the family as an institution has been questioned because it has all too often forced people to live together in a narrow inward looking atmosphere where there is little love and much oppression. Bahá'ís believe that when a family is based on sound moral and spiritual principles it will make an invaluable contribution to the development of all concerned; husband, wife, parents, children, and to society as a whole. The contribution of the family is an essential element in the development of a just society and it is believed that there is no substitute for it. It seems therefore appropriate to say something of the Bahá'í concept of the family before passing on to the wider institutions of society.

The last chapter discussed Bahá'í teachings on equality between all members of the human race. This theme permeates the idea of the Bahá'í family. Of particular importance is belief in the equality of men and women — one of the basic principles of the Bahá'í Faith. Women, in some respects, have different areas of capacity than men and a distinctive viewpoint; partly, of course, as a result of upbringing, but partly also from the very difference in physical make-up and their unique function in society. The capacity and the contribution they can make to the general good of society are just as important as the capacity and contribution men make. Consequently, when women are prevented from reaching their full potential, society is thrown off balance and suffers accordingly.

"The happiness of mankind will be realized when women and men coordinate and advance equally, for each is the complement and helpmeet of the other." 'Abdu'l-Bahá.[1]

It is the purpose of Bahá'í teachings to ensure that women play their full role in society and that they find a true pride in their femininity. Bahá'ís believe that women should be given equal legal rights with men, equal social treatment and respect, and equal opportunities, and they should have equal hearing in councils of government.

'Abdu'l-Bahá said that the key to achieving equality for women in society was to ensure that their education was the same as for men. In fact, He went further and said that in view of the critical part women played in the raising of children, the generation of the future, their education should be given the higher priority. The following extract from a talk He gave in 1912 at Philadelphia is representative of many talks given in the West on this subject:

"In proclaiming the oneness of mankind, He (Bahá'u'lláh) taught that men and women were equal in the sight of God and there is no distinction to be made between them. The only difference between them now is due to lack of education and training. If woman is given equal opportunity of education, distinction and estimate of inferiority will disappear. The world of humanity has two wings as it were, one is the female, the other is the male. If one wing be defective the strong perfect wing will not be capable of flight. The world of humanity has two hands. If one be imperfect, the capable hand is restricted and unable to perform its duties. God is the creator of mankind. He has endowed both sexes with perfections and intelligence, given them physical

[1] Bahá'í World Faith, p. 241 (USA).

members and organs of sense, without differentiation or distinction as to superiority; therefore why should woman be considered inferior? This is not according to the plan and justice of God. He has created them equal; in His estimate there is no question of sex. The one whose heart is purest, whose deeds are most perfect, is acceptable to God, male or female . . . Furthermore, the education of women is of greater importance than the eduation of men, for they are the mothers of the race and mothers rear the children. The first teachers of children are the mothers. Therefore they must be capably trained in order to educate both sons and daughters. There are many provisions in the words of Bahá'u'lláh in regard to this.

He promulgated the adoption of the same course of education for man and woman. Daughters and sons must follow the same curriculum of study, thereby promoting unity of the sexes. When all mankind shall receive the same opportunity of education and the equality of men and women be realized, the foundations of war will be utterly destroyed. Without equality this will be impossible because all differences and distinction are conducive to discord and strife. Equality between men and women is conducive to the abolition of warfare for the reason that women will never be willing to sanction it. Mothers will not give their sons as sacrifices upon the battlefield after twenty years of anxiety and loving devotion in rearing them from infancy, no matter what cause they are called upon to defend. There is no doubt that when women obtain equality of rights war will entirely cease among mankind."[1]

At another time He said:

"The world in the past has been ruled by force, and man has dominated over woman by reason of his more forceful and aggressive qualities both of body and mind. But the balance is already shifting; force is losing its dominance, and mental alertness, intuition, and the spiritual qualities of love and service, in which woman is strong, are gaining ascendancy. Hence the new age will be an age less masculine and more permeated with the feminine ideals, or to speak more

---

[1] Promulgation of Universal Peace, pp. 169-170 (USA).

exactly, will be an age in which the masculine and feminine elements of civilization will be more evenly balanced."[1]

These principles apply both in society at large and within the family. Though a man and a woman may not necessarily perform the same functions in the day-to-day life of the family, there should be equal treatment and the affairs of the family should be conducted on the basis of consultation giving equal consideration to the views of both men and women.

It is of interest to note that the teaching concerning equality of men and women was one cause for the antagonism with which the Faith was often greeted by the ignorant and prejudiced in its early years in Persia. Fifty years before the suffragette movement became a force in the West, a young woman named Ṭáhirih, who has subsequently been recognized as one of the great poets of Persian literature practised the new teachings in the face of a fiercely hostile society and eventually lost her life for her beliefs (see Chapter eight).

B — *Marriage*

The core of the family is marriage. In Bahá'í Writings it is said that the first purpose of marriage is procreation and the raising of children: in short, the continuation of the species. But this is not all. It is also an instrument for the spiritual development of all members of the family, living together in intimacy with persons of a different sex and different age groups, learning to appreciate the beauty in the variety of life, and learning the responsibilities of protecting the young and weak. The Bahá'í concept of marriage is therefore much more than a legal contract between two individuals. It is more a social and spiritual contract covering all members of the family.

Bahá'u'lláh described the Bahá'í marriage laws as *"a fortress for well being and salvation."*[2] The qualities and experiences of marriage and the family are of the utmost

---

[1] Bahá'u'lláh and the New Era, p. ,141 (UK).
[2] Bahá'í Prayers, p. 44, Section Two (UK).

importance in learning how to live in the wider family of the community of the human race.

"If love and agreement are manifest in a single family, that family will advance, become illumined and spiritual; but if enmity and hatred exist within it destruction and dispersion are inevitable ... When love is realized and the ideal spiritual bonds unite the hearts of men, the whole human race will be uplifted, the world will continually grow more spiritual and radiant and the happiness and tranquility of mankind be immeasurably increased." 'Abdu'l-Bahá.[1]

Marriage and the family should provide an open home for the community, a haven and a place of love for all, including those who are deprived and lost. This is the outward-looking family giving every opportunity for the spiritual growth of its members, and of those who visit it. This is the family setting the example of how a community should be.

So rewarding are the fruits of marriage for the individual and for society in general that Bahá'u'lláh said that all should marry if they are able and can find the right partner. He specifically deplored professional celibacy which, though never advocated by any of the great Educators, has become nevertheless a tradition in many religions.

"... Seclude not yourselves in churches and cloisters: come forth by My leave and occupy yourselves with that which will profit your souls and the souls of men ... Enter ye into wedlock, that some one may fill your place...." Bahá'u'lláh.[2]

In the past there were circumstances, as was recognized by Muhammad when polygamous marriages might be necessary in the interest of society because strife had so upset the natural balance in numbers between men and women that there was an overriding need for the protection of women and for an increase in population. However, as man progresses and a peaceful balanced society is established, monogamy becomes the most satisfactory basis for the family, for only then can there be real equality between

---

[1] Bahá'í World Faith, p. 229 (USA).
[2] Bahá'u'lláh and the New Era, p. 163 (UK).

man and woman.* Monogamy is a logical biological unit for the human species as such a union is best made for the full development of the complementary qualities of the marriage partners and for the provision of a stable, balanced, responsible and loving background for the rearing of children — the only sort of background which can give a child a true sense of identity. If, as happens in some societies, a man who already has several wives becomes a Bahá'í he is not obliged to divorce any of them. He must undertake, however, to do his best to assure equality of treatment within his household.

A monogamous marriage does not mean a narrow family. The Bahá'í family is much more than just parents and children. Every effort should be made to keep vigorous the ties with the wider family: grandparents, cousins and, as suggested earlier, the other members of the community. Grandparents often have a special relationship with children because they have become perhaps less active and more reflective, and are happy to talk to children of their own childhood. Their very presence strengthens awareness of the rights of all members of the family.

"According to the teachings of Bahá'u'lláh, the family being a human unit must be educated according to the rules of sanctity. All the virtues must be taught the family. The integrity of the family bond must be constantly considered and the rights of the individual members must not be transgressed. The rights of the son, the father, the mother, none of them must be transgressed, none of them must be arbitrary. Just as the son has certain obligations to his father, the father likewise has certain obligations to his son. The mother, the sister and other members of the household have their certain prerogatives. All these rights and prerogatives must be conserved, yet the unity of the family must be sustained. The injury of one shall be considered the injury of all; the comfort of each the comfort of all; the honour of one the honour of all." 'Abdu'l-Bahá.[1]

Marriage is the most important relationship in the

* The Bahá'í Faith is the first of the world's religions to specifically lay down monogamy as the only basis for marriage. It will be recalled that Jesus did not mention this subject.

[1] Promulgation of Universal Peace, p. 163 (USA).

92

average person's life insofar as it is the most long lasting and the most intimate. The opportunities which it offers are indeed rewarding, but such opportunities do not come without the deepest commitment. One of the most important tests of marriage is learning to consult together in a fruitful manner. The partners should recognize their own weaknesses and determine to put them right. They should at the same time make a full commitment to make it as easy as possible for the spouse to overcome his or her limitations. When a marriage is fully based on consultation of this sort there will be less chance of painful confrontations, nagging or trials to place blame for past events. Prayer plays a most important role in developing the most constructive attitudes in marriage because it lifts the spirit to a higher plane of detachment and perspective. Rúḥíyyih Rabbani, widow of Shoghi Effendi, has given the following most realistic advice on what is required to achieve a successful marriage:

"Do not expect too much of marriage, or too little. Water cannot rise above its own level. Your union cannot produce more than you two contribute to it. If you are full of imperfections, intolerant, impatient, exacting, dictatorial, suspicious, short-tempered, selfish, do not imagine that these characteristics are going to make your marriage happy or that by changing your partner a new union will be more successful! Marriage, like all our other relationships in life, is a process which, among other things, serves to grind the sharp edges off us. The grinding often hurts, the adjustment to another person's character is difficult at first, that is why love is needed here more than in any other relationship. Love, being essentially a divine force, binds; it leaps like a spark the gap between people's thoughts and conflicting desires, between perhaps widely different temperaments. It heals the wounds we all inflict on each other whether inadvertently or in moments of rage, jealousy or spite. To the influence of love in marriage is gradually added another powerful catalyst: habit. The common home, the daily association, produces a common framework, and habit, one of the most powerful forces in life, begins to knit husband and wife together. It acts

as a wonderful stabilizer; if love is allowed to fail, habit itself may be strong enough to preserve the union."[1]

As marriage is such an important relationship, Bahá'ís place great emphasis on careful choice of a marriage partner. The Bahá'í view is that this involves becoming thoroughly acquainted with both one's own character and that of the proposed partner, so that both can be assured that there is the required maturity of outlook for marriage on both sides.

"They must show forth the utmost attention and become informed of one another's character . . . if the union is merely from the physical point of view unquestionably it is temporal and at the end separation is inevitable.

"Consequently when the people of Bahá desire to enter the sacred union of marriage, eternal connection and ideal relationship, spiritual and physical association of thoughts and conceptions of life must exist between them." 'Abdu'l-Bahá.[2]

A person who is mature enough for marriage will be loyal, faithful, honest and trustworthy in all dealings with others; will be of a generous, not a jealous, possessive or domineering spirit; will be ready to work hard and will have a balanced attitude on family economics, being neither wasteful nor overly concerned about saving every penny for the future. Such a person will have the strength to handle the hard as well as the easy times of life.

"Anybody can be happy in the state of comfort, ease, health, success, pleasure and joy, but if one will be happy and contented in the time of trouble, hardship and prevailing disease, it is the proof of nobility." 'Abdu'l-Bahá.[3]

A good sign of maturity is a sense of humour and an ability to laugh *with* others, not *at* others. A marriage relationship has the best chance of success if each partner is appreciative, sensitive and fundamentally at one with himself or herself.

Such a careful approach to marriage is not always easy in present-day Western society. Conventional romantic prac-

[1] Prescription for Living, by Rúḥíyyih Rabbani, p. 69, George Ronald, London, 1950.
[2] Bahá'í World Faith, pp. 372-373 (USA).
[3] Bahá'í World Faith, p. 363 (USA).

tice tends to throw two young people together more or less by themselves and almost inevitably an undue and artificial emphasis is placed on physical relationships, an occurrence which is made all the more likely by current values. What is learnt about the character and spiritual qualities of the other person is often shallow and incomplete because each seeks to present an attractive front which the other is all too ready to accept and, in any case, has little real opportunity to verify.

A Bahá'í will often find a marriage partner within the Bahá'í community where there are no artificial or unhealthy pressures and where there are opportunities to see possible partners working and relating to others in a relaxed but highly motivated setting. Clearly for a Bahá'í to marry another Bahá'í has many advantages, giving as it does family unity on the raising of children and the general purpose of life.

If the partner is found within the Bahá'í community there is quite a strong possibility, the community being as diverse as it is, that he or she will be of another class, nation or race. Though in present-day society this may present particular tests which should be realistically assessed before making a decision, there is nothing to prevent such a union — on the contrary, it is to be welcomed as a positive demonstration of the Bahá'í belief in the unity of mankind.

"If it be possible, gather together these two races, black and white, into one Assembly, and put such love into their hearts that they shall not only unite but even inter-marry. Be sure that the result of this will abolish differences and disputes between black and white." 'Abdu'l-Bahá.[1]

When a marriage partner has been found Bahá'í Writings call for certain conditions to be observed before the marriage takes place. The intent of these conditions is to ensure as far as possible a sound basis for marriage. First, it is required that the free consent of both partners to the proposed marriage be given.

"First you must select one (a marriage partner), and then it depends on the consent of the father and mother. Before

[1] Bahá'í World Faith, p. 359 (USA).

your selection they have no right of interference."
'Abdu'l-Bahá.[1]

To a Westerner this may seem a little unnecessary. However, it should be remembered again that the Bahá'í Faith is for the whole world, and in many societies marriages are still arranged by families without reference to those who are to be married. Secondly, it is required that consent be given to the marriage by all of the living (and mentally capable) parents of the couple.*

"As We desired to bring about love and friendship and the unity of the people, therefore, We made it conditional upon the consent of the parents also, that enmity and ill feeling might be avoided." Bahá'u'lláh.[2]

This requirement lays the basis for unity within the marriage itself and the larger family, too, and is a way of making use of the often sound and more detached judgment of those who love but who are not so passionately involved. Bahá'í parents are enjoined to take this duty very seriously.

"When the parents are Bahá'ís they should, of course, act objectively in withholding or granting their approval. They cannot evade this responsibility by merely acquiescing into their child's wish . . . ."[3]

Sometimes, of course, this condition can result in long delays in the marriage, but if the intended partners really are sure of themselves they will endure and most likely the parents, impressed with such standards, will eventually see that their reservations were unnecessary. This law has served to educate the parents as well as the intended partners to a higher spiritual level, as has been shown, for instance, in those cases where parents who are not Bahá'ís have at first refused an inter-racial marriage out of prejudice, overt or otherwise, and then have relented when they have seen the stalwart spiritual strength of the intended partners in face of this severe test. The feeling of family unity which comes from this requirement of

[1] Tablets of 'Abdu'l-Bahá, p. 563.

* In informing parents who are not Bahá'ís of this requirement it is made clear that their consent will not be read in any way to imply approval of the Bahá'í Faith, as such.

[2] Bahá'u'lláh and the New Era, p. 164 (UK).

[3] Letter of Universal House of Justice, dated February 1, 1968. The Universal House of Justice is today the supreme body of the Bahá'í Faith (see chapter six).

Bahá'u'lláh contrasts with the frequent bitterness and shallowness of marriages which in conventional society are forced through against the wishes of the parents.

A Bahá'í who wishes to marry must have a Bahá'í ceremony to ensure that the Bahá'í conditions of marriage are carried out. If he does not he is breaking Bahá'í law and as a result will be deprived of certain rights as a member of the community. The conditions for the Bahá'í marriage ceremony itself are very simple. There should be at least two witnesses who are acceptable to the Local Spiritual Assembly or the National Spiritual Assembly as appropriate (see Chapter six for a description of Bahá'í administration). It should be dignified and before completion the bride and bridegroom shall each repeat the vow:

"We will all, verily, abide by the Will of God."[1]

This vow clearly emphasizes the wide responsibilities of marriage and that neither partner is subject to the other but that both will strive to follow a much higher law. If the marriage requires a second ceremony, because of the requirements of the local government, or because one partner is not a Bahá'í, then both ceremonies must take place on the same day. In some countries, the civil law requires that the legally recognized ceremony come first.

It is not necessary for the couple to be Bahá'ís to have a Bahá'í marriage. In fact many couples who are not Bahá'ís are married each year in a Bahá'í ceremony because they are attracted to the Bahá'í concept of marriage. Although the following passage, attributed to 'Abdu'l-Bahá, is not authenticated, it does capture the spirit of what is meant by the Bahá'í concept of marriage:

"The bond that unifies hearts most pefectly is loyalty. True lovers once united must show forth the utmost faithfulness one to another. You must dedicate your knowledge, your talents, your fortunes, your titles, your bodies and your spirits to God, to Bahá'u'lláh and to each other. Let your hearts be spacious, as spacious as the universe of God!

Allow no trace of jealously to creep between you, for jealously, like unto poison, vitiates the very essence of love.

[1] Bahá'í Prayers, p.44 of Section Two (UK).

Let not the ephemeral incidents and accidents of this change-ful life cause a rift between you. When differences present themselves, take counsel together in secret, lest others magnify a speck into a mountain. Harbour not in your hearts any grievance, but rather explain its nature to each other with such frankness and understanding that it will disappear, leaving no remembrance. Choose fellowship and amity and turn away from jealously and hypocrisy.

Your thoughts must be lofty, your ideals luminous, your minds spiritual, so that your souls may become a dawning-place for the Sun of Reality. Let your hearts be like unto two pure mirrors reflecting the stars of the heaven of love and beauty.

Together make mention of noble aspirations and heavenly concepts. Let there be no secrets one from another. Make your home a haven of rest and peace. Be hospitable, and let the doors of your house be open to the faces of friends and strangers. Welcome every guest with radiant grace and let each feel that it is his own home.

No mortal can conceive the union and harmony which God has designed for man and wife. Nourish continually the tree of your union with love and affection, so that it will remain ever green and verdant throughout all seasons and bring forth luscious fruits for the healing of nations.

O beloved of God, may your home be a vision of the paradise of Abhá, so that whosoever enters therein may feel the essence of purity and harmony, and cry out from the heart: "Here is the home of love! Here is the palace of love! Here is the nest of love! Here is the garden of love!"

Be like two sweet-singing birds perched upon the highest branches of the tree of life, filling the air with songs of love and rapture.

Lay the foundation of your affection in the very centre of your spiritual being, at the very heart of your consciousness, and let it not be shaken by adverse winds.

And when God gives you sweet and lovely children, conse-crate yourselves to their instruction and guidance, so that they may become imperishable flowers of the divine rose-garden, nightingales of the ideal paradise, servants of the world of humanity, and the fruit of the tree of your life.

Live in such harmony that others may take your lives for an example and may say to one another: "Look how they live like two doves in one nest, in perfect love, affinity and union. It is as though from all eternity God had kneaded the very essence of their beings for the love of one another."

Attain the ideal love that God has destined for you, so that you may become partakers of eternal life forthwith. Quaff deeply from the fountain of truth, and dwell all the days of your life in a paradise of glory, gathering immortal flowers from the garden of divine mysteries.

Be to each other as heavenly lovers and divine beloved ones dwelling in a paradise of love. Build your nest on the leafy branches of the tree of love. Soar into the clear atmosphere of love. Sail upon the shoreless sea of love. Walk in the eternal rose-garden of love. Bathe in the shining rays of the sun of love. Be firm and steadfast in the path of love. Perfume your nostrils with the fragrance from the flowers of love. Attune your ears to the soul-entrancing melodies of love. Let your aims be as generous as the banquets of love, and your words as a string of white pearls from the ocean of love. Drink deeply of the elixir of love, so that you may live continually in the reality of Divine Love."[1]

Nothing can be guaranteed in life and even after the most careful preparation a marriage can go wrong. This is certainly true in present society where there are so many forces at work which are likely to have a divisive effect on a marriage. The Bahá'í Writings recognize that this is so and make compassionate provision for dealing with marriages which run into difficulty. When a couple feel that they need help to keep their marriage going they are encouraged to consult with their Local Spiritual Assembly (see next chapter). This body will do all in its power to reconcile them. If reconciliation at that time seems impossible there is then a period of separation during which time husband and wife should not live together. During this time they will have the opportunity to reflect and gain perspective on their situation away from the arena of

[1] Bahá'í Prayers, UK revised edition, 1951, PL II, pp. 47-50.

conflict. If after a year of separation the couple are still unreconciled then they will be allowed to divorce, as it is not the intent to force people to live together in unhappiness, provided only that such a divorce is in accordance with local law (obedience to government is a Bahá'í teaching which will be discussed in the next chapter).

Though the Bahá'í Writings are compassionate about divorce, the subject of marriage and divorce is not taken lightly and it is pointed out that someone who breaks up a marriage through malice, thoughtlessness or selfishness bears a very heavy burden indeed:

"The friends (Bahá'ís) must strictly refrain from divorce unless something arises which compels them to separate because of their aversion for each other; in that case, with the knowledge of the Spiritual Assembly, they may decide to separate. They must then be patient and wait one complete year. If during this year harmony is not re-established between them, then their divorce may be realized. . . . The foundation of the Kingdom of God is based upon harmony and love, oneness, relationship and union, not upon differences, especially between husband and wife. If one of these two become the cause of divorce, that one will unquestionably fall into great difficulties, will become the victim of formidable calamities and experience deep remorse." 'Abdu'l-Bahá.[1]

There is nothing to prevent a Bahá'í from remarrying if he wishes. However, before making such an undertaking he will consider carefully just what limitations in his character contributed to the failure of his first marriage and whether or not those limitations still exist.

C — Chastity

So far, marriage has been discussed primarily as a spiritual union, which is appropriate, as the Bahá'í view is that this is the real and most lasting aspect of marriage, reflecting the fact that man is essentially, a spiritual being. However, Bahá'í Writings affirm that the physical side of

[1] Bahá'u'lláh and the New Era, p. 165 (UK).

marriage is also of great importance. Sex is not only the means of procreation, which in itself is one of the main purposes of marriage, but it is one of the most beautiful channels for the expression of the spiritual union which should exist between husband and wife. The pleasure which is found in using this channel to strengthen the bond of love in marriage is one of the great joys of nature and is so appreciated in Bahá'í teaching.

However, sex, as is true of every other physical aspect of nature quickly loses its beauty when it becomes an end in itself, and when it is used outside its proper bounds it can and does become an ugly and a destructive force. The Bahá'í view is that the proper bounds are the marriage bond. The following extract from a letter written in 1938 on behalf of Shoghi Effendi summarizes the Bahá'í position:

"The Bahá'í Faith recognizes the value of the sex impulse, but condemns its illegitimate and improper expressions such as free love, companionate marriage and others, all of which it considers positively harmful to man and to the society in which he lives. The proper use of the sex instinct is the natural right of every individual, and it is precisely for this very purpose that the institution of marriage has been established. The Bahá'ís do not believe in the suppression of the sex impulse but in its regulation and control."[1]

There are those who maintain that pre-marital sex is necessary to determine whether or not a man and a woman are compatible. This point of view overlooks the fact that true marriage is a spiritual union and that if a couple have really discovered each other's character and love what they see, then sex cannot be a fundamental problem. If they love each other and there should turn out to be sexual difficulty after marriage, which is unlikely, then they will wish to solve the problem together in tenderness and love, with, if necessary, medical help. If they do not love each other, then pre-marital sex is not going to make any difference and to base a marriage on any sexual pleasure which may be found before marriage is to invite disaster. Furthermore, indulgence in pre-marital sex on these grounds will surely

[1] National Bahá'í Review, No. 4, 1968, p. 1 (USA).

take away some of the beauty from marriage: there will be, even if subconsciously, a devaluation of the marriage itself, perhaps a sense of hypocrisy, and a feeling of having started the marriage on less than the highest ideal.

As a response to the frequent failure of marriage in present-day society, there is a school of thought which maintains that men and women are not naturally monogamous and that during a lifetime it is normal to love many people either singly or simultaneously. The more consistent advocates of this point of view live with others without getting married or enter into marital communes. Others use it as an excuse for both pre-marital and extra-marital sexual relations and for divorce roundabouts. A true spiritual union between a man and a woman gives the opportunity for the greatest fulfilment for both parties and when this intimate relationship is diluted by bringing in others, no matter how "cool and broadminded" the parties may seem about the matter, a great deal will be lost, which can never be recovered. Once a sense of emotional security and trust is undermined what can and will be given by each party to the other will decline drastically and it is unrealistic to think that this can be compensated for elsewhere: two or more shallow relationships can never equal one profound one in terms of fulfilment. One of the most unpleasant side effects of the polygamous philosophy is that it almost inevitably leads to comparisons, with the partners having developed different levels of sexual expectation and appetite. Then, indeed, there is likely to be a problem of incompatibility. The argument confuses intimate love between man and woman, which is both spiritual and physical, with the purely spiritual love which should exist between all mankind. The greater number a man loves the first way the poorer he is; the more the second way the richer he will be.

An even more frank argument against the concept of marital chastity is put forward by those who believe that sex does not have to be connected to love; that it is a physical sensation complete in itself which should be enjoyed by all like any other material commodity. This is a logical development of the materialistic philosophy. It has direct connection with the fear of death and the desperate cult of youth to fend off the thought of death. Those who pursue sex for its own sake find after a time that conventional forms become boring and, in order to satisfy their demand for excitement, search for more and more variations. The variations become progressively more sadistic and bestial and quite unidentifiable with the human spirit. As with the unbridled pursuit of any other form of sensual pleasure, happiness is not found, only a painful longing for what cannot be reached. And, ironically, for those who seek eternal youth, unlimited sexual promiscuity brings death to the spirit and they lose forever the possibility of a real relationship and progressive fulfilment.

"Despair both here and hereafter is all you will gain from self-indulgence." 'Abdu'l-Bahá.[1]

The loss is even deeper than that. For those who can treat their own and other peoples' bodies as supermarket commodities by definition coarsen and brutalize their whole attitude to their fellow human beings. In short, it is believed that unlimited sexual freedom is not compatible with lasting respect and love between human beings and while such a philosophy prevails there is not a chance of achieving a just and spiritually-progressive society.

These conventional arguments in favour of sexual promiscuity have been gradually extended to include defence of homosexuality. Homosexuality is now regarded by many as acceptable and natural sexual behaviour. Bahá'ís deeply deplore the past savage persecution of homosexuals, whom they regard as having a sickness which requires not persecution for its cure, but compassion and all the medical and spiritual assistance that a society can give. However, physically and spiritually people of the same sex are not complementary in the same sense that people of the opposite sex are, and a homosexual relationship is therefore seen by Bahá'ís as an artificial creation which in the long run destroys rather than augments the spiritual qualities of those involved. The following statement written on behalf of

[1] The Secret of Divine Civilization, p. 105 (USA).

Shoghi Effendi summarizes the Bahá'í position on this subject:

"Homosexuality, according to the Writings of Bahá'u'lláh, is spiritually condemned. This does not mean that people so afflicted must not be helped and advised and sympathized with. It does mean that we do not believe that it is a permissible way of life. . . .

". . . No matter how devoted and fine the love may be between people of the same sex, to let it find expression in sexual acts is wrong. Immorality of every sort is really forbidden by Bahá'u'lláh, and homosexual relationships He looks upon as such, besides being against nature.

". . . But through the advice and help of doctors, through a strong and determined effort, and through prayer, a soul can overcome this handicap." Shoghi Effendi.[1]

Despite the prevalence of the permissive view of sex, young people becoming Bahá'ís seem to grasp very quickly the significance of the idea of chastity in the overall scheme of Bahá'í philosophy: that chastity is an essential attribute of a just race of men and women.

"As to a chaste and holy life it should be regarded as no less essential a factor that must contribute its proper share to the strengthening and vitalization of the Bahá'í community upon which must in turn depend the success of any Bahá'í plan or enterprise." Shoghi Effendi.[2]

They understand that chastity is in reality a state of mind, a spiritual concept, and that it involves not only reserving sexual relationships for marriage, but the way we think about others and the way we want other people to think about ourselves. Chastity is conveyed in our general bearing, and in the conduct of social relations.

"A chaste and holy life must be made the controlling principle in the behaviour and conduct of all Bahá'ís, both in their social relations and with the members of their own community, and in their contact with the world at large. It must adorn and reinforce the ceaseless labours and meritorious exertions of those whose enviable position is to

[1] National Bahá'í Review, No. 3, 1968, p. 2 (USA).
[2] The Advent of Divine Justice, p. 25 (USA).

propagate the Message, and to administer the affairs, of the Faith of Bahá'u'lláh. It must be upheld, in all its integrity and implications, in every phase of the life of those who fill the ranks of that Faith, whether in their homes, their travels, their clubs, their societies, their entertainments, their schools, and their universities. . . .

Such a chaste and holy life, with its implications of modesty, purity, temperance, decency and clean-mindedness, involves no less than the exercise of moderation in all that pertains to dress, language, amusements, and all artistic and literary avocations. It demands daily vigilance in the control of one's carnal desires and corrupt inclinations. It calls for the abandonment of a frivolous conduct, with its excessive attachment to trivial and often misdirected pleasures. It requires total abstinence from all alcoholic drinks, from opium, and from similar habit-forming drugs. It condemns the prostitution of art and literature, the practices of nudism and of companionate marriage, infidelity in marital relationships, and all manner of promiscuity, of easy familiarity, and of sexual vices. It can tolerate no compromise with the theories, the standards, the habits and the excesses of a decadent age. Nay rather it seeks to demonstrate, through the dynamic force of its example, the pernicious character of such theories, the falsity of such standards the hollowness of such claims, the perversity of such habits, and the sacrilegious character of such excesses." Shoghi Effendi.[1]

D — *The Raising of Children*

Earlier in this chapter it was mentioned that one of the main purposes of the family is the raising of children. This task is of such importance that it requires some further discussion before passing on to the next chapter. To a Bahá'í the responsibility is not only the normally-accepted one of a parent protecting and educating another innocent and defenceless human being, but one of helping to raise up a new race of men and women on whom depends future world society. Bahá'ís believe that those parents who are

[1] The Advent of Divine Justice, p. 25 (USA).

negligent of their children's education have committed an unforgivable act:

"... *It is enjoined upon the father and mother, as a duty, to strive with all effort to train the daughter and the son, to nurse them from the breast of knowledge and to rear them in the bosom of sciences and arts. Should they neglect this matter, they shall be held responsible and worthy of reproach in the presence of the stern Lord.*

This is a sin unpardonable, for they have made that poor babe a wanderer in the Sahara of ignorance, unfortunate and tormented; to remain during a lifetime a captive of ignorance and pride, negligent and without discernment." 'Abdu'l-Bahá.[1]

Bahá'í Writings point out that the spiritual and intellectual growth of the child, as well as its physical growth starts in the womb, and that the mother should bear this in mind whilst pregnant. There is the suggestion that the more serene and spiritual the mother is during this time, the better it will be for the baby as well as for herself.

From the time when the baby is born the parents must be ever conscious of their responsibility and their power to influence the character of the child in their care. If their own lives are corrupt and conducted at standards lower than the highest, they must expect that this condition will become a part of the character of their children. In this connection it is worth drawing particular attention to one failing which is so common, that of backbiting (see previous chapter). It has been said that backbiting does more to stunt the spiritual growth of children than probably any other element in the average "good" household. Children should be brought up in a home where there is warmth of feeling for all people, a sense of reverence for all things, an attitude of prayer to God.

In the early month's of the child's life its formal education should begin and there should be applied those two great principles of all education: reward and punishment.

"*O People of God! That which traineth the world is justice, for it is upheld by two pillars, reward and punishment. These*

[1] Tablets of 'Abdu'l-Bahá, Vol. III, pp. 578-579.

two pillars are the sources of life to the world." Bahá'u'lláh.[1]

This implies love hand-in-hand with a constant firmness right from the beginning. At an early age a child is highly sensitive and will cry merely when he senses anger in the home, and will normally respond to a gentle but firm voice. Such firmness should be consistent between both parents. A child quickly learns to exploit a situation in which one parent contradicts the firmness of the other with an attitude of weakness. If there is a true atmosphere of love in the household a child will want to make its parents happy and will normally desist from an action merely by being told that it will hurt the father or mother. If these principles are applied early enough there should be no need for physical chastisement. Should stern measures in fact have to be taken, they should never reach the point of physical beating or tongue-lashing as such punishments would soon make a child hate his own home. Essentially, however, the emphasis should be on the positive. A properly educated child will receive more praise for the things he does well than chastisement for the things he should not do.

In Bahá'í teachings there is no compromise on the role of the parents. All members of the family have rights as human beings and part of the right of parents is their authority which comes from their greater experience and maturity. That authority is most easily held if they have the respect of their children which, it is suggested, rests on at least two requisites. First, the parents must practise what they preach. How many millions of parents have forbidden smoking and drinking to their children and openly consume such drugs themselves. Double talk is one of the most effective ways of undermining a child's sense of values. Secondly, they must teach constantly what is reasonable and just. This does not mean that it is necessary to have a long discussion each time there is a point at issue; on the contrary, the child should learn soon to take on trust, from experience, the reasonableness of the parents' position. When a child is treated with justice and empathy, he can

[1] The Advent of Divine Justice, p. 23 (USA).

confide in his parents without fear, and the barriers between generations will not arise.

As the child grows up, an important part of his education is diversity of experience. He should have continuous access to his parents in both formal learning and in play, and if possible, to his grandparents and other adults. If he is left overmuch solely in the company of his peers he is likely to develop a narrower view of life. It is partly to this end that a Bahá'í home should be always a centre of hospitality. This practice has the benefit of allowing the child to see his everyday experience, and from an early age, the highest principles of universal brotherhood in action.

The prime object of the education of the child as he grows older is to give him the tools to think freely for himself and to think wisely. This objective is partly achieved by seeing to it that he receives a balanced schooling in the teachings of all religions and other systems of ethics. Such an approach, however, does not in any way imply restraint in teaching the child about the Faith. In the Bahá'í view it would be hypocritical and unfair to the child:

". . . A Bahá'í child must be trained according to the moral precepts of Bahá'u'lláh, he must be taught daily of the love of God, the history of the Faith must be read to him, the love of humanity must be inculcated into every fibre of his being and the universal principles be explained to him in as easy a manner as possible to be devised. Then the power of great faith will take possession of his heart. But if these supreme precautions are not taken in the earliest states of the child's growth, it will be most difficult to curb later on his growing manifold appetites. For then he will live according to the requirements of the world of nature and uncontrolled self. Once the lower and sensual habits of nature take hold of him, it will be very hard to return him by any human agencies. Hence children must be brought under the control of the love of God and spiritual influence from their earliest youth. . . ."
'Abdu'l-Bahá.[1]

Bahá'ís believe that a child has reached the age of maturity at the age of fifteen. By then his basic character

[1] Star of the West, Vol. VII, p. 143.

is formed and he is capable of searching for the truth himself. If he has not had a good foundation in education by then, life is likely to be hard for him. When a branch has become hard and stiff it is very hard to straighten. It is at this age that a child can decide for himself whether he wishes to declare his faith as a Bahá'í. No pressure is to be applied: the decision must be of his own free choice. If it were otherwise the whole point of Bahá'í teachings would be lost.

CHAPTER VI

A JUST SYSTEM OF GOVERNMENT

A — *The Administrative Order*

HAVING discussed the institution of the family it is now appropriate to widen the frame of reference to the institutions of the greater family of the human race. The first chapter mentioned some of the major inadequacies of present methods of government. The major challenges which man faces are worldwide in scale and their solution requires action on a universal basis. Yet present institutions tend to strengthen factionalism and to stultify the generous and long-range concepts of society in favour of the superficial and selfish. Bahá'ís believe that these institutions are so fundamentally obsolete and destructive of man's potential that they will not be the vehicle for the establishment of a new civilization.

"Humanity, whether viewed in the light of man's individual conduct or in the existing relationships between organized communities and nations, has, alas, strayed too far and suffered to great a decline to be redeemed through the unaided efforts of the best among its recognized rulers and statesmen — however disinterested their motives, however concerted their action, however unsparing in their zeal and devotion to its cause. No scheme which the calculations of the highest statesmanship may yet devise; no doctrine which the most distinguished exponents of economic theory may hope to advance; no principle which the most ardent of moralists may strive to inculate, can provide, in the last resort, adequate foundations upon which the future of a distracted world can be built." Shoghi Effendi.[1]

As noted before, there are many, especially among the young, who are totally disillusioned with present day institutions. Their emotional conclusion is that life would be a great deal more pleasant without institutions and that

[1] World Order of Bahá'u'lláh, pp. 33-34 (USA).

basically everything would be well if all were allowed to live without restraint. Those who think in this way are generally gentle and, within the limits imposed by their culture, well disposed toward their fellow human beings, and they assume that everyone else is too. Though superficially attractive, this view is surely unrealistic and basically regressive. When men live together there are many facets of their existence about which they have to consult, agree, and work together in order to make the best of their lives; indeed, often in order to survive. This means organization, it means institutions and government. Some of the more obvious areas where cooperation is required are the protection of the weak, medical care, the development of education and the sciences, communications, and the use of scarce resources. When government is diverted from its true purpose of service to the community, of channelling the collective abilities of the community toward the greatest achievements for the good of all, and instead becomes an instrument of oppression, the answer is not to regress and deny that there is a need for government, but rather to search for the ways by which government can be made just and fruitful.

The Bahá'í view is that in order to create a new, just civilization, man needs a new spiritual outlook and a new system of government through which that spiritual outlook may be most effectively put into action. New wine requires new bottles. These two features of the new civilization must develop together, interacting on one another to create a progressive spiral. A just form of government will not be possible if the new spirit does not develop; the new spirit will be frustrated and stunted if there is not a just form of government. Our experience affords ample evidence for the realism of this view. On the one hand, contemporary events show how democratic institutions, which look fine on paper, break down when those in politics are spiritually immature and cannot abide by the necessary minimum rules of moderation and tolerance; on the other hand, many a spiritually-creative man wishing to carry out reforms for the good of all society, has become corrupted and diverted from his original aims by the requirements of the political game.

". . . the Spirit breathed by Bahá'u'lláh upon the world . . . can never permeate and exercise an abiding influence upon mankind unless and until it incarnates itself in a visible order, which would bear His name, wholly identify itself with His principles and function in conformity with His laws." Shoghi Effendi.[1]

". . . The administration of the Cause is to be conceived as an instrument and not a substitute for the Faith of Bahá'u'lláh, . . . it should be regarded as a channel through which His promised blessings may flow. . . ." Shoghi Effendi.[2]

To promote the development of a world civilization, Bahá'u'lláh designed a new system of government which is known as the Bahá'í Administrative Order. This Order is worldwide in its embrace, yet at the same time it is intimate and on a human scale when put into practice. Its structure is simple, flexible and adaptable to all cultures, ranging from the most primitive tribe to the most sophisticated of technological societies. Its features make it supremely responsive to orderly change and to the needs of those whom it serves.

". . . The machinery of the Cause has been so fashioned, that whatever is deemed necessary to incorporate into it in order to keep it in the forefront of all progressive movements can, according to the provisions made by Bahá'u'lláh, be safely embodied therein." Shoghi Effendi.[3]

The Administrative Order does not have individual leaders but is designed to obtain universal participation in the process of government. As pointed out in the first chapter most systems of government in the past have placed far too great a reliance on individual leaders with resulting problems of succession, inflated egos, personal corruption, and narrowness of view. In Bahá'í administration, authority rests solely with the elected institutions. No part

---

[1] World Order of Bahá'u'lláh, p. 156 (USA).
[2] World Order of Bahá'u'lláh, p. 9 (USA).
[3] World Order of Bahá'u'lláh, pp. 22-23 (USA).

of that authority becomes associated in any way with the individuals who serve on the institutions. A person serving on a Bahá'í institution receives no special privilege and derives no prestige from his office. The reward of office is the inner hope of having done all in one's power to serve the community.

". . . Personalities should not be made centres around which the community may revolve but . . . they should be subordinated under all conditions and however great their merits to the properly constituted Assemblies." Shoghi Effendi.[1]

". . . there is a distinction of fundamental importance which should be always remembered in this connection, and this is between the Spiritual Assembly as an institution, and the persons who comprise it. These are by no means supposed to be perfect, nor can they be considered as inherently superior to the rest of their fellow believers. It is precisely becaue they are subject to the same human limitations that characterize the other members of the community that they have to be elected every year. . . ." Letter written on behalf of Shoghi Effendi.[2]

One type of leader prominent in history has been the priest. Bahá'í Writings, while recognizing that priests have served a useful purpose in the past in teaching the principles of religion to largely illiterate societies, also show that they have frequently displayed all the weaknesses of other individual leaders and have done as much as any group to pollute the original pure stream of the religion for which they lived. Bahá'u'lláh specifically forbade the creation of a priesthood in the Bahá'í Faith,[3] in keeping with His teaching that in this age, when universal education is both possible and necessary, man must, in order to grow spiritually, seek the truth about life for himself in his own reading and experience. This is one reason why there is so much emphasis in Bahá'í teaching plans in having Bahá'í books translated into as many

---

[1] Principles of Bahá'í Administration, p. 69 (UK).
[2] The Local Spiritual Assembly, p. 9 (USA).
[3] God Passes By, p. 214 (USA).

languages as possible so that all can read for themselves.*

All the collective institutions of the Administrative Order are elected democratically by secret ballot. However, there is a difference from the normal democratic theory in that the elected institutions are required to be responsible not to their constituents but to God. This means that their whole outlook is directed to the good of society as a whole, not to factional interest, and society is understood in the widest sense, including not merely the present generations but also the generations past and future.

The Administrative Order has institutions at three distinct levels. To look after the affairs of each town or village where there are at least nine adult Bahá'ís there is a Local Spiritual Assembly.

Where there are a sufficient number of Local Spiritual Assemblies which have a common historical, cultural and geographic background a co-ordinating and directing National Spiritual Assembly is formed. The areas of jurisdiction of the National Spiritual Assemblies coincide in many instances with existing national boundaries, but in other areas there are variations because present state boundaries are accidents of politics. Bahá'í Writings describe the Local and National Spiritual Assemblies as the bedrock of the new World Order.

In 1982 there were 133 National Spiritual Assemblies in existence throughout the world and over twenty-four thousand Local Spiritual Assemblies (see Appendix I).

Crowning the Order, is the third level, the supreme legislative body of the Faith, the Universal House of Justice. Its seat is at Haifa, in Israel, the meeting point of East and West, crossroads between Europe, Africa and Asia, home of man from earliest times, Holy Land for many of the world's great religions, in short, the hub of the world. The Universal House of Justice unites and directs the whole Bahá'í world. To Bahá'ís it is an embryonic world government — a sign of the future.

---

* By 1968 Bahá'í literature was available in 411 languages (see Appendix III). By 1973 the number was 571.

B — *Elections and Consultation*

The effectiveness of the Administrative Order as a device for establishing a just society rests not only on a structure which is unified on a world scale with roots going to every local community, but also on how that structure works. Two extremely important aspects of Bahá'í Administration are the method of election and the method of consultation and decision making. The method of election is designed to ensure that all in the community are given every facility for truly independent choice, that at the time when they make their choice they are fully aware of their responsibility, and finally that those elected are the most qualified to serve the community. The system of consultation directs the community toward consideration of all points of view in a spirit of unity and in a logical step-by-step fashion with the object of arriving at the very best decision for the whole community.

Local Spiritual Assemblies, National Spiritual Assemblies and the Universal House of Justice each have nine members. The Local Spiritual Assembly is elected once a year on April 21 by all the adult Bahá'ís in the assembly area of jurisdiction. All of the adult Bahá'ís on the electoral list of the local community are eligible for election to the Assembly. There is a moral obligation on every member of the community to vote. Not to vote implies lack of interest in the establishment of a just society:

"These Local Spiritual Assemblies will have to be elected directly by the friends, and every declared believer of twenty-one years and above, far from standing aloof and assuming an indifferent or independent attitude, should regard it his sacred duty to take part conscientiously and diligently, in the election, the consolidation and the efficient working of his own local Assembly." Shoghi Effendi.[1]

Such a moral obligation would not apply if a Bahá'í feels he cannot make an intelligent choice; as he might, for instance, if he has only just arrived in the area.

"The distinguishing right . . . does not carry with it nor

[1] Bahá'í Administration, p. 39 (USA).

*does it imply an obligation to cast his vote if he feels that the
circumstances under which he lives do not justify or allow
him to exercise that right intelligently and with understanding.*" Shoghi Effendi.[1]

To be eligible to vote in a Bahá'í election and to serve on
a Bahá'í Assembly, a Bahá'í must be twenty-one years old
or more. This rule can be important in those countries
where the law makes such a requirement of incorporated
bodies. It will be recalled from the last chapter that in
Bahá'í teachings the age of spiritual maturity is fifteen.
Bahá'ís between the ages of fifteen and twenty-one enrolled
and declared as Bahá'í Youth are greatly encouraged to
serve on appointed committees of Assemblies so that they
can gain administrative experience and so that the
community can tap their youthful enthusiasm and vigour.

Though there is provision for absentee balloting, the
preference is for the community to meet together for the
election. At the election meeting the community reviews
together the provisions of the Bahá'í method of election.
This is often an important step in helping those in the
poorest and least educated communities, for without such
provision many might not acquire the habit of carrying out
their responsibility as voters. Then there are readings from
Bahá'í Writings which describe the importance of the
system of administration in establishing a new society, and
the sort of qualities which are required of those who are to
be part of that administration. There follows a time of
prayer for spiritual guidance, a time for calmness, reflection
and self-searching. Then, and only then, does the actual
process of casting the secret ballot take place.

The National Spiritual Assembly is also elected once a
year by a National Convention which serves as both an
electoral body and as a representative assembly to bring
forward ideas and suggestions for consultation with the
National Spiritual Assembly. The area of jurisdiction of the
National Spiritual Assembly is divided into regions, or
localities, each of which elects a number of delegates to the
National Convention in proportion to the number of Bahá'ís

[1] Bahá'í Administration, p. 198 (USA).

in its area. The election of the National Spiritual Assembly by a National Convention rather than directly by the whole national community allows for the election to be held at one meeting with all the advantages that this method affords which were mentioned above. Any adult Bahá'í in good standing in the national community is eligible for election to the National Spiritual Assembly.

The Universal House of Justice is elected — every five years at the present time — by an International Convention which meets in Haifa. The International Convention is very similar in nature and function to the National Convention. Its delegates are the members of all the National Spiritual Assemblies throughout the world. Any man in the whole world community may be elected to the House of Justice, with the very few exceptions referred to later in the chapter.*

The Bahá'í election has several other significant features. First, there are no nominations and no political campaigns. In conventional democracy such procedures are considered necessary because otherwise the electors would have no idea for whom to vote. However, the price of such practices is high, as is clear to anyone interested in politics. It can be an opportunity for manipulation by the rich and powerful vested interests. In many countries as, for example, in the United States, few but the rich can be elected to the most important offices because only the rich can afford the cost of campaigns. In nearly all countries the emphasis tends to be on the image rather than on reality. A man's record, which in any case is so often hard to define, counts for less than his public appearance and soft words. As a result the electors never really know for whom they are voting. Worst of all, the campaign system creates a leadership cult, with all the consequences that such cults imply. Clearly, such practices make the formation of a just government all but impossible.

In Bahá'í Administration the emphasis is on a community

---

* The rule that only men may serve on the Universal House of Justice may appear to abrogate the principle of equality between men and women. 'Abdu'l-Bahá stated that the reason for this rule would become apparent in the future.

which is like a family, constantly meeting and coming to know its own members in a loving atmosphere.

"What the friends should do is to get thoroughly acquainted with one another, to exchange views, to mix freely and discuss among themselves the requirements and qualifications for such a membership [on an assembly] without reference or application, however indirect, to particular individuals. We should refrain from influencing the opinion of others, of canvassing for any particular individual, but should stress the necessity of getting fully acquainted with the qualifications of membership . . . and of learning more about one another through direct, personal experience rather than through the reports and opinions of our friends." Shoghi Effendi.[1]

In the local community during the course of the year a Bahá'í will almost certainly come to know all the other friends at the regular Nineteen Day Feast (described later in this section) and at other community occasions, and in consequence there is no need for nominations or election campaigns. Of course, in the wider national and international communities it is not possible to know everyone. Yet, in practice the system works very effectively because delegates to national and international conventions tend to be amongst the most active Bahá'ís. Activity brings experience of the wider community and an opportunity to obtain informal ideas on which persons, because of their spiritual qualities and services, are best qualified to be elected to help guide the affairs of the community. With no false pressures from nominations and campaigns the Bahá'í elector is free

". . . to consider without the least trace of passion and prejudice, and irrespective of any material consideration, the names of only those who can best combine the necessary qualities of unquestioned loyalty, of selfless devotion, of a well-trained mind, of recognized ability and mature experience. . . ." Shoghi Effendi.[2]

Another important feature of the Bahá'í election is that

[1] Principles of Bahá'í Administration, p. 59 (UK).
[2] Bahá'í Administration, p. 88 (USA).

each elector votes for a complete Assembly, that is, he votes for nine persons rather than one. This feature protects the community against undue emphasis on particular individuals. It also helps the elector think about the whole Assembly and the range of qualities and diversity of background it needs to function most effectively. Besides choosing the most loyal, able and mature, a Bahá'í will be also conscious of the need to have a balanced and fully representative selection of the community on the Assembly:

"The Assembly should be representative of the choicest and most varied and capable elements in every Bahá'í community." Shoghi Effendi.[1]

An example of a balance already achieved is the National Spiritual Assembly for the USA at the time of writing. Racially the Assembly has three Whites, three Blacks, one Navajo Indian, one Oriental and one with Persian/Russian background. Six of the nine are men and three are women; typically, the balance in most years is five and four. Such a balance was achieved not through any constitutional device allocating proportions of seats to certain minorities, but directly and spontaneously from the growing maturity of ther American Bahá'í community. This philosophy reflects the fundamental aim of the Bahá'í Faith to base its unity on diversity.

"Unlike the nations and peoples of the earth, be they of the East or of the West, democratic or authoritarian, communist or capitalist, whether belonging to the Old World or the New, who either ignore, trample upon, or extirpate, the racial, religious or political minorities within the sphere of their jurisdiction, every organized community, enlisted under the banner of Bahá'u'lláh should feel it to be its first and inescapable obligation to nurture, encourage, and safeguard every minority belonging to any faith, race, class or nation within it." Shoghi Effendi.[2]

This principle is further reflected in the practice concerning ties for ninth place. Normally a second ballot is cast to decide between those who were in the tie but if one should

[1] Bahá'í Electoral Process, p. 26 (USA).
[2] The Advent of Divine Justice, p. 29 (USA).

be clearly from a minority group he or she is given preference.

"*So great and vital is this principle that in such circumstances, as when an equal number of ballots have been cast in an election, or where the qualifications for any office are balanced as between the various races, faiths or nationalities within the community, priority should unhesitatingly be accorded the party representing the minority.*" Shoghi Effendi.[1]

Once elected, a Bahá'í should not resign his office, unless there are most exceptional circumstances. He has been shown the confidence of the community and has a spiritual obligation to render the service which has been asked of him.

"*. . . Under special circumstances, such as illness, one may do so (resign), but only after, and never before he has been elected to the membership of the Assembly. Personal differences and disagreements among Assembly members surely afford no sufficient ground for such resignation, and certainly cannot justify absence from assembly meetings. Through the clash of personal opinions, as 'Abdu'l-Bahá has stated, the spark of truth is often ignited, and divine guidance revealed.*" Shoghi Effendi.[2]

After the election of the Assembly, it in turn will elect its own officers and thereafter appoint the various committees it will need to assist in the running of the day-to-day affairs of the community. The chief officers: chairman, vice-chairman, secretary and treasurer, are elected one by one by majority vote for all the members of the Assembly. These officers perform much the same function as in conventional organizations except that the chairman is more of a co-ordinator than a leader. He has one vote and normally gives his opinion last. The chairmanship of the Universal House of Justice is rotated on a regular basis, perhaps to avoid all suggestion of a head of the world institution. All committees are appointed by the Assembly and there is a limit placed on the responsibility which may be delegated to

---

[1] The Advent of Divine Justice, pp. 29-30 (USA).
[2] The Local Spiritual Assembly, p. 21 (USA).

them. These are important administrative details because they further add to the strength and unity of the Order.

As the members of an Assembly are conscious of the fact that their only ambition is to serve God and the community, and that they have not fought an election campaign against one another to win office, they start with a potential for spiritual unity and friendship. Of course, sometimes there are certain clashes of temperament which may cause difficulty, but normally with the aid of prayer with which every Assembly meeting begins, with the awareness of the need to look on others in a spirit of brotherhood, and with the concerted help of all the other members of the Assembly, such difficulties are usually overcome.

In the conduct of its affairs the Assembly is urged to consult together, not to make speeches or to debate with one another. All must speak out frankly, for as 'Abdu'l-Bahá said, from the clash of opinion will come the spark of truth. Direct speech, however, should be couched in gentle, courteous language, in a spirit of friendship, and there should be no recriminations, argument or bitterness.

"They must . . . proceed with the utmost devotion, courtesy, dignity, care and moderation to express their views. They must in every matter search out the truth and not insist upon their own opinion, for stubbornness and persistence in one's views will lead ultimately to discord and wrangling and the truth will remain hidden. The honoured members must with all freedom express their own thoughts, and it is in no wise permissible for one to belittle the thought of another. . . ." 'Abdu'l-Bahá.[1]

When an Assembly member has put forward an idea in consultation, he should not regard it as his own to be defended at all costs because of pride, but as just one of the many ideas which belong to the Assembly. If an Assembly is working well together it is often the case that a member will be impressed by the points raised by the others and as a result may himself speak later against his own original suggestion and not feel that this is in any way out of the ordinary. This is true objectivity and intellectual integrity.

[1] Bahá'í Administration, p. 22 (USA).

"*The purpose is to emphasize the statement that consultation must have for its object the investigation of truth. He who expresses an opinion should not voice it as correct and right but set it forth as a contribution to the consensus of opinion. . . . Man should weigh his opinions with the utmost serenity, calmness and composure. Before expressing his own views he should carefully consider the views already advanced by others. If he finds that a previously expressed opinion is more true and worthy, he should accept it immediately and not wilfully hold to an opinion of his own. By this excellent method he endeavours to arrive at unity and truth.*"
'Abdu'l-Bahá.[1]

It is not only a Bahá'í's responsibility to give his own ideas, he must also make sure, regardless of whether or not he is chairman, that all the other members of the Assembly are given the opportunity, and indeed encouraged to give their ideas. It is most important to avoid dominance by one or two forceful characters. This practice has particular significance in these early days of development when, as often occurs, there are on an Assembly poor people who in the conventional world are used to keeping quiet and letting the rich, the middle class and white do all the talking. Not only is there an important principle here of complete participation, with its implication of real unity, but it often turns out that the poor have a much closer grasp of reality in everyday life than the protected, fast-talking, middle class, and to miss the advice of the poor is to limit severely the collective wisdom of the Assembly. The most fruitful attitude toward consultation was summed up by 'Abdu'l-Bahá as follows:

"*The prime requisites for them that take counsel together are purity of motive, radiance of spirit, detachment from all else save God, attraction to His Divine Fragrances, humility and lowliness amongst His loves ones, patience and long-suffering in difficulties and servitude to His exalted Threshold.*"[2]

In its consultation the Assembly is enjoined to follow a

---

[1] Promulgation of Universal Peace, p. 69 (USA).

[2] Bahá'í Administration, p. 21 (USA).

logical sequence of thought so as to handle its affairs most efficiently. The usual pattern in fact is very similar to normal procedures followed for scientific enquiry. First, it should agree on the exact nature of the problem; second, ascertain the relevant facts; third, agree upon the spiritual or administrative principles involved; fourth, conduct a full and frank discussion of the case, leading up to the offering of a resolution when appropriate; and fifth, vote upon the resolution. The true end to the process is when the action required by the resolution has been completed. It sounds very simple and perhaps obvious. But where else is this done?*

The consultations of an Assembly are confidential and under no circumstances will Assembly members discuss consultations outside the confines of an Assembly meeting. This is a rule which helps the consultations to be most frank, gives a feeling of unity and family confidence, and of course it is one more defence against old style electioneering.

When a vote is taken it is preferable that it be unanimous. The Universal House of Justice feels its responsibility to be so weighty that it has only acted on important issues when all nine members have been present, and so far all decisions on such issues have been unanimous. It sometimes postpones decisions when it is felt that the correct decision is not forthcoming. However, as a general rule, an Assembly is permitted to act on the basis of a majority decision. When the decision is made, it is the decision of all the Assembly, including those who voted against it.

"Bahá'ís are not required to vote on an assembly against their consciences. It is better if they submit to the majority view and make it unanimous. But they are not forced to. What they must do, however, is to abide by the majority decision, as this is what becomes effective. They must not go around undermining the Assembly by saying they disagreed

---

* It is of interest to note that in an experiment carried out at Harvard University a group of non-Bahá'í students trained in the rudiments of Bahá'í consultation performed significantly better than other groups working on the same problems (P. Christensen, *The Unity-Diversity Principle and its Effect on Creative Group Problem Solving: An Experimental Investigation,* 1969).

with the majority. In other words, they must put the Cause first and not their own opinions." Shoghi Effendi, through his secretary.[1]

The unity of the Assembly and community take precedence over individual opinions because, so Bahá'ís believe, unity is ultimately the only basis for a new just society. This is of far more importance than the possibility of an error on a particular issue. While errors can always arise, they should be rare if the spirit of consultation has been properly followed and, in any case, decisions can usually be reviewed later.

"If they agree upon a subject, even though it be wrong, it is better than to disagree and be in the right, for this difference will produce the demolition of the divine foundations. Though one of the parties may be in the right and they disagree, that will be the cause of a thousand wrongs, but if they agree and both parties are in the wrong, as it is in unity, the truth will be revealed and the wrong made right." 'Abdu'l-Bahá.[2]

Accordingly all members of an Assembly will work hard for the implementation of decision even if they did not vote for it personally.

If a member of a community feels deeply that his Assembly has made a mistake he has recourse to an orderly system of appeal which avoids destroying the sense of unity in the community. He can make an appeal to the Assembly asking it to reconsider its decision at its next meeting or, should this fail to satisfy him, he may make an appeal to the National Spiritual Assembly. If he is unhappy with the answer he may then appeal to the Universal House of Justice. The correct way to make appeals to higher bodies is not directly but through the channel of his own Assembly.

It might be noted in passing that the number of nine on every Assembly, though not fixed for all time, has proved advantageous. On the one hand, it is sufficiently large enough to give a wide cross-section of experience and views, and on the other, it is a small enough number to allow

---

[1] Bahá'í News, December 1947, p. 3 (USA).
[2] Principles of Bahá'í Administration, p. 60 (UK).

efficient and speedy discussion — especially when there is a strong sense of unity and purpose.

Though an Assembly conducts its consultation in confidence it keeps in very close contact with its community so that it can explain its decisions and obtain as wide a spectrum of community views as possible.

"The duties of those whom the friends have freely and conscientiously elected as their representatives are no less vital and binding than the obligations of those who have chosen them. Their function is not to dictate, but to consult, and consult not only among themselves, but as much as possible with the friends whom they represent. They must regard themselves in no other light but that of chosen instruments for a more efficient and dignified presentation of the Cause of God. They should never be led to suppose that they are the central ornaments of the body of the Cause, intrinsically superior to others in capacity or merit, and sole promotors of its teachings and principles. They should approach their task with extreme humility, and endeavour, by their open-mindedness, their high sense of justice and duty, their candour, their modesty, their entire devotion to the welfare and interests of the friends, the Cause, and humanity, to win, not only the confidence and the genuine support and respect of those whom they serve, but also their esteem and real affection. They must, at all times, avoid the spirit of exclusiveness, the atmosphere of secrecy, free themselves from a domineering attitude, and banish all forms of prejudice and passion from their deliberations. They should, within the limits of wise discretion, take the friends into their confidence, acquaint them with their plans, share with them their problems and anxieties, and seek their advice and counsel." Shoghi Effendi.[1]

Every nineteen days at the beginning of each Bahá'í month the community gathers together to celebrate the Nineteen Day Feast. The spirit of the Feast is set with prayers from Bahá'í Writings. With the spirit of unity and warmth established, the community then turns to a discussion of its business and to consultation on matters to be

[1] Bahá'í Administration, p. 64 (USA).

presented to the Assembly. As in the Assembly itself, the idea is to try to have as many contribute to the discussion as possible — universal participation is the first watchword of the Bahá'í system of administration.

"In the human body, every cell, every organ, every nerve has its part to play. When all do so the body is healthy, vigorous, radiant, ready for every call made upon it. No cell, however humble, lives apart from the body, whether in serving it or receiving from it. This is true of the body of mankind in which God "has endowed each humble being with ability and talent," and is supremely true of the body of the Bahá'í world community, for this body is already an organism, united in its aspirations, unified in its methods, seeking assistance and confirmation from the same Source, and illumined with the conscious knowledge of its unity. Therefore, in this organic, divinely guided, blessed, and illumined body the participation of every believer is of the utmost importance, and is a source of power and vitality as yet unknown to us." Universal House of Justice.[1]

After the consultation on business matters there is a time for informal socializing when the bonds of unity in the community are further strengthened by personal friendships. The importance of the Feast in the life style of Bahá'í society cannot be overestimated. It is both a significant spiritual event for every individual Bahá'í and it is also the most basic administrative device for the unity and growth of the local community. It is a genuine exercise in grassroots democracy. Here every nineteen days a local governing body comes together with all its community to openly discuss public affairs. It is more than that, however. The ideas which come up at such meetings, if of more than local application, may be passed on to the National Spiritual Assembly and even to the Universal House of Justice. In short, it is one of the more important ways in which all levels of Bahá'í Administration keep in touch with the community at large.

Mention has been made that the Feast takes place at the beginning of every Bahá'í month and it would seem appro-

[1] Wellspring of Guidance, pp. 37-38 (USA).

priate before going on to the next section to mention something of the Bahá'í calendar. Each of the main religions: Christianity, Islám, Judaism, Buddhism, Hinduism, as well as other cultures, has its own calendar which, of course, has a considerable impact on the daily life and thinking of a society. When mankind is united as one family there will be a practical need for the whole family to live by one calendar and what more appropriate than a calendar recalling the teachings of the Faith which brings together in unity all religions and cultures.

The Bahá'í calendar dates from the declaration of the Báb, (1844), which marks the beginning of the Bahá'í era. The calendar is based on the solar year which begins on the March Equinox and is divided into nineteen months of nineteen days each, with four intercalary days to make up the year, except in leap years when a fifth intercalary day is added. Each day starts at sunset. The months are named after attributes of God and are as follows:

Month	Arabic Name	Translation	First day*
1	Bahá	Splendour	March 21
2	Jalál	Glory	April 9
3	Jamál	Beauty	April 28
4	'Aẓamat	Grandeur	May 17
5	Núr	Light	June 5
6	Raḥmat	Mercy	June 24
7	Kalimat	Words	July 13
8	Kamál	Perfection	August 1
9	Asmá'	Names	August 20
10	'Izzat	Might	September 8
11	Mashíyyat	Will	September 27
12	'Ilm	Knowledge	October 16
13	Qudrat	Power	November 4
14	Qawl	Speech	November 23
15	Masá'il	Questions	December 12
16	Sharaf	Honour	December 31
17	Sulṭán	Sovereignty	January 19
18	Mulk	Dominion	February 7
19	'Alá'	Loftiness	March 2

*Gregorian calendar.

127

The Intercalary Days are from February 26 to March 1, inclusive. These days known as Ayyám-i-Há are a time of rejoicing, devoted to hospitality, gift-giving and acts of charity. They precede the fast.

There are nine days in each year in which Bahá'ís refrain from work. Seven of these Holy Days are times of celebration and joy, and the two others commemorate the passing of the Báb and Bahá'u'lláh. The nine days are:

March 21 *(Naw-Rúz)*	New Year's Day (the spring equinox). This is also the day on which the period of fasting ends.
April 21 *(Ridván)* April 29 May 2	These three days, the most important on the Bahá'í calendar, are in remembrance of Bahá'u'lláh's Declaration of His Mission in 1863, in the garden of Ridván, Baghdád (See Chapter eight).
May 23	The Báb's Declaration of His Mission (1844).
May 29	The passing of Bahá'u'lláh (1892).
July 9	The martyrdom of the Báb (1850).
October 20	The birth of the Báb (1819).
November 12	The birth of Bahá'u'lláh (1817).

'Abdu'l-Bahá said of the Feast of Naw-Rúz (the Bahá'í New Year):
"Undoubtedly the friends of God, upon such a day must leave tangible philanthropic or ideal traces that should reach all mankind and not pertain only to the Bahá'ís."[1]

---

[1] *Bahá'u'lláh and the New Era*, p. 169 (UK).

There are two other anniversaries in the Bahá'í calendar which are not treated as days when work should be suspended:

November 26 The Day of the Covenant.
       To commemorate Bahá'u'lláh's Covenant with the Bahá'ís that (after his death) they should follow 'Abdu'l-Bahá. (See next part of this Chapter).

November 28 The passing of 'Abdu'l-Bahá.

Many Bahá'í communities also observe World Religion Day (third Sunday in January), Race Unity Day (June 10), World Peace Day (September 17), United Nations Day (October 24) and Human Rights Day (December 10).

C — Functions and Authority

Today the Administrative Order is the backbone of the world Bahá'í community. In future Bahá'ís envisage that it will be the basis for government in society as a whole. At that time local and national bodies now called Spiritual Assemblies would become known as Houses of Justice to denote their wider function.

"The friends must never mistake the Bahá'í administration for an end in itself. It is merely the instrument of the spirit of the Faith. This Cause is a Cause which God has revealed to humanity as a whole. It is designed to benefit the entire human race, and the only way it can do this is to reform the community life of mankind, as well as seeking to regenerate the individual. The Bahá'í administration is only the first shaping of what in future will come to be the social life and laws of community living. As yet the believers are only first beginning to grasp and practise it properly. So we must have patience if at times it seems a little self conscious and rigid in its workings. It is because we are learning something very difficult but very wonderful — how to live together as a community of Bahá'ís according to the glorious teachings." Shoghi Effendi, (through his secretary).[1]

Some comment on the role of Bahá'í administration in the

[1] The Local Spiritual Assembly, p. 28-29 (USA).

wider context will be made in the next chapter on "World Civilization". Here comment will be mostly confined to its present role within the Bahá'í community. Even this role is of significance to all mankind. The very existence of a working and world-wide Bahá'í administration means that there is in embryo an alternative system of government to the chaos of conventional institutions, a system which is ready to serve the whole society when there is a major breakdown of those institutions. Further, it means that when eventually such a system is accepted by mankind there will be a great body of practical experience in how it should function.

Bahá'ís today have two overriding but closely related objectives. They have to spread as widely as possible knowledge of Bahá'u'lláh and of His teachings for the creation of a new civilization. The task is enormous and the numbers of Bahá'ís few. However, Bahá'ís do not feel overwhelmed because teaching works on the basis of the multipler: one teaches one, then two teach two, then four teach four and so on. They have also continually to increase their own understanding of these teachings and put them into practice in their own lives. This applies not only to their personal lives but, just as important, in the way the community grows in its practice of unity, justice and brotherhood. These are the obligations of a community looking not to itself as such, but to the welfare of all humanity.

The Local Spiritual Assembly is responsible for directing and supervising the teaching of the Bahá'í Cause in its area of jurisdiction. The methods used are numerous, differing according to the type of society in the area, but they all have certain common features. First, the approach must be dignified and respectful of the intelligence and feelings of the listener: there must be no misleading sales pitch, nor must the Cause be thrust upon those who do not wish to listen. The approach should be as if "offering a gift to a king" with love and genuine concern for those addressed. Often the approach is to let the other person do most of the talking at first so that he can empty himself of his pent-up feelings. After that he is more likely to be receptive to new ideas which can be introduced as relevant responses to the problems and anxieties and hopes which he has expressed:

"To teach is, to a great extent, the art of listening. If you will listen to the one you want to teach and find out what he wants and needs to hear then you can start your treatment by giving him, from our teachings, the right answer, the right remedy. ...

Teaching is excellent discipline for the personal ego, for to teach successfully you have to put yourself in the background and subdue your will and self-expression enough to be a sensitive receiving instrument that will pick up the seeker's correct wave length. If you tune into that person you can commune with him and through that sympathetic thought you can begin to let the light of the Cause into his mind, you cannot force yourself into another person's soul or pound the truth into him just through sheer conviction that you are right." Rúḥíyyih Rabbani.[1]

As part of their teaching effort Assemblies will sometimes, if practical, keep in touch with the local authorities. This practice at a minimum reassures the authorities that the Bahá'í community is in no way "subversive" (see section D of this chapter). It can also lead to fruitful consultation with the authorities and as a result increased public interest in Bahá'í proclamation and teaching. A most effective method of presenting the Cause is to teach as a group, for then others may observe something of the unity of the Bahá'ís. Furthermore, this method serves as a corrective when as occasionally happens new Bahá'ís confuse Bahá'í teachings with some of their own "old world" ideas. Another well-tried and successful way of teaching is to invite friends into one's home, to hold a "Fireside". The relaxed and secure atmosphere of a warm Bahá'í home is more conducive than most other backgrounds to the true heart-to-heart discussion appropriate to matters of such significance in all our lives.

When people hear of what the Bahá'í Faith stands for, many want to become a part of it and help build a new civilization. Some come to this decision after a great deal of

[1] *"Success in Teaching"*, pp. 11-13 (USA).

study and heart-searching. This is encouraged in the Bahá'í teaching that all should independently investigate the truth. Others, most often those who have suffered in life, such as the poor, the oppressed, the outcasts, intuitively know that this is what they have wanted all their lives. It is the duty of the Local Spiritual Assembly to enroll new Bahá'ís and in so doing it is to make sure that each one knows what he is about: that he accepts Bahá'u'lláh as the Manifestation of God for this Age and that he will undertake to follow with all his strength the Bahá'í teachings and obey the Bahá'í institutions.

"*. . . In the process of declaring themselves they must, in addition to catching the spark of faith, become basically informed about the Central Figures of the Faith, as well as the existence of laws they must follow and an administration they must obey.*"

Universal House of Justice.[1]

The other main function of the Local Spiritual Assembly is to consolidate the unity, sense of purpose and general practice of the Bahá'í way of life in the community. This function has several aspects. One important responsibility which follows from the teaching effort is to make sure that there is a continuous follow up in the deepening of all members of the community in the knowledge of what the Cause fully signifies. Enrollment is not significant in itself; what is important is how individuals grow spiritually thereafter. Meetings should be held regularly to teach and discuss the Bahá'í Writings and members of the community should be encouraged to make prayer and meditation a part of their daily life. However, another most effective way of acquiring real knowledge of what the Faith means is to teach it to others. Teaching provokes questions which have to be answered and forces a Bahá'í to develop his own understanding in order to do this. This is a process which adds greatly to the spiritual strength of the community as well as to that of the individual.

Another responsibility of the Assembly in the area of community consolidation is the sponsorship and develop-

[1] Wellspring of Guidance, p. 32 (USA).

ment of what might be called family or social services. Of particular importance is the Assembly's concern for the welfare and education of children. In the last chapter it was pointed out that the education of children is one of the greatest responsibilities of society and under no circumstances must it be allowed to pass by default. The Local Spiritual Assembly is directly responsible for the upbringing of any orphans in the community. Classes should be provided for all children of Bahá'ís in the area. Children of those who are not Bahá'ís are, of course, welcome to attend. In a disintegrating society there are many parents who, though not willing to commit themselves to the Faith, send their children to Bahá'í schools because they know they will be taught the highest standards of morality and an enlightened and progressive view of the human race and its environment.

The Local Spiritual Assembly should see to it that the sick, old and handicapped are properly cared for by the community and that they are given all the love and attention which might be expected of a good close-knit family. The poor should be helped in every way to overcome their difficulties so that they are more able to help themselves.

Community members must be made to feel that they can turn to the Local Spiritual Assembly for help when they have personal problems, especially of a spiritual nature, and that all problems will be treated with the utmost confidence. As noted earlier one important aspect of this work is consulting with friends who are experiencing marital or family difficulties* Though some problems clearly require professional attention, it is also true that a Local Spiritual Assembly of nine elected Bahá'ís dedicated to the good of the community and to complete objectivity will be able to offer advice and help of a quality which cannot be had anywhere else. As with every other service provided, the more experience the Assembly has, the more ability and unity is

---

* Confession is prohibited in the Bahá'í Faith.

"*It is not allowable to declare one's sins and transgressions before any man, inasmuch as this has not been, nor is, conducive to securing God's forgiveness and pardon. At the same time such confession before the creatures leads to one's humiliation and abasement, and God . . . does not wish for the humiliation of His servants.*" Bahá'u'lláh, Bahá'í World Faith, pp. 193-194 (USA).

created for yet greater service to the community. In some countries where government services are particularly corrupt, people who are not Bahá'ís have come to Local Spiritual Assemblies to ask for settlements of their disputes, such has become the reputation of Bahá'í Assemblies for dedicated objectivity and justice. In serving the community the Assembly should not always passively wait for problems to be brought forward. Where there is dissension, for instance, or a member of the community seems estranged, the Assembly must do all in its power to heal the wounds, to make all feel that they are wanted and loved.

Two specific social services which are supervised by the Local Spiritual Assembly are the Bahá'í ceremonies for marriage and burial which occur in its areas of jurisdiction. The Assembly's function is to see that the ceremonies are conducted in accordance with the requirements of Bahá'í laws, and to make proper record in the community's archives.

The Local Spiritual Assembly must be aware of what is going on in the wider world community and of its role in that wider community as well as looking to its responsibilities within its own locality. The Local Spiritual Assembly serves as a channel of communication between its own community and the national Assembly; it will often work together with other Assemblies on regional projects; and sometimes it may be even serving the Universal House of Justice directly by supporting projects in other parts of the world.

The Local Spiritual Assemblies are given guidance and support by the National Spiritual Assembly. The National Spiritual Assembly watches over the activities of the national community and is empowered to give or withhold recognition of Local Assemblies and of enrollment of new Bahá'ís. It has power to adjudicate on local boundaries and to hear appeals against the decisions of Local Assemblies. The National Spiritual Assembly gives general guidelines and goals to be followed by all the national community at the local level. In directing the national teaching effort it is a major responsibility of the National Spiritual Assembly to see that there is a balanced approach to all sections of the population.

"In countries where teaching the masses has succeeded, the Bahá'ís have poured out their time and effort in village areas to the same extent as they had formerly done in cities and towns. The results indicate how unwise it is to solely concentrate on one section of the population. Each national assembly therefore should so balance its resources and harmonize its efforts that the Faith of God is taught not only to those who are readily accessible but to all sections of society, however remote they may be." Universal House of Justice.[1]

In those regions of a country where no Local Assemblies are formed, the National Spiritual Assembly takes direct responsibility for the development of the Faith, usually through appointed regional committees. Finally, though much of the work in a national community is done at the local level, there are certain services which are now best done centrally by the National Spiritual Assembly. Such services include the production of publications and other material on the Faith, and the organization of nationwide summer schools.

The responsibility of the National Spiritual Assembly lies not only inward to the Bahá'í community. It is also responsible for presenting the Faith to the national government and to the national, as distinct from local, news media. Further, the National Spiritual Assembly is a strong link in the bond which links the individual Bahá'í through his local community to the Universal House of Justice. The National Spiritual Assemblies have been described as the pillars of the Universal House of Justice because they make up collectively the International Convention which elects the House, and because they have the major part of the task of organizing the execution of programmes of the Universal House of Justice for the development of the worldwide Bahá'í community. In so doing National Spiritual Assemblies, especially the strongest and best established, will be given tasks far outside their own national field of juris-

---

[1] Wellspring of Guidance, pp. 31-32 (USA).

diction, so adding to the sense of cooperation and oneness throughout the Bahá'í world community.

Directing, coordinating, and safeguarding the Bahá'í world community is the Universal House of Justice. This body has executive, judicial and legislative functions.

As an *executive* body it draws up the long range plans for the growth and development of the Faith and it allocates goals in these plans to the various National Spiritual Assemblies. As an executive body it administers the Bahá'í properties associated with the World Centre, and keeps in constant contact with the government of Israel. It is also in contact with the United Nations. The Bahá'í International Community is an accredited non-governmental organization with consultative status to the Economic and Social Council of the United Nations and an office is maintained in New York for a permanent representative. Through this representative the Universal House of Justice brings to the attention of the assembled nations' representatives the Bahá'í concepts of world brotherhood. Bahá'í representatives have, for instance, suggested amendments to the United Nations Charter to make it a more effective and democratic instrument for world peace.

As a *judicial* body the Universal House of Justice is the final Court of appeal in the Faith. It lays down boundaries for the jurisdiction of National Assemblies and has sole authority to recognize new National Assemblies.

The Bahá'í Writings provide guidelines for a world society over a long period of time and in consequence they are stated as broad principles rather than as detailed laws to meet every conceivable situation. Neither the Universal House of Justice nor any other person or body has the authority to formulate official interpretations of them. This fundamental rule of the Bahá'í Faith is of great significance because it provides protection against the sort of corruption of the basic teachings of the Faith which has occurred in other religions. However, in those areas of policy which have not been specifically dealt with in the Bahá'í Writings, the Universal House of Justice in its *legislative* role may institute new laws for the Bahá'í world community which are in keeping with the spirit and principles laid down in the Writings:

"[the Universal House of Justice has] exclusive right and prerogative ... to pronounce upon and deliver the final judgment on such laws and ordinances as Bahá'u'lláh has not expressly revealed." Shoghi Effendi.[1]

It also has the power to repeal laws which it has established.

". . . Inasmuch as this House of Justice hath power to enact laws that are not expressly recorded in the Book and bear upon daily transactions, so also it hath power to repeal the same . . ." 'Abdu'l-Bahá.[2]

In addition to the National Spiritual Assemblies and various committees the Universal House of Justice has the assistance of groups of men and women chosen for their dedication and distinguished service to the Bahá'í Cause. Those who were appointed by Shoghi Effendi during the period of his guardianship of the Faith (1921-1957) are known as Hands of the Cause of God and they are held in particularly high esteem by the Bahá'í community because of their personal qualities and the services which they have rendered individually, and also because of the critical part they played collectively in the evolution of the Administrative Order following the death of Shoghi Effendi (see chapter eight). The others are Counsellors appointed by the Universal House of Justice and grouped into five Continental Boards, each with responsibility for a region of the world. Each Continental Board of Counsellors is assisted at the regional level by Auxiliary Board Members. Free from the general duties of administration, Hands of the Cause and the Counsellors travel about the world helping to deepen Bahá'í communities in the meaning of the Faith. They are specifically enjoined to watch over the security of the Faith and to report to National Spiritual Assemblies and to the Universal House of Justice when they find problems. The Universal House of Justice has agreed to a request of the Hands of the Cause that they not

[1] World Order of Bahá'u'lláh, p. 150 (USA).
[2] Will and Testament of 'Abdu'l-Bahá, p. 18 (UK).

be voted for. Counsellors may be voted for, but if elected to an Assembly must choose to resign from one institution or the other.*

The Writings are very direct concerning the authority of the Universal House of Justice and the other institutions of the Bahá'í World Order. In a unique way the Bahá'í institutions have built into them the strongest protection against the abuse of power. In consequence many conventional devices for restricting the influence of government are not required and Bahá'í administration is free to put all its untrammeled energy into its work for the good of all society. The relationship between community and institution is one of mutual love and harmony rather than the suspicion and disputation which is so often the case with political institutions. It is fundamental to the Bahá'í way of life to view loyalty and obedience to elected institutions of the Administrative Order as essential for the establishment of a united, peaceful, and just society. In other words, it is the path of freedom.

"True liberty consisteth in man's submission unto My commandments, little as ye know it. Were men to observe that which We have sent down unto them from the Heaven of Revelation, they would, of a certainty, attain unto perfect liberty. ... The liberty that profiteth you is to be found nowhere except in complete servitude to God, the Eternal Truth. Whoso hath tasted of its sweetness will refuse to barter it for all the dominion of earth and heaven." Bahá'u'lláh.[1]

The law of obedience applies to individuals and to institutions alike. Local Spiritual Assemblies follow the guidance of National Spiritual Assemblies and all follow the word of the Universal House of Justice. Within the "constitution" of the Bahá'í scriptures the authority of the Universal House of Justice is supreme and Bahá'ís understand that its actions are for the good of all humanity, and that it is the instrument of the Will of God on earth.

". . . The members of the Universal House of Justice . . . are

---

* However a Hand or Counsellor may serve temporarily on a Local Spiritual Assembly if its continued existence depends upon such service, as for instance when there are only nine adults, including the Hand or Counsellor, in the local Bahá'í community.

[1] Gleanings, p. 335 (UK).

not . . . responsible to those whom they represent, nor are they allowed to be governed by the feelings, the general opinion, and even the convictions of the mass of the faithful, or of those who dircetly elect them . . . They may, indeed they must, acquaint themselves with the conditions prevailing among the community, must weigh dispassionately in their minds the merits of any case presented for their consideration, but must reserve for themselves the right of an unfettered decision. . . . They, and not the body of those who either directly or indirectly elect them, have thus been made the recipients of the divine guidance which is at once the lifeblood and ultimate safeguard of this Revelation." Shoghi Effendi.[1]

The formal base for obedience of Bahá'ís to the institutions of the Administrative Order are in the Wills of Bahá'u'lláh and 'Abdu'l-Bahá. In His Will (known as the *Book of Covenant*) Bahá'u'lláh told the Bahá'ís that after His death they must be obedient to 'Abdu'l-Bahá, Whom He appointed the Centre of the Covenant. Furthermore, He said that 'Abdu'l-Bahá would have sole authority to interpret His teaching.

The *Will and Testament* of 'Abdu'l-Bahá, which Shoghi Effendi said

"called into being, outlined the features and set in motion the processes of this Administrative Order."[2]

indicated that after 'Abdu'l-Bahá's death, the Bahá'ís must turn to the Guardian (Shoghi Effendi) and the Universal House of Justice in accordance with the Plan of Bahá'u'lláh.

"To none is given the right to put forth his own opinion or express his particular convictions. All must seek guidance and turn unto the Centre of the Cause and the House of Justice. And he that turneth unto whatsoever else is indeed in grievous error."[3]

The place of obedience to the elected institutions in the Bahá'í way of living is of such importance that something should be said at this point on what happens should the subject be brought into question. Abiding by Bahá'í laws

[1] World Order of Bahá'u'lláh, p. 153 (USA).

[2] God Passes By, p. 325.(USA).

[3] Will and Testament of 'Abdu'l-Bahá, pp. 20-21 (UK).

concerning personal morality is a matter of private conscience up to the point when public and flagrant breaking of the laws brings the community into disrepute. So long as a person is genuinely struggling to follow the Bahá'í law, the institutions will do all in their power to assist and there will be no question of sanctions. However, continued and flagrant public display of disobedience to the laws must call forth action to protect the unity and good name of the community. In such cases, after all attempts to induce a change have failed, the National Spiritual Assembly may deprive the person in question of his administrative rights. The deprivation of this right means that he is not allowed to attend Feasts, though he may still meet with individual Bahá'ís, he may not vote in Bahá'í elections, he is ineligible to be elected to Bahá'í institutions, and he is not permitted to contribute to Bahá'í funds (see below). By the standards of the outside world these may not sound like very impressive sanctions, but to a Bahá'í who receives much joy and spiritual nourishment from his community this is a severe blow, so severe that the institutions are only too anxious to have the rights restored as soon as the person concerned shows willingness to try again. The same deprivation of rights may be applied to those who cause continuous and vicious dissension in the community and to those who break community laws, such as those on marriage and backbiting, as distinct from personal laws.

To attack, disobey or attempt to undermine the central authorities of the Bahá'í Faith, i.e. Bahá'u'lláh, 'Abdu'l-Bahá, Shoghi Effendi or the Universal House of Justice, is the most serious offence for this stabs at the very heart of the purpose of the Cause, the unification of mankind. In such cases every effort is made to help the person concerned to see the destructive nature of his position and so come back into the community. If this fails then the Universal House of Justice has the authority to expel such a person from the Bahá'í community, an action which is in reality a formalization of a position he has already adopted. Such "Covenant-breakers" must be shunned by all Bahá'ís.

"Bahá'u'lláh and the Master ('Abdu'l-Bahá) in many places and very emphatically have told us to shun entirely all Covenant-breakers as they are afflicted with what we might try and define as contagious spiritual disease; they have also told us, however, to pray for them. These souls are not lost forever. . . . God will forgive any soul if he repents. . . .

. . . Also, it has nothing to do with unity in the Cause; if a man cuts a cancer out of his body to preserve his health and very life no one would suggest that for the sake of "unity" it should be reintroduced into the otherwise healthy organism! On the contrary, what was once a part of him has so radically changed as to have become a poison." Shoghi Effendi (through his secretary).[1]

So strict is this rule to protect the community from such a disease that anyone who continues to associate with the Covenant-breaker, including members of his own family, may be also expelled from the community. It must be emphasized that there is no element of vindictiveness in such sanctions. As in the case of deprivation of voting rights, the Universal House of Justice is ever ready to welcome a Covenant-breaker back into the world community with love and without recrimination as soon as he has made genuine submission to its authority and expressed regret for the past. It should be also stressed that the law refers specifically to those who maliciously try to destroy the Faith. Those who voluntarily leave the Faith for other reasons will continue to be treated by Bahá'ís in as warm and friendly a fashion as any other human being.

One last subject should be mentioned before closing this section and that is the question of the financing of the Faith. The major part of the work of the Faith is done on a voluntary basis and is therefore never recorded as a financial expense. However, there are significant activities in the community which do require financial support. The work of the Universal House of Justice and of many of the National Spiritual Assemblies requires the services of a full-time staff which must be paid for, though the rate of pay which prevails has to be very low by normal standards.

[1] Principles of Bahá'í Administration, p. 34 (UK).

Major expense is also incurred in connection with the maintenance and development of Bahá'í properties, and support of summer schools and other teaching programmes. Books and other materials have to be supplied to many parts of the world at prices which put them within reach of all who need them, including the poorest, and this often means at below cost. The Faith does not have fully-paid missionaries but it does need "pioneers" to go from strong communities to help establish new centres and, just as important, to give administrative and other assistance to fledgling communities. Such pioneers should be self-supporting but often in the initial period following a move it is difficult to obtain work, especially in those countries which for nationalistic reasons are reluctant to allow "foreigners" to work in their country. During these difficult periods financial assistance is given from the Bahá'í funds. Travel-teaching, as pointed out earlier, is a most succesful way of maintaining a sense of world community. Few Bahá'ís are rich enough to be able to pay for all such travel out of their pockets and help has to be given from central funds. In short, the provision of funds is vital to the life of the Faith and will become even more so as it grows.

"The supply of funds, in support of the National Treasury, constitutes, at the present time, the life-blood of those nascent institutions which you are labouring to erect. Its importance cannot, surely be overestimated." Shoghi Effendi.[1]

Funds are usually collected at the local level. Each Local Spiritual Assembly will have its own budget which provides for regular amounts to be sent to the National Spiritual Assembly and for its own needs. In turn the National Spiritual Assembly will have a budget which includes an allocation for the Universal House of Justice's International Fund. In addition Bahá'ís may send contributions directly to the national and international funds, and may earmark them for specific programmes.

It is fundamental to the Bahá'í spiritual approach to

[1] Messages to America, p. 5 (USA).

administration that giving to the Bahá'í fund is purely voluntary.

"I feel urged to remind you of the necessity of ever bearing in mind the cardinal principle that all contributions to the Fund are to be purely and strictly voluntary in character. It should be made clear and evident to everyone that any form of compulsion, however slight and indirect, strikes at the very root of the principle underlying the formation of the Fund ever since its inception. While appeals of a general character carefully worded and moving and dignified in tone are welcome under all circumstances it should be left entirely to the discretion of every conscientious believer to decide upon the nature, the amount, and purpose of his or her own contribution for the propagation of the Cause." Shoghi Effendi.[1]

This does not mean, however, that it is a matter of indifference whether or not a Bahá'í gives to the Fund. For a Bahá'í, giving to the Fund is a strong moral obligation. Every penny given is in support of the greatest enterprise of all time: the building of a just society for all mankind, and therefore must have the highest priority on any Bahá'í unencumbered resources.*

"Let us try to enlarge our realization of the great work that the Cause is doing for humanity. We are trying to save mankind from destruction and the means and agencies for so doing to bring about this result have been revealed to us and we have been given the privilege of establishing them and maintaining them. So the budget, from first to last, is a spiritual rather than a material obligation."[2]

Giving to the Bahá'í funds is also a privilege because only Bahá'ís may do so.

"Moreover, we should, I feel, regard it as an axiom and guiding principle of Bahá'í administration that in the conduct of every specific Bahá'í activity, as distinct from undertakings of a humanitarian, philanthropic or charitable character, which may in future be conducted under Bahá'í

[1] Principles of Bahá'í Administration, p. 104 (UK).
* Bahá'ís should not contribute to the Fund to the detriment of paying off any debt which they may have.
[2] Bahá'í News, October 1956. Article by Horace Holley.

143

auspices, only those who have already identified themselves with the Faith and are regarded as its avowed and unreserved supporters should be invited to join and collaborate." Shoghi Effendi.[1]

When a person who is not a Bahá'í insists on giving to the Fund the contribution is used only for charitable services. This rule is strictly enforced no matter how great the material needs of the Faith.

Bahá'ís believe that universal participation in regular giving to the Fund is of far greater significance for the spiritual growth of the community than the giving of large amounts by a few rich people. Further, the spiritual growth will be even greater when giving involves sacrifice. Sacrifice, that is making sacred, means a positive commitment to this greatest of causes, and that in itself entails its own spiritual reward.

"*We must be like the fountain or spring that is continually emptying itself of all that it has and is continually being refilled from an invisible source. To be continually giving out for the good of our fellows undeterred by the fear of poverty and reliant on the unfailing bounty of the Source of all wealth and all good — this is the secret of right living.*" Shoghi Effendi.[2]

D — *The Old World Order*

For several important reasons Bahá'ís completely avoid taking part in politics. Whilst recognizing that certain progress in the human condition has been made and may still be made through politics, especially as Bahá'í principles become more generally accepted, it is the Bahá'í view that the really fundamental changes which are needed for the establishment of a truly just world society will not be achieved by these means, a theme which was touched upon in the first chapter and again at the beginning of this chapter. They feel that it would be a misuse of their time to struggle to cure symptoms of the world's problems in the

[1] Bahá'í Administration, p. 182 (USA).
[2] Principles of Bahá'í Administration, p. 107 (UK).

political arena and that all their energy should be devoted to dealing with the root of the problem by means of the spiritual and scientific tools of government provided by the Bahá'í Faith. Bahá'ís draw an analogy which shows the present political and social system to be like an old tumbledown house standing on rotten foundations. The political reformer is one who runs from room to another, painting a little here, doing a small repair there. The Bahá'í is the one who goes outside the old house and starts to build a new strong one on the soundest foundations — that is the World Order of Bahá'u'lláh. The point is given added force when it is remembered that the Bahá'ís are at present only a small proportion of the world's total population. Every bit of time, energy and skill that those few have is desperately needed for the immense but absolutely essential long-run task of building a new world civilization. The world simply cannot afford to have Bahá'ís give any of their precious energy to other but narrower progressive movements, no matter how worthy they may seem.

There is another consideration even more important. It is a characteristic of politics that they divide, and it is believed that no matter how well motivated Bahá'ís might be they too would soon become divided if they went into politics, and in consequence the whole Bahá'í community would be weakened on the very issue for which it stands: the unity of man. It is not difficult to imagine that the unity of feeling between, say, a Russian Bahá'í and an American Bahá'í, would not be the same if one were to join the Communist party and the other the Republican party.

"We Bahá'ís are one the world over; we are seeking to build up a new World Order, divine in origin. How can we do this if every Bahá'í is a member of a different political party — some of them diametrically opposite to each other? Where is our unity then? We would be divided, because of politics, against ourselves, and this is the opposite of our purpose. Obviously if one Bahá'í in Austria is given freedom to choose a political party and join it, however good its aims may be, another Bahá'í in Japan or America, or India has the right to do the same thing and he might belong to a party the very *opposite in principle to that which the Austrian Bahá'í belongs to. Where would be the unity of the Faith then? These two spiritual brothers would be working against each other because of their political affiliations (as the Christians of Europe have been doing in so many fratricidal wars). The best way for a Bahá'í to serve his country and the world is to work for the establishment of Bahá'u'lláh's World Order, which will gradually unite all men and do away with divisive political systems and religious creeds.*" Shoghi Effendi (through his secretary).[1]

Avoidance of politics for Bahá'ís means not taking part in political campaigns or in any way identifying themselves with a political party; not giving financial assistance to political parties, and not holding political office. However, Bahá'ís may hold office in government if it is genuinely non-political.

"It is their duty to strive to distinguish, as clearly as they possibly can, and if needed, with the aid of their elected representatives such posts and functions as are either diplomatic or political from those that are purely administrative in character." Shoghi Effendi.[2]

They may also cast their vote in the secret ballot of a normal democratic election.

"The friends may vote if they can do it, without identifying themselves with one party or another. . . . It remains for the individuals to so use their right to vote as to keep aloof from party politics, and always bear in mind that they are voting on the merits of the individual, rather than because he belongs to one party or another." Shoghi Effendi.[3]

Though Bahá'ís keep out of politics they have not withdrawn from the present world to work on some future Utopia. They are deeply concerned to do all they can to ameliorate present conditions, consistent with the building of the new world society, which they believe is the ultimate answer. As mentioned before, Bahá'ís in their private lives tend to gravitate to those professions, trades and occu-

[1] Principles of Bahá'í Administration, p. 43 (UK).
[2] World Order of Bahá'u'lláh, pp. 64-65 (USA).
[3] Principles of Bahá'í Administration, pp. 41-42 (UK).

pations which most directly are of real service to humanity; for instance, medicine, agriculture, teaching, the protection of the environment, and the social services:

"It should be made unmistakably clear that such an attitude implies neither the slightest indifference to the cause and interests of their own country, nor involves any insubordination on their part to the authority of recognized and established governments. . . . It indicates the desire cherished by every true and loyal follower of Bahá'u'lláh to serve, in an unselfish, unostentatious and patriotic fashion, the highest interests of the country to which he belongs, and in a way that would entail no departure from the high standards of integrity and truthfulness associated with the teachings of the Faith." Shoghi Effendi.[1]

Furthermore, though careful to avoid political entanglements Bahá'ís will take up many issues which are the particular concern of progressive movements such as minority rights, women's rights, justice for the poor as well as rich, improved education, a world government. For instance, in recent years the Bahá'ís of the United States have sponsored, in cooperation with the United Nations, such programmes as "International Human Rights Year" (1968) and the "International Education Year" (1970). The Bahá'í world community was also represented at the "Stockholm Conference on the Human Environment" (1972), the "World Conference of the International Women's Year" in Mexico City (1975), the "World Conference to Combat Racism and Racial Discrimination" held in Geneva (1978) etc.

The principle of non-involvement in politics clearly has bearing on the Bahá'í approach to established governments. Bahá'ís believe that existing forms of governments will fade away of their own accord in the course of time, dying out like the dinosaur because they have outlived their time. However, whilst the present political system exists Bahá'ís must practise a positive neutrality by demonstrating total loyalty to all established governments.

"In every country or government where any of this

[1] World Order of Bahá'u'lláh, p. 65 (USA).

community reside, they must behave toward that government with faithfulness, trustfulness and truthfulness." Bahá'u'lláh.[1]

The principle of loyalty to government has very important long-run significance. Bahá'ís believe obedience to be the very foundation of the institutions of a new World Order. Unless this principle is deeply imbedded in the consciousness of all world-citizens, the creation of a new civilization is out of the question. So important is this point that Bahá'ís have to be seen practising it at all times, even if it means accepting a government whose actions are causing great harm to the people it rules. Bahá'ís who wish to bring about universal law and order, cannot now be identified with the division and disorder which would follow from opposition to government. They must be seen to be completely trustworthy on both an individual and a social level.

Loyalty to government is also important from the short-run point of view. The Bahá'í community has had to undergo many, many trials in pursuing its great enterprise including many unjust persecutions from state and church. It does not make much sense to seek additional tribulations by wantonly provoking the hostility of established governments. Picking quarrels with governments is not going to bring a new civilization any nearer; quite the contrary. The Bahá'í community needs as much peace as it can get so that it can devote all its energies to teaching and building up the World Order. Bahá'ís believe that, as on the personal level, more is achieved by friendly example and persuasion than by hostile confrontation.

Obedience to government means submitting to all its laws and regulations (except any demand to deny the Faith):

"To all administrative regulations which the civil authorities have issued from time to time, or will issue in the future in that land [Persia], as in all other countries, the Bahá'í community, faithful to its sacred obligations towards its government, and conscious of its civic duties, has yielded,

[1] Bahá'í World Faith, p. 192 (USA).

and will continue to yield implicit obedience." Shoghi Effendi.[1]

This is so even if it means that Bahá'ís are not allowed to carry out their activities.

"If local, state or federal authorities prohibit Bahá'í life or some aspect of it, then Bahá'ís must submit to these requirements in all cases. . . ." Universal House of Justice.[2]

Loyalty to government does not imply approval nor does it mean obsequiousness. Bahá'ís may petition with the maximum vigour allowed by the law against those acts which are considered illegal or unjust. The only exception to the law of obedience to government is that Bahá'ís cannot be forced by a government to renounce their Faith as noted above. No government has the right to dictate what individuals may believe.

"In matters, however, that vitally affect the integrity and honour of the Faith of Bahá'u'lláh, and are tantamount to a recantation of their Faith and repudiation of their innermost belief, they are convinced and are unhesitatingly prepared to vindicate by their lifeblood the sincerity of their conviction, that no power on earth, neither the arts of the most insidious adversary nor the bloody weapons of the most tyrannical oppressor, can ever succeed in extorting from them a word or deed that might tend to stifle the voice of their conscience or tarnish the purity of their faith." Shoghi Effendi.[3]

Many young Bahá'ís are first affected by the principle of loyalty to government when they are faced with compulsory military service. As the reader no doubt expects, Bahá'í teachings are emphatically against any form of personal violence. Bahá'u'lláh wrote:

"Beware lest ye shed the blood of any one."[4]

'Abdu'l-Bahá said that though a Bahá'í may defend his life if attacked, he should not retaliate even against a blood-thirsty enemy.

"From the texts you already have available it is clear that Bahá'u'lláh has stated that it is preferable to be killed in the

[1] God Passes By, p. 372 (USA).
[2] National Bahá'í Review, August 1970, p. 1.
[3] Bahá'í Administration, p. 162 (USA).
[4] Epistle to the Son of the Wolf, p. 25 (USA).

path of God's good-pleasure than to kill, and that organized religious attack against Bahá'ís should never turn into any kind of warfare, as this is strictly prohibited in our Writings.

"*A hitherto untranslated Tablet from 'Abdu'l-Bahá, however, points out that in the case of attack by robbers and highwaymen, a Bahá'í should not surrender himself, but should try, as fas as circumstances permit, to defend himself, and later on lodge a complaint with the government authorities. In a letter written on behalf of the Guardian, he also indicates that in an emergency when there is no legal force at hand to appeal to, a Bahá'í is justified in defending his life. In another letter the Guardian has further pointed out that the assault of an irresponsible assailant upon a Bahá'í should be resisted by the Bahá'í, who would be justified, under such circumstances, in protecting his life.*

"*The House of Justice does not wish at the present time to go beyond the guidelines given in the above-mentioned statements. The question is basically a matter of conscience, and in each case the Bahá'í involved must use his judgement in determining when to stop in self-defence lest his action deteriorate into retaliation.*" Universal House of Justice.[1]

Throughout the Writings war is condemned in the severest terms. For example, 'Abdu'l-Bahá wrote:

"*Peace is light whereas war is darkness. Peace is life; war is death. Peace is guidance; war is error. Peace is the foundation of God; war is satanic institution. Peace is the illumination of the world of humanity; war is the destroyer of human foundations.*"[2]

Therefore, wherever possible within the law, Bahá'ís must do all in their power to avoid being placed in a position in which there is an obligation to kill:

"*. . . It would be unthinkable for [Bahá'ís] to willingly place themselves in a position where they must take human life.*" Universal House of Justice.[3]

Accordingly, in those countries where it is legal, Bahá'ís who are drafted should apply for "conscientious objector"

---

[1] National Bahá'í Review, August 1970, p. 3 (USA).

[2] Bahá'í World Faith, p. 231 (USA).

[3] National Bahá'í Review, August 1969, p. 2 (USA).

status so that they may do "alternative service" or perform "non-combatant" duties.

"It is immaterial whether such activities would still expose them to dangers either at home or in the front, since their desire is not to protect their lives, but to desist from any acts of wilful murder." Shoghi Effendi.[1]

However, in those countries where there is no legal choice, then Bahá'ís are obliged to go through with their military service even in combatant units. This is a different position from that of the pacifist. To the Bahá'í, deplorable as it is to have to serve in the armed forces, rebellion is worse because in the long run acceptance of the idea of disloyalty will make more difficult the establishment of a just world government and lasting peace. Shoghi Effendi said:

"Extreme pacifists are thus very close to the anarchists, in the sense that both of these groups lay an undue emphasis on the rights and merits of the individual. The Bahá'í conception of social life is essentially based on the subordination of the individual will to that of society. It neither suppresses the individual nor does it exalt him to the point of making him an anti-social creature, a menace to society. As in everything, it follows the 'golden mean'." Shoghi Effendi, through his secretary.[2]

He went on:

"The other main objection to the conscientious objectors (i.e., pacifists) is that their method of establishing peace is too negative. Non-cooperation is too passive a philosophy to become an effective way for social reconstruction. Their refusal to bear arms can never establish peace. There should first be a spiritual revitalization which nothing, except the Cause of God, can effectively bring to every man's heart."[3]

It should be noted, too, that the Bahá'í position on force differs from the pacifist in another respect. Though all wars in the present circumstances are condemned, and Bahá'ís believe that when a just world government is established its authority will be for the most part based on the moral

---

[1] Principles of Bahá'í Administration, p. 108 (UK).
[2] National Bahá'í Review, August 1969, p. 3 (USA).
[3] National Bahá'í Review, August 1969, pp. 3-4 (USA).

maturity of the peoples of the world, they also recognize that there could be occasions when there would be violent attacks on society and such attacks would have to be restrained by force. In these circumstances Bahá'ís believe that failure to resist such attacks would be a gross injustice.

"When Christ said: 'Whosoever shall strike thee on the right cheek, turn to him the left one also,' it was for the purpose of teaching men not to take personal revenge. He did not mean that if a wolf should fall upon a flock of sheep and wish to destroy it, that the wolf should be encouraged to do so. No, if Christ had known that a wolf had entered the fold and was about to destroy the sheep, most certainly He would have prevented it." 'Abdu'l-Bahá.[1]

Consequently, as will be seen in the next chapter, one of the arms envisaged for a future world government is a peace-keeping international police force.

[1] Some Answered Questions, p. 270 (USA).

CHAPTER VII

A WORLD CIVILIZATION

A — *The Most Great Peace*

THE Bahá'í community is distinguished from all other groups, social, political, and religious, in that it is totally dedicated to the building of a new world civilization in which there will be opportunity for and encouragement of spiritual growth and fulfilment for all men, free from the oppression of hatred, prejudice, violence and injustice.

"*Let there be no mistake. The principle of the Oneness of Mankind — the pivot round which all the teachings of Bahá'u'lláh revolve — is no mere outburst of ignorant emotionalism or an expression of a vague and pious hope. . . . It does not constitute merely the enunciation of an ideal, but stands inseparably associated with an institution adequate to embody its truth, demonstrate its validity, and perpetuate its influence. It implies an organic change in the structure of present-day society, a change such as the world has not yet experienced. It constitutes a challenge, at once bold and universal, to outworn shibboleths of national creeds — creeds that have had their day and which must, in the ordinary course of events as shaped and controlled by Providence, give way to a new gospel, fundamentally different from, and infinitely superior to, what the world has already conceived. It calls for no less than the reconstruction and the demilitarization of the whole civilized world — a world organically unified in all the essential aspects of its life, it political machinery, its spiritual aspiration, its trade and finance, its script and language, and yet infinite in the diversity of the national characteristics of its federated units.*" Shoghi Effendi.[1]

Bahá'ís believe that a new world civilization will be reached in two stages. The first, or transitional, stage will be a state which is called the 'Lesser Peace' in which there

[1] World Order of Bahá'u'lláh, pp. 42-43 (USA).

will be general agreement to settle disputes without resort to war. In this stage many of the basic illnesses of society will be still present and the establishment of a civilization permanently at peace with itself, both materially and spiritually, will only come with the second stage, which is called the 'Most Great Peace'. The 'Most Great Peace' will be achieved when there is a world-wide acceptance of the teachings of Bahá'u'lláh. Even the 'Lesser Peace' will, to a significant degree, depend on many Bahá'í principles being accepted by the majority of the peoples and governments of the world, whether consciously or unconsciously.

This is one reason why Bahá'ís feel the urgency of spreading knowledge of Bahá'u'lláh and His teachings as widely and as quickly as possible.

"Bestir yourselves, O people, in anticipation of the days of Divine Justice, for the promised hour is now come. Abandon that which ye possess, and seize that which God, Who layeth low the necks of men, hath brought. Know ye of a certainty that if ye turn not back from that which ye have committed, chastisement will overtake you on every side, and ye shall behold things more greivous than that which ye beheld aforetime."[1]

Bahá'u'lláh warned that if men did not change their way of conducting affairs there is the gravest danger of terrible disasters before the "Lesser Peace" is established.

Though doing everything in their power to change attitudes and so avert such catastrophes, Bahá'ís have to be prepared for the possibility that the political and social system will not respond quickly enough. This gives added reason for Bahá'ís to learn as quickly and as deeply as possible the principles of the World Order of Bahá'u'lláh and for them to spread evenly throughout the world so that in the event of major catastrophes they will be ready to help build a new civilization out of the ruins of the old.*

---

[1] The Promised Day is Come, p.3 (USA).

* Bahá'ís are urged not only to go to all parts of the world but to pay particular attention to rural as well urban areas. The main reason is that Bahá'ís wish to reach peoples of all backgrounds. A second reason is that in today's conditions those who live in rural areas by and large tend to have more time and interest in spiritual matters and consequently are often more immediately responsive to Bahá'í teachings. In the present context it should be noted that this practice makes it more likely that some of the Bahá'í community would survive, say a nuclear holocaust than if they all stayed in the big cities.

To describe the "Most Great Peace" is clearly a difficult task as we are barely able to comprehend even remotely what it would be like to live in a civilization based on spiritual principles.

"In this present cycle there will be an evolution in civilization unparalleled in the history of the world. The world of humanity has heretofore been in the stage of infancy; now it is approaching maturity. Just as the individual human organism having attained the period of maturity reaches its fullest degree of physical strength and ripened intellectual faculties, so that in one year of this ripened period there is witnessed an unprecedented measure of development, likewise the world of humanity in this cycle of its completeness and consummation will realize an immeasurable upward progress . . ." 'Abdu'l-Bahá.[1]

However, the attempt should be made; because not to do so would be to give a very incomplete picture of what the Faith signifies.

To a large extent much of what we know about the "Most Great Peace" has been said in previous chapters. These chapters dealt with principles and teachings not only for today's community, but for the world civilization into which it will grow. However, in addition, the Bahá'í Writings include other teachings which relate more specifically to the time when the major part of society is Bahá'í and there is a Bahá'í system of government in that society. These additional teachings might be put into two groups: those which deal directly with the strengthening of world unity, and secondly those which have more to do with justice and harmony at the local community level. The first group are discussed in the next section, and the second group in the third and last section of this chapter.

B — *The World Community*

The first principle which will have bearing on the nature of the new civilization is the necessity for a world system of government. This would be similar in many ways to the

[1] Promulgation of Universal Peace, p. 35 (USA).

Administrative Order crowned by the Universal House of Justice which is the backbone of the present Bahá'í community, developed to take account of vastly expanded responsibilities.

"*And as the Bahá'í Faith permeates the masses of the peoples of East and West, and its truth is embraced by the majority of the peoples of a number of the Sovereign States of the world, will the Universal House of Justice attain the plentitude of its power, and exercise, as the supreme organ of the Bahá'í Commonwealth, all the rights, the duties, and responsibilities incumbent upon the world's future superstate.*" Shoghi Effendi.[1]

Such principles of the Administrative Order as the methods of election and consultation would be clearly essential features. The exact details of a world system of government will be unfolded in response to the circumstances of the time but a general picture of the system can be obtained from the following statement of Shoghi Effendi.

"*The unity of the human race as envisaged by Bahá'u'lláh implies the establishment of a world commonwealth in which all nations, races, creeds and classes are closely and permanently united, and in which the autonomy of its state members and the personal freedom and initiative of the individuals that compose them are definitely and completely safeguarded. This commonwealth must, as far as we can visualize it, consist of a world legislature, whose members will, as the trustees of the whole of mankind, ultimately control the entire resources of all the component nations, and will enact such laws as shall be required to regulate the life, satisfy the needs and adjust the relationships of all races and peoples. A world executive, backed by an international Force, will carry out the decisions arrived at, and apply the laws enacted by, this world legislature, and will safeguard the organic unity of the whole commonwealth. A world tribunal will adjudicate and deliver its compulsory and final verdict in all and any disputes that may arise between the various elements constituting this universal system . . .*

"*A world federal system, ruling the whole earth and*

[1] World Order of Bahá'u'lláh, p. 7 (USA).

exercising unchallengeable authority over its unimaginably vast resources, blending and embodying the ideals of both the East and the West, liberated from the curse of war and its miseries, and bent on the exploitation of all the available sources of energy on the surface of the planet, a system in which Force is made the servant of Justice, whose life is sustained by its universal recognition of one God and by its allegiance to one common Revelation — such is the goal toward which humanity, impelled by the unifying forces of life, is moving." Shoghi Effendi.[1]

The role of government will be set to a large extent by the spiritualization of world society — that is, the practice in daily life by all of true religious principles. On the other hand, the spiritual nature of government methods will contribute to the spiritual growth and development of society. This is obviously so different from most of our experience that it is difficult to draw parallels with present or past institutions. However, the writer would like to venture the following remarks.

From studying Bahá'í methods and administration it seems that there will be the minimum of bureaucracy and the prevailing spirit will be to rely on voluntary compliance with the rulings of the world government, and in consequence a great deal of responsibility will be delegated to national and local bodies.

"The worldwide law of Bahá'u'lláh ... repudiates excessive centralization on one hand, and disclaims all attempts at uniformity on the other. Its watchword is unity in diversity ... The principle of the oneness of mankind ... calls for ... a world organically unified in all the essential aspects of its life ... infinite in the diversity of the national characteristics of its federated units." Shoghi Effendi.[2]

As in all open societies, there would be room for great diversity of view and discussion. However, this is only possible when there is acceptance by all of the basic premises of society. Recent history is full of examples of

[1] World Order of Bahá'u'lláh, pp. 203-204 (USA).
[2] World Order of Bahá'u'lláh, pp. 41-43 (USA).

what happens to open societies when the basic rules are no longer followed.

In some respects it might be true to say that the national level will be less important than it is within the present political framework which gives the national state more or less unrestricted sovereignty. On the one hand, general direction will be given to national governments by the world institutions, and on the other there will be a devolution of much responsibility to the local community where most of the day-to-day affairs will be conducted.

The "Force" referred to by Shoghi Effendi in the last but one quotation is an international peacekeeping police force which would be the only significant armed group permitted. It would be probably very small by comparison with present day national forces and it would be sufficient only to defend the world community against attack by any selfish interest which might arise. Local communities would have their police forces sufficient to maintain law and order and additionally there may be some need for a small central group under each national government. The important point, of course, is that such police forces would be protectors of society, and they would have the wholehearted support of those whom they protect.

An important function of the world government would be to strengthen the sense in all men of belonging to one world family. The chief instrument for the development of such an awareness would be study of Bahá'í Writings whose main message is the three unities: God is one, Religion is one, Mankind is one. There would be a universal system of compulsory education which would place equal emphasis on spiritual growth along the lines indicated in Bahá'í Writings, and on objective scientific investigation. Spiritual studies would act as a unifying force which would give meaning to the whole education process and provide the universal principles which apply in science and other branches of learning. The whole concept is quite different from present-day systems of education which are lacking in unity of purpose and which are morally confusing. The system of education would also restore the balance between intellectual learning and manual skills, giving recognition to the importance of each in the fully rounded man. The object would be to raise up a new Race of Man, spiritually mature, and with an ever-inquiring view of the universe in its every aspect.

It is interesting to note with regard to education, the great importance which is placed on the role of the teacher in the new society by Bahá'u'lláh and 'Abdu'l-Bahá — a role which contrasts with the reality of today, despite protestations to the contrary.

Bahá'í interest in the development of a more balanced system of education has already begun to bear fruit not only within the community itself but also in the world at large. In the United States Bahá'ís are making valuable contributions to the development of the theory and practice of education,* and it is a Bahá'í who is the founder and driving force behind the well known Harlem Preparatory School which has successfully motivated drop-outs to continue their education and go on to college, and so help break further the vicious circle of poverty which has held back the black people of America for so long.

An important part of the curricula of the world system of education would be the teaching of a universal auxiliary language and script.

"The day is approaching when all the peoples of the world will have adopted one universal language and one common script. When this is achieved, to whatsoever city a man may journey it shall be as if he were entering his own home. These things are obligatory and absolutely essential."
Bahá'u'lláh.[1]

Quite apart from the practical necessity of a world language for smooth and rapid communication, it is clear that language plays an important part in the growth of a sense of oneness in a people. The universality of Latin in the Roman Empire added much to the strength of that state, as has English to the unity of the United States. Disagreement

---

* A summary account may be found in the 'Anisa Model', *World Order.* Spring 1972.
[1] Gleanings, pp. 248-249 (UK).

over the principle of one language has been a source of major concern for India.

The Bahá'í Writings do not specify what the world language will be. 'Abdu'l-Bahá praised the aim and purpose of Esperanto* but did not say whether or not it would become the world language of the future.

"Regarding the subject of Esperanto; it should be made clear to the believers that while the teaching of that language has been repeatedly encouraged by 'Abdu'l-Bahá, there is no reference either from Him or from Bahá'u'lláh that can make us believe that it will necessarily develop into the international auxiliary language of the future. Bahá'u'lláh has specified in His Writings that such a language will either have to be chosen from one of the existing languages, or an entirely new one should be created to serve as a medium of exchange between the nations and peoples of the world. Pending this final choice, the Bahá'ís are advised to study Esperanto only in consideration of the fact that the learning of this language can considerably facilitate inter-communication between individuals, groups and Assemblies throughout the Bahá'í world in the present stage of the evolution of the Faith. Shoghi Effendi[1]

It is to be stressed that in addition to a universal auxiliary language use of ethnic language would be encouraged in the Bahá'í system of education so as to ensure the continuing vitality of local culture, which is so important an aspect of the Bahá'í concept of world civilization.**

Other means of communication will also be on a world basis. Shoghi Effendi wrote of the establishment of a world communications system which would facilitate rapid conversation and movement to and from all parts of the world in the most efficient manner. This might suggest a world network of international transportation, cable, telephones, postal, radio and television services. In

---

[1] Directives from the Guardian, p. 23, Bahá'í Publishing Trust, India.

* The daughter of Dr. Zamenhof, the inventor of Esperanto, was a Bahá'í. Her life story is told in the book. *"Lidia: the Life of Lidia Zamenhof, Daughter of Esperanto"*, by Wendy Heller (George Ronald, Oxford, 1985).

** The United Nations Educational, Scientific and Cultural Organization (UNESCO) estimates that today there are some five thousand eight hundred languages and dialects throughout the world.

addition, of course, there would be local and national systems. The news media, though decentralized, would have a world view point and be conscious of their responsibilities.

"Newspapers are as a mirror, which is endowed with hearing, sight and speech; they are a wonderful phenomenon and a great matter. . . . But it behoveth the writers thereof to be sanctified from the prejudice of egotism and desire and to be adorned with the ornament of equity and justice; they must inquire into matters as much as possible, in order that they might be informed of the real facts, and commit the same to writing." Bahá'u'lláh[1]

Another important function of the world government will be to ensure that the world's resources are used efficiently for the benefit of all mankind, not just for privileged classes and nations as at present.

"The economic resources of the world will be organized, its sources of raw materials will be tapped and fully utilized, its markets will be coordinated and developed, and the distribution of its products will be equally regulated. . . . Destitution on the one hand, and gross accumulation of ownership on the other, will disappear. The enormous energy dissipated and wasted on war, whether economic or political, will be consecrated to such ends as will extend the range of human inventions and technical development, to the increase of the productivity of mankind, to the extermination of disease, to the extension of scientific research, to the raising of the standard of physical health, to the sharpening and refinement of the human brain, to the exploitation of the unused and unsuspected resources of the planet, to the prolongation of human life, and to the furtherance of any other agency that can stimulate the intellectual, the moral, and spiritual life of the entire human race." Shoghi Effendi.[2]

A fair distribution of resources, and such other Bahá'í teachings as universal compulsory education, equality of men and women, the creation of a universal sense of social responsibility and awareness, have significance with regard

---

[1] Bahá'í World Faith, p. 171 (USA).
[2] World Order of Bahá'u'lláh, p. 204 (USA).

to the problem of world population growth. Thus at the United Nations World Population Conference held in Bucharest in 1974 it was agreed that in the long run population problems would be ultimately solved only when all peoples have escaped from the crushing burden of poverty.

A fair distribution of the world's resources would be partly achieved by the creation of a unified world economy. Barriers preventing the free movement of trade and peoples would be abolished, so that, for instance, commerce between Spain and Australia would be as free as it now is between Florida and Wisconsin. A spiritual society will have more rational methods of protecting its members from economic hardship than restrictions on movement of trade and peoples which cause gross inequalities and inefficiencies in the economic system.

There will be a uniform system of weights and measures and, more important, a world currency. It is not part of the Bahá'í concept that in a more spiritual society there will be somehow no need for money. This is a theory that is sometimes taken up by social idealists who see money as cause of evil in itself and who like to see it replaced by reversion to a barter-system. Money is the most convenient and flexible means of measuring wealth and is therefore an essential instrument for a world government which is seeking to establish economic justice.

Devaluation and inflation rob a currency of these properties, undermine confidence and frequently penalise the most productive elements in society. This is clearly neither efficient not just, and it is reasonable to assume that in a future World Commonwealth the world currency would be carefully regulated so that it would have a more or less constant value.

It is interesting to note that the nations of the world through such instruments as the General Agreement on Tariffs and Trade, and the Special Drawing Rights at the International Monetary Fund are slowly moving under the pressure of events, albeit with much grumbling and selfish argument, toward these principles of free trade and a world currency which Bahá'u'lláh laid down over a hundred years ago as necessary for the world's economic health.

Today the economies of many capitalist countries depend to a large extent on the continued creation of increasingly frivolous consumer goods and on built-in obsolescence. In other countries all is sacrificed for the economic and military power of the state. In a spiritual world society such factors, which are so utterly irrelevant to the well being of mankind, will not be present. Instead there will be, hand in hand with the concern for a fair distribution of wealth, a careful husbanding of available resources: a recognition of man's role as steward of the world, charged to protect nature both for its own sake and for the benefit of future generations. At long last men today are coming to realize that the protection of the world's environment and resources is ultimately the function of one world authority. Thus at the 1972 United Nations Conference on the Human Environment it was recognised that one of the most useful roles which the United Nations would have in the future would be the coordination and supervision of the development of those resources which lie beneath the oceans and the establishment and monitoring of basic controls for the preservation of a healthy environment.

C — *The Local Community*

Present-day society is dominated by the megalopolises, huge, ugly, dirty blotches on the landscape which have grown far beyond the "human scale", and which crush the human spirit. There are many signs that these growths are reaching a completely unmanageable size and that they will die of their own weight and rigidity. Bahá'í Writings seem to indicate that a future world society will be more balanced and that the city will have less dominating a role. Certainly there may be economic and sociological reasons for thinking this may be the development of the future. The megaloplis has grown partly as a result of the need for large numbers of workers to man vast mass-production factories, and partly — ironically now — to facilitate rapid communication, in government, commerce and the arts. There are indications that the age of mass-production may be passing its peak and that in future industrial plants will be small and will be designed to use highly specialized skills, and quality craftsmanship. If so, dispersal will become practical as well as attractive. What mass-production will still be required will undoubtedly be automated for the most part and so require relatively few workers, as is already the case with oil refining and is becoming so in the steel industry. The tendency toward dispersal might be strengthened by developments in communications. It is now possible to conceive that in the not too distant future we will be able to converse instantly, cheaply and extensively with others in any part of the globe, and that people will be able to travel to the other end of the earth without thinking more about it than they now do to go down to the next town. When this happens the pull of the giant city will be even less.

This impression that society will be more decentralized in future is strengthened by statements in the Bahá'í Writings to the effect that agriculture with its associated activities will reassert itself as the first industry of society and that man's occupations and way of life in general will become more harmonized with nature. It has been pointed out that a world economy built around a scientifically managed agriculture would eliminate the worst ecological abuses of present-day industry. For instance it is foreseen that it would be possible to develop and grow materials on the land which could be substituted for plastics and other industrial synthetics which now rely so heavily on oil and other limited mineral resources.

This all suggests that the typical local community of the future will be either a relatively small and 'human-sized' city or an agricultural village. Each town or village would have a community centre at the heart of which would stand the place of worship, a domed nine-sided building surrounded by trees, fountains and gardens. The house of worship is known as the Mashriqu'l-Adhkár or Dawning Place of God's Praise. Other public buildings in the town or village would be the seat of the Local House of Justice, the community assembly hall, schools, a university, a library, scientific research laboratories, hospitals and auxiliary medical units, homes for the aged, the orphaned and the handicapped.

"The Mashriqu'l-Adhkár has important accessories which are accounted of the basic foundations. These are: school for orphan children, hospital and dispensary for the poor, home for the incapable, college for the higher scientific education, and hospice. In every city a great Mashriqu'l-Adhkár must be founded after this order. In the Mashriqu'l-Adhkár services will be held every morning. There will be no organ in the Temple. In buildings nearby, festivals, services, conventions, public meetings and spiritual gatherings will be held, but in the Temple the chanting and singing will be unaccompanied. Open ye the gates of the Temple to all mankind."

When these institutions, college, hospital, hospice and establishment for the incurables, university for the study of higher sciences, giving post-graduate courses, and other philanthropic buildings are built, the doors will be opened to all the nations and religions. There will be absolutely no line of demarcation drawn. Its charities will be dispensed irrespective of colour or race. Its gates will be flung wide open to mankind; prejudice towards none, love for all. The central building will be devoted to the purpose of prayer and worship. Thus . . . religion will become harmonized with science, and science will be the handmaid of religion, both showering their material and spiritual gifts on all humanity." 'Abdu'l-Bahá.[1]

Though the Mashriqu'l-Adhkár will be the spiritual and social centre of the community it will not be the only place where there is worship of God as is made clear in the affirmation:

"Blessed is the spot, and the house, and the place, and the city, and the heart, and the mountain, and the refuge, and the cave, and the valley, and the land, and the sea, and the

[1] Bahá'u'lláh and the New Era, pp. 173-174 (UK).

island, and the meadow where mention of God hath been made, and His praise glorified." Bahá'u'lláh.[1]

The public facilities of the centre will have the highest social priority in contrast to what happens in most capitalist societies where, as Kenneth Galbraith put it, there is "private affluence and public squalor". Being human-sized communities, the sick, the aged, the orphans and the students who are served at the centre will not have to suffer from faceless institutions which seem to be a characteristic of very nearly every "advanced" society today but will feel the warmth of participation in a living family.

The local community will have a major role to play with regard to anti-social behaviour. Crime today is predominantly associated with the uneducated and those who are rootless, particularly in the big city. In a Bahá'í community, social cohesiveness and an emphasis on a full spiritual and material education for all will greatly reduce the likely incidence of crime. Nevertheless, it is recognized that there will be some who will break the law. The Bahá'í Faith has come to bring justice to all men and a necessary aspect is punishment of those who attack and oppress other members of society. 'Abdu'l-Bahá made the following comment on the treatment of criminals:

"There are two sorts of retributory punishments. One is vengeance, the other chastisement. Man has not the right to take vengeance, but the community has the right to punish the criminal; and this punishment is intended to warn and to prevent, so that no other person will dare to commit a like crime. This punishment is for the protection of man's rights, but it is not vengeance; vengeance appeases the anger of the heart by opposing one evil to another. This is not allowable; for man has not the right to take vengeance. But if criminals were entirely forgiven, the order of the world would be upset. So punishment is one of the essential necessities for the safety of communities, but he who is oppressed by a transgressor has not the right to take vengeance: on the contrary, he should forgive and pardon, for this is worthy of the world of man.

[1] Bahá'í Prayers, Frontispiece (USA).

The communities must punish the oppressor, the murderer, the malefactor, so as to warn and restrain others from committing like crimes. But the most essential thing is that the people must be educated in such a way that no crimes will be committed; for it is possible to educate the masses so effectively that they will avoid and shrink from perpetrating crimes, so that crime itself will appear to them as the greatest chastisement, the utmost condemnation and torment. Therefore no crimes which require punishment will be committed. . . .

. . . . Communities are day and night occupied in making penal laws, and in preparing and organizing instruments and means of punishment. They build prisons, make chains and fetters, arrange places of exile and banishment, and different kinds of hardship and tortures, and think by means to discipline criminals; whereas, in reality, they are causing destruction of morals and perversion of characters. The community, on the contrary, ought day and night to strive and endeavour with the utmost zeal and effort to accomplish the education of men, to cause them day by day to progress and to increase in science and knowledge, to acquire virtues, to gain good morals and to avoid vices, so that crimes may not occur. At the present time the contrary prevails; the community is always thinking of enforcing the penal laws, and of preparing means of punishment, instruments of death and chastisement, places for imprisonment and banishment; and they expect crimes to be committed. This has a demoralizing effect.

But if the community would endeavour to educate the masses, day by day knowledge and sciences would increase, the understanding would be broadened, the sensibilities developed, customs would become good, and morals normal; in one word, in all these classes of perfections, there would be progress, and there would be fewer crimes."[1]

Today the treatment of criminals in many countries is a disgrace to civilization. Poorly paid and poorly educated police are often corrupt and brutal, the courts slow, legal professions self-serving and detached from reality, and

[1] Some Answered Questions, pp. 307, 308 & 311 (USA).

prisons hells on earth. The system seems almost consciously designed to ensure that anyone who falls foul of the law will be deeply and permanently depraved. Dostoevski once said with some justice that the degree of civilization in a society can be judged by entering its prisons. In a Bahá'í society the lawbreaker, like the member of any other sick or deprived group, would be the responsibility, and in the care of, his family community.

It is generally agreed that much of the crime in present day society stems from extreme injustice with regard to inequalities of wealth. Though Bahá'ís believe complete equality is neither desirable, practical, nor capable of attainment, one of the more important of their objectives is to abolish extremes of wealth and poverty, to see that the basic needs of all peoples are met and that additional riches are given for service and not according to the accident of birthplace or race or family;

"The arrangement of the circumstances of the people must be such that poverty shall disappear, that everyone, as far as possible, according to his rank and position, shall share in comfort and well being.

We see amongst us men who are overburdened with riches on the one hand, and on the other those unfortunate ones who starve with nothing; those who possess several stately palaces, and those who have nowhere to lay their head . . . .

This condition of affairs is wrong, and must be remedied. Now the remedy must be carefully undertaken. It cannot be done by bringing to pass absolute equality between men.

Equality is a chimera! It is entirely impracticable! Even if equality could be achieved it could not continue — and if its existence were possible, the whole order of the world would be destroyed. The law of order must always obtain in the world of humanity. Heaven has so decreed in the creation of man . . . .

It is important to limit riches as it is also of importance to limit poverty. Either extreme is not good." 'Abdu'l-Bahá.[1]

Many of the laws and principles of the Faith which have been already discussed have bearing on economic justice, for

[1] Paris Talks, pp. 151-153 (UK).

instance, compulsory universal education, the equality of men and women, the emergence of the true family spirit, the idea that work in the spirit of service is worship, the fact that begging is forbidden, the awareness of being members of one world family, the concept of a fair distribution of the world's resources amongst all nations. There are many others of which perhaps the more important are those dealing with industrial organization, inheritance and taxation.

The Writings lay down basic principles affecting economic organization but leave the details for the Universal House of Justice to decide according to the circumstances of the time. Clearly, from the very nature of Bahá'í teachings on community co-operation, there will be many industrial and commercial enterprises organized on a genuine co-operative basis. It is to be expected, too, that enterprises on critical importance will be under the aegis of the world government and others will be run by national governments. However, there will certainly be also a place for individual initiative and enterprise, as this is so clearly for the benefit of all society. The difference from the present is that enterprise would be seen as service, not an opportunity to exploit. There would be fair prices and those who acquire wealth from their enterprise would count it an honour to be able to give on a voluntary basis to serve the community's needs.

"The time will come in the near future when humanity will become so much more sensitive than at present that the man of great wealth will not enjoy his luxury, in comparison with the deplorable poverty about him. He will be forced, for his own happiness, to expend his wealth to procure better conditions for the community in which he lives."
'Abdu'l-Bahá.[1]

The idea of consultation would not be confined to government but would be a normal feature of all organizations, including commercial enterprises. Those enterprises which are not co-operatives will have a far-reaching profit-sharing programme which would be supervised by local or national governments to make sure that the sharing was equitable.

[1] Star of the West, Vol. VIII, pp. 4-5 (USA).

"Therefore, laws and regulations should be established which would permit the workmen to receive from the factory owner their wages and a share ... of the profits, or in some other way the body of workmen and the manufacturers should share equitably the profits and advantages ... It would be well ... that laws be established, giving moderate profits to manufacturers, and to workmen the necessary means of existence and security for the future. Thus, when they become feeble and cease working, get old and helpless, and die leaving children under age, these children will not be annihilated by excess of poverty. And it is from the income of the factory itself, to which they have a right, that they will derive a little of the means of existence." 'Abdu'l-Bahá.[1]

Another powerful device for ensuring economic justice will be the application of both a progressive income tax and a negative income tax. Each person will have his income free of tax up to the point where it exceeds his basic needs, thereafter a genuine progressively heavier tax will be levied.

"Now, if his income be equal to his expenditure, from such a farmer nothing whatever will be taken. That is, he will not be subjected to taxation of any sort needing as he does all his income. Another farmer may have expenses running up to one thousand dollars we will say, and his income is two thousand dollars. From such a one a tenth will be required, because he has a surplus.* But if his income be ten thousand dollars and his expenses one thousand dollars or his income twenty thousand dollars he will have to pay as taxes one fourth. If his income be one hundred thousand dollars and his expenses five thousand, one third will he have to pay because he has still a surplus since his expenses are five thousand and his income one hundred thousand. If he pays, say thirty five thousand dollars, in addition to the expenditure of five thousand he still has sixty thousand left. But if his expenses be ten thousand and his income two hundred thousand, then he must give an even half because

[1] Some Answered Questions, pp. 315-316 (USA).

* 'Abdu'l-Bahá made it clear that these figures were for illustration only and had no particular significance.

ninety thousand will be in that case the sum remaining. Such a scale as this will determine allotment of taxes. . . ." 'Abdu'l-Bahá.[1]

When Bahá'u'lláh wrote, progressive income tax was virtually unknown. Since then there has been widespread lip-service to the idea, though in practice there are so many qualifications and loopholes to so-called progressive tax systems that there is probably not a system in the world which meets the Bahá'í standards of equity.

Another Bahá'í teaching to prevent extremes of riches and poverty is that concerning wills. These teachings have been summarised as follows:

"Bahá'u'lláh states that a person should be free to dispose of his possessions during his lifetime in any way he chooses, and it is incumbent on everyone to write a will stating how his property is to be disposed of after his death. When a person dies without leaving a will, the value of the property should be estimated and divided in certain stated proportions among seven classes of inheritors, namely, children, wife or husband, father, mother, brothers, sisters, and teachers, the share of each diminishing from the first to the last. In the absence of one or more of these classes the share which would belong to them goes to the public treasury . . . .

There is nothing in the law of Bahá'u'lláh to prevent a man from leaving all his property to one individual if he pleases, but Bahá'ís will naturally be influenced, in making their wills, by the model Bahá'u'lláh has laid down for the case of intestate estates, which ensures distribution of the property among a considerable number of heirs."[2]

Bahá'ís believe that only religion has the power to inspire society to support enthusiastically and equitable distribution of wealth and that such enthusiasm is required to ensure success. Past attempts to achieve an equitable distribution of wealth have failed because they have been made by governments in face of important groups in society

---

[1] Star of the West, Vol. XIII, pp. 228-229 (USA).
[2] Bahá'u'lláh and the New Era, p. 138-139 (UK).

which have been at best indifferent and at worst extremely hostile to the idea.

With regard to public finance, generally the objective would be to make each community self-supporting. Besides income from taxes, estates and gifts, 'Abdu'l-Bahá mentioned also that the community would receive royalty rights over all minerals and treasure trove in its area of jurisdiction, and certain property taxes. Some of the community income would be earmarked as in the present Bahá'í Administration for national and international government, which would additionally have other sources of income. It will probably take a considerable time for all local communities to reach a sufficient degree of prosperity to be able to support community services to the required level and therefore, during this period, the poorer communities will need assistance from either national or international finances resources.

One last thing should be said about the new civilization. It is envisaged that it will inspire the greatest renaissance in the arts. This will find expression in local culture freed from prejudice and glorying in positive patriotism. More important, it will be shown in a new world culture. In the arts today there is an overwhelming emphasis on the ugly which reflects the reality of our society, and this perhaps more healthy than presenting a fake veneer of beauty. It might be argued, however, that the tendency has become excessive and that the movement has lost its original genuineness and is now preoccupied with the bleak side of life for its own sake, that it is merely a hollow fashion. Be that as it may, Bahá'í artists having a vision of the "Promised Day" have a different view, and it is this view which it is believed will blossom in the new age. Then the subjects and styles of the arts will shine in reflection of a just and progressive civilization at one with itself and nature, and wholeheartedly committed to the worship of God in all His Glory.

CHAPTER VIII

THE BEGINNING

A — *The Báb*

SO FAR the discussion has been confined basically to the teachings of the Bahá'í Faith. Clearly, however, the teachings of a religion do not come fully alive or acquire their real significance until related to the Founder. Furthermore, in a more general sense, history is an essential factor in judging the genuiness and practicality of the ideas of any movement. There have been many movements whose ideas sounded fine on paper but which in practice became a terrible perversion of the original ideal. Other apparently attractive ideas remained just that — too unrealistic to make any impact on the lives of ordinary people. Such experiences have made some who admire the high principles of the Bahá'í Faith sceptical as to whether they could ever become the standards of mankind. In response to these points this chapter is devoted to a brief outline of the history of the Faith from its beginnings in 1844 to the present day.

As mentioned earlier Bahá'u'lláh was born in Persia and it was in this land that most of the early events of the Faith took place. Persia* is bounded by Russia and the Caspian Sea in the north, Afghánistán and Pákistán in the east, the Persian Gulf in the south and 'Iráq and Turkey in the west. It has an area of about six hundred and thirty thousand square miles which makes it some three times the size of France and a little larger than Alaska. It is mainly a semi-arid plateau with high mountain ranges and a considerable amount of barren desert. The Caspian coastal

---

* Persia is the name which has been most often used in the West since the time of the Greeks and derives from the ancient peoples of Persis, an area of Southwest Persia which is now the province of Fárs. The people of the country call it Írán (land of the Aryans). Though Írán is the official name, the Íránian Government has indicated that it will not object to the term Persia being used.

173

region is semi-tropical and fertile. The Persian Gulf is characterized by extreme heat and general aridity.

Today Persia has a population of nearly forty million. In the time of Bahá'u'lláh it was probably less than ten million. The chief areas of population are around the capital of Ṭihrán, the southern shores of the Caspian Sea and the eastern part of the province of Ádhirbáyján in the northwest. The majority of the population is of mixed ancestry, part Indo-European and part Arab. Most belong to the Shí'ih sect of Islám.* Minority groups include the Qashqá'ís and Bakhtíyárí tribes of the Southwest, Kurds who for the most part belong to the Sunni sect, Armenians and Assyrians, many of whom are Christians; Jews and a few Zoroastrians.

Persia has had a long and distinguished history. First united in the sixth century, B.C. by the Achaemenids, the Persians conquered most of what is today the Middle East; Babylon, Assyria and Egypt, and they even entered Europe. The Empire of the Achaemenids was enlightened in many respects and displayed tolerance for the local cultures and religions of all its subject peoples. Under Persian rule the Jews were allowed to return to Jerusalem from the Babylonian Exile and the first Suez Canal was completed.

In the first century, B.C., Parthia, which represented a renaissance of Persian civilization after a period of decline, successfully withstood the onslaught of the Roman Empire at the height of the latter's power, and inflicted on it one of the worst defeats it was ever to suffer at the battle of Carrhae (53 B.C.). There was another great flowering of civilization under the Sásáníyán kings around the third century, A.D. In the centuries following the Arab conquest (seventh century, A.D.) when Islám replaced Zoroastrianism as the main religion of Persia, the peoples of this land reached their highest point of achievement, creating poetry,

---

* The Shí'ih sect is one of the two great divisions of Islám, the other being the Sunní sect. The main distinctive feature of the Shí'ih belief is that the succession to the leadership of Islám was vested in 'Alí Muḥammad's son-in-law, and his descendants, the Imáms, and not in others who claimed to be the caliphs. Most Arabs, Turks, Afgháarís and Pákistánís belong to the Sunní sect.

handicrafts, and architecture possibly as beautiful as anything ever produced by man.

This period came to an end in the thirteenth century when the land was ravaged by Chingiz Khán (Ghengis Khán) and other invaders from the East, including in the fourteenth century, Tímúr-i-Lang (Tamburlaine). Some order was reestablished in the sixteenth century by Sháh 'Abbás, first of the Safaví dynasty, who made the Shí'ih sect the official faith of the country. Thereafter Persian society went into rapid decline with only a brief moment of military glory in the eighteenth century when Nádir Sháh temporarily conquered northern India.

By the beginning of the nineteenth century Persian civilization had sunk to a very low level, indeed. The government was in the hands of Sháhs of the Qájár dynasty who kept themselves in power by violence and intrigue, by reserving all government positions for their numerous progeny and by an incredibly intricate and all-pervading system of bribery and corruption. Ordinary people had little protection from the law and brigandage was rife. Culturally the country had become a backwater and like so many other declining societies in the East was impotent in face of the technology and vigour of the invading Westerners. Poverty, illiteracy and the deepest ignorance of all save their immediate surroundings was the lot of most of the population. Religious leadership which had a very powerful influence on both the court and the general population, was a force for reaction and repression. For the most part it was obscurantist, ridden with ritual and superstition and fiercely intolerant of those who professed different views. It was typical of the time that Islám, whose original social teachings emphasized tolerance and equality, should be used to justify the practice of treating women as property.*

In the midst of this spiritual and material desolation there was a small but growing number of educated and perceptive Persians who recognized that a spiritual renaissance and radical social reform had to come. They believed that such reform would come within the framework

* Many religious leaders taught that women did not have souls.

of a revitalized religion. In the West, by contrast, the most influential advocates of social and political reform at this time tended to be secular and anti-clerical. The most distinguished and most respected of the new thinkers was Shaykh Aḥmad-i-Ahsá'í (1743-1826). At about the age of forty Shaykh Aḥmad settled in the Shí'ih holy city of Karbilá in 'Iráq and began to teach that in response to the needs of the time there would soon come a return in spirit of the twelfth Imám,* the Promised One. In his talks and lectures he would show that not all the events described in the Qur'án were to be taken literally and that they had a far more profound meaning if read in a spiritual sense. The French historian Nicolas described his teachings as "powerful and enlightened liberalism". Shaykh Aḥmad's learning, his kindness and deep humanity as compared with the sterility of conventional religious thought soon attracted to his side many of the most enlightened in Persian Society. As he travelled from town to town in Persia he was greeted with warmth, and even the Sháh and his relations begged him to visit them.

When Shaykh Aḥmad died his followers turned to his appointed successor Siyyid Kázim-i-Rashtí (1793-1843) for guidance. Siyyid Kázim urged them to become free of material concerns and to prepare for the coming of the Promised One. He drew attention to Shaykh Aḥmad's prediction that the Promised One would be "like a trumpet blast" to warn men against their nonspiritual ways and that He would be followed almost immediately by Another who would "quicken and revive" mankind. The power and urgency of Siyyid Kázim's teachings caused some resentment amongst reactionary Muslim leaders but they also won passionate approval from those who longed for a better world.

It is perhaps interesting to compare the Shaykhí movement in Persia with those groups who were their contemporaries in the West who were expecting the Second Coming

* It was Shí'ih tradition that in the 'day of the end' the twelfth and last Imám would return to save Man. As mentioned earlier, all the great religions have the tradition of the return of a great Prophet at a critical time in history.

of Christ. Though similar to the Shaykhís in that they grasped that they lived at a critical time in history, they were different in that they interpreted the prophecies of the Second Coming in a quite literal sense; they expected to witness the return of a physical Christ sitting on a cloud. Like the Jews at the time of Augustus who read their traditions literally to mean that the Messiah would be a great political leader who would sit on the throne of David, they missed the real significance of what was happening and were inevitably disappointed.

Toward the end of his life Siyyid Kázim sent Mullá Husayn-i-Bushrú'í, a young and outstanding follower, to Persia to present to some of the more distinguished religious leaders the point of view of the Shaykhís. Mullá Husayn's fervour and skill in discussion won him much respect from those he met. Having completed his mission he returned to Karbilá only to find that the Siyyid had died a short time before in December 1843. After a period of meditation Mullá Husayn determined to devote his life to the search for the Manifestation of God foretold by Siyyid Kázim and Shaykh Ahmad, and advised his friends to do likewise.

So saying he set out for Persia, going first to the port of Búshihr on the Persian Gulf. Then he turned inland and, following his intuition, made his way towards Shíráz, city of the great poets of the past, Háfiz and Sa'dí. Arriving in the city in late afternoon, hot and weary after the long climb from the coast under the broiling sun, he was amazed and then overwhelmed by the warmth of greeting he received from a distinguished looking young stranger, who wore a green turban, denoting that he was a Siyyid or descendant of the Prophet Muhammad. The young stranger whose name was Siyyid 'Alí-Muhammad invited him to go to his house for refreshments.

Over refreshments Mullá Husayn told of his quest which brought him to Shíráz. As Mullá Husayn finished the young man declared that He was the One foretold, the Herald or Gate (Báb in Arabic) of God. Mullá Husayn was at first shocked and dumbfounded by this claim, but then realized that his Host fitted the description of the Promised One given by Siyyid Kázím.* Furthermore, he was deeply impressed by the Young Man's courtesy, sincerity, learning and wisdom. As he listened to his Host he remembered that Siyyid Kázím had once said that one proof of the Manifestation of God would be His ability to deliver a profound commentary on the meaning of the súrih of Joseph, one of the most difficult passages in the Qur'án. Unasked, the Báb delivered that night the first part of such a commentary** and Mullá Ḥusayn without further hesitation passionately offered his acceptance of the Báb's claim. The discussion ended in the early hours of the morning with the Báb saying that He would not proclaim His mission until seventeen others came to Him and accepted Him of their own volition.

The Declaration of the Báb took place on the night of May 22-23, 1844. Bahá'ís believe that this event marked the beginning of a new age in the evolution of man and for that reason the Bahá'í calendar has its beginning in this year. It is interesting to remember that the claim of the Báb took place in the very year in which the Millerites and others, working on calculations made from prophecies in the Bible, were expecting the return of Christ. It has been remarked too that on May 24, 1844, Samuel Morse sent the very first telegraph message from Washington, D.C. to Baltimore. The message was: "What hath God wrought".***

At the time of His Declaration the Báb was twenty-five years old having been born on October 20, 1819. His father died when He was a child and He had been brought up by His maternal uncle who was a merchant in the city. As a child He was an outstanding pupil. All who were acquainted with Him loved Him for His gentleness, humility, piety and nobility of person and respected Him for His instinctive grasp of the essence of things. Even his uncle and other older relatives turned to Him auto-

---

* Siyyid Kázím had predicted that the Promised One would be descended from Muḥammad, would be between the ages of twenty and thirty, would be endowed with great knowledge, would be a nonsmoker and free from bodily blemishes.

** The Báb said that Joseph signified the new Educator for this Age who would deliver His Message despite the bitter attacks of His own brother.

*** Numbers XXIII:23.

matically for advice. At the age of seventeen He joined his uncle in his business and soon earned a reputation for just dealings in which He would neither allow others to overcharge Him nor allow them to overpay Him for His goods. His private life was full of happiness, only marred by the death of His one child in infancy. At this time, He had a comfortable house and was living in a close-knit family in which the favourite pastime was the study and appreciation of good literature.

After forty days had elapsed sixteen men and one woman accepted the Báb's claim. The last one was a young man later surnamed Quddús whose ability and passionate devotion won for him a special place in the heart of the Báb. The woman was a remarkable young person later surnamed Ṭáhirih, the Pure One, who was the daughter of one of the leading priests in the city of Qazvín in north Persia. She had read widely and deeply and became aware of the hypocrisy and corruption of religion and society. Much to the chagrin of several members of her family, she did not keep her views to herself. She was particularly outspoken in her denunciation of the way women were used, and demanded that they should be treated as equals by men. Her deepest feelings were expressed in poetry which has since been recognized as amongst the most distinguished written in nineteenth century Persia. She became profoundly influenced by the views of the Shaykhís and she entered into correspondence with Siyyid Kázim. In 1843, despite the opposition of her family, she set out to visit him. She arrived in Karbilá in December, a few days after his death. Later Ṭáhirih gave a sealed letter to her brother-in-law, another follower of Shaykh Aḥmad, just as he was about to set out on the same quest as Mullá Ḥusayn, and asked him to deliver it to the Promised One when he found Him. The brother-in-law found the Báb and became the sixteenth follower. The Báb recognized Ṭáhirih as His seventeenth follower because her letter acknowledged His claim.

The Báb gathered His followers together and bade them scatter across the country to spread the news of His claim.

To indicate their role. He called them the "Letters of the Living". He told them to speak with wisdom, and not to arouse antagonisms. Mullá Ḥusayn had a special mission. He was to visit several cities, including Ṭihrán, which the Báb intimated had a special significance. Soon after arriving in Ṭihrán, Mulla Ḥusayn met a man from the nearby district of Núr, and in conversation mention was made of Mírzá Buzurg-i-Núrí, who had been one of the most distinguished ministers of the crown and who came from Núr.* Mullá Ḥusayn learned that Mírzá Buzurg's eldest son, Mírzá Ḥusayn 'Alí, though still a young man had become widely known for his kindness and spirituality. Mullá Ḥusayn right away resolved to send a message to Mírzá Ḥusayn 'Alí telling him of the claim of the Báb. When Mírzá Ḥusayn 'Alí, who was later to be designated by the name of Bahá'u'lláh (the Glory of God), received the Message He signified His acceptance of the Báb's claim without a moment's hesitation.

Bahá'u'lláh was born on November 12, 1817. Like the Báb, He was a brilliant child and it is recorded that on one occasion when He was only seven he had presented and won a legal case at the royal court. Though He had no formal training everything seemed to indicate He would follow in his father's footsteps. However, early in life He rejected court society and politics and devoted His life to helping the poor, and to meditation and learning. When His father died, the resulting vacant post in the government was offered to Him by the S̲h̲áh. No offence was taken when the offer was gently refused. The Grand Vazír is said to have remarked that Mírzá Ḥusayn 'Alí was intended for greater things. This was typical of His relations with His peers. Though He had rejected their way of life, this was not done arrogantly and they continued to respect Him for His knowledge and for His considerate and gentle manners.

Having heard of Bahá'u'lláh's acceptance, the Báb, accompanied by Quddús set out in October 1844 for Mecca, centre of the world of Islám to make a formal announcement

* The family of Mírzá Buzurg was one of the oldest in Persia and was descended from the Sásáníyán kings.

of His claim. Involved in their routine everyday affairs, men fail to observe the truly significant event when it occurs in front of their eyes. This was the case when the Báb went to Mecca. Public pronouncements and a letter to the Sharíf of the city were alike ignored.

News of the Báb's claim had a somewhat different reception in Persia Having returned to Búshihr in early 1845, the Báb sent Quddús on ahead to Shíráz. Learning of the presence of followers of the Báb in the city several priests set up an outcry. Soon afterwards Quddús and two other Bábís were arrested and tortured by agents of the provincial governor. The governor also gave orders for the Báb to be brought to Shíráz under guard (July 1845). After a strong appeal for clemency from the Báb's family the governor was persuaded to release Him on parole.*

Meanwhile the work of the Letters of the Living was bearing fruit and many came to Shíráz from all over Persia to give their allegiance to the Báb. Those who came were from all classes of society: peasants, herdsmen, merchants, scholars and the more liberal clergy. Word of the Báb swept across the country like wildfire, so much so that it attracted the concern of the court. Muḥammad Sháh, then thirty-seven years old and the ruler of the county since 1834, became anxious to learn the nature of this new movement and sent Siyyid Yaḥyáy-i-Dárábí (later known as Vaḥíd), the most distinguished and trusted scholar at this court to question the Báb. At first Vaḥíd adopted a superior manner toward the Báb but within the space of three interviews he became a changed man, conquered by the courtesy, gentleness and profound knowledge and spirit of the Báb. He wrote to the Sháh that the Báb was indeed the One He claimed to be and that he was going to stay at His side.

The governor, angered at these developments, ordered the chief constable of Shíráz to re-arrest the Báb. At this time (September 1845) there was a serious outbreak of cholera in the city. The chief constable's son became ill and then recovered after the Báb had been asked for His help. There-

---

* The first mention in the Western press of the new Faith was a report on these events which appeared in the London "Times" for November 1, 1845.

upon the constable wrote to the governor and persuaded him to release the Báb provided that He left the city.

Banished from his home city the Báb went northward to Iṣfáhán where there was a small group of His followers. Manúchihr Khán, the Governor of Iṣfáhán, a friend of the Sháh and in times past an able if sometimes cruel general, proved to be sympathetic to the Báb's Cause and gave Him protection against the clergy who, like their compatriots in Shíráz, tried to stir up antagonism against Him. Frustrated in their first violent designs, the priests sought to win the support of the central government by hinting that the followers of the Báb were a revolutionary party bent on the overthrow of the monarchy.

Their insinuations fell on receptive ears. The government of that time was more than usually incompetent, corrupt, and insecure. Ḥájí Mírzá Áqásí, the Grand Vazír or Prime Minister, was also the Sháh's religious counsellor and his former tutor. While Ḥájí Mírzá Áqásí was Prime Minister this once proud country had been severely humiliated in quarrels with the Ottoman Empire and England and had been shaken by a whole series of internal disturbances. Money intended to pay the army was regularly diverted into private pockets (often those of members of the Sháh's family) with the consequence that this essential prop of the government was not very reliable.

Ḥájí Mírzá Áqásí saw the Báb as a threat to the regime and in particular to his personal influence over the Sháh, and earlier he had plotted with the governor in Shíráz to have the Báb murdered. While the Báb was in the protection of Manúchihr Khán, however, there was little he could do except frustrate any attempt to bring the Báb to the Sháh. Then in February 1847 Manúchihr Khán died and the Prime Minister saw his opportunity. He persuaded the Sháh to order the Báb to be sent to Ṭihrán. Though knowing what was intended, the Báb set out for the capital. Meanwhile the weakwilled Sháh was persuaded that this was not an appropriate time for a meeting after all and new orders were sent to the Báb's escort to take Him as a prisoner to the fortress of Máh-Kú high up in the mountain wilderness near the Russian frontier in the northwest of Persia. This part of Persia was inhabited by Kurds who were Sunní Muslims and who were traditionally hostile to Persians. The Prime Minister calculated that in such a place the Báb would be completely isolated and that His influence would soon wane.

From the beginning the Prime Minister's calculations were upset. On the way to the fortress the Báb had to pass through the city of Tabríz and there excited crowds turned out to meet Him. At the prison-fortress the wardens soon came to have high regard for the Báb and allowed many to come and visit Him. Alarmed at these developments and under pressure from the Russian minister who feared trouble in this sensitive region near the Russian-Persian frontier, the Prime Minister issued orders for the removal of the Báb from Máh-Kú. In April 1848 the Báb was transferred to the fortress of Chihríq which is some hundred miles to the south of Máh-Kú and which was under the command of a brother-in-law of the Sháh. The story was repeated. All who were in contact with the Báb came to love Him and His teachings. Seeing the failure of his plans, Hájí Mírzá Áqásí then decided to try to discredit the Báb by having Him publicly interrogated before a court of senior priests presided over by Násiri'd-Dín Mírzá, the Crown Prince. The examination which was staged in Tabríz in July 1848 was a disaster for the government. The commanding presence and authority of the Báb, despite His status as a prisoner, threw His opponents into confusion and before the crowded audience He made once again His claim to be the "Promised One". The government hastily terminated the proceedings and sent the Báb back to Chihríq.

During the Báb's imprisonment, the work of spreading knowledge of His claim to all classes and regions was continued by His followers. The most well known of His followers were Bahá'u'lláh, who was working in the area to the northeast of Tihrán, Quddús and Mullá Husayn in Mashhad, a city in the northeast of Persia, and Táhirih in Karbilá.

At this time in response to a call from the Báb, His

followers began to make their way to the province of Khurásán in the northeast of Persia. Ṭáhirih left Karbilá and travelled northward teaching on the way in Baghdád, Kirmánsháh and Hamadán. Finally she reached her home city of Qazvín. Here she was subjected to intense harassment by members of her family, paticularly her boorish husband and his father. When her father-in-law was murdered in the mosque she was immediately accused by the heirs of the murdered man of plotting the murder and she would undoubtedly have been condemned if the real murderer had not confessed. As it was, the local extremists used the murder as a device for exciting a mob into going out to savagely butcher several Bábís who were in the city — the first to die in Persia in the name of the Cause.* Soon afterwards Ṭáhirih was able to escape from the city as a result of plans made by Bahá'u'lláh, and she continued on her way to the first conference of the Báb's followers.

This conference, which was called by the Báb and arranged by Bahá'u'lláh, was held in June 1848 in the small hamlet of Badasht. There were two main subjects on the agenda. The first was how best to seek the release of the Báb. Events were soon to make any move in this direction impossible. The second was to discuss the significance of the Báb's Declaration and how His teachings related to Islámic Law. During the conference the participants came to see that the Báb was not just a reformer within Islám but that a new Revelation for a new age had been born. Symbolic of the break with the past was the unprecedented appearance at one meeting of a woman, Ṭáhirih, without a veil, which caused violent shock to many of those present. Few have heard of the conference of Badasht and probably most think of 1848 as the year of revolution in Europe. Nevertheless Bahá'ís believe that in the long run this conference will be recognised as being one of the most important events of that year and a significant stage in the evolution of a new civilization.

* The first Bábí to lose his life for the Cause was one of the Letters of the Living, Mullá 'Aly-i-Basṭámí, who was arrested and imprisoned for several months in Baghdád. Late in 1844 orders were given for his transfer to the capital. However, it is apparent that the lost his life en route as he was never heard of again after passing through the city of Mosul.

During his imprisonment in C̲h̲ihríq the Báb set down the outline of His teachings in the *"Bayán"*. In this work He stated that the new Manifestation of God would appear within a short time after the end of His own life. It was the duty of all to obey that Educator who would bring a new world order. For the first time there was a direct reference as to who this would be.

"Well it is with him who fixeth his gaze upon the order of Bahá'u'lláh and rendereth thanks unto his Lord. For He will assuredly be made manifest. God hath indeed irrevocably ordained it in the Bayán."[1]

The Báb upheld the station of Muḥammad but to fit the conditions of the time, pending the coming of the Promised One, He abrogated certain Muslim laws on fasting, marriage, and prayer, and made others to protect women and the poor, to promote education and useful crafts, and to prevent the scourge of alcohol and opium. Besides the *Bayán* the Báb wrote a constant stream of letters to His followers. He also wrote to the S̲h̲áh and the Sultán of the Ottoman Empire to record His claim to the title of the "Báb".

After the Tabríz trial, the government seemed to lose whatever direction it had once had with regard to the Bábís. Its vacillation was compounded by the effect of the sudden decline in the health of the S̲h̲áh. The possibility of a new reign had all the ministers thinking about thier own immediate careers rather than the larger world outside the court. In September 1848 Muḥammad S̲h̲áh died and was succeeded by his seventeen-year-old son, Náṣiri'd-Dín Mírzá, who was then the Governor of the province of Ád̲h̲irbáyján. Ḥájí Mírzá Áqásí was dismissed and a new government was formed under Amír-Niẓám Mírzá Taqi K̲h̲án.

The new government proved to more vigorous and modern than the one it replaced. It was to encourage the establishment of the first newspapers in Persia and the founding of a polytechnic institute in Ṭihrán. There was a serious attempt to reduce nepotism, which took some

[1] God Passes By, p. 25 (USA).

courage as it earned the new Prime Minister the hatred of the Sháh's mother and of the royal hangers on. For the first time in many years the army was paid regularly.

There was also a dark side to the government's policy. Though it was evident to all who made even the most cursory investigation that the teachings of the Báb gave promise of real modernization and true peace for the country the new Prime Minister, like his predecessor, chose to see the Bábís as a popular and dangerous threat to the monarchy and his own position. He soon decided that the Bábís would have to be crushed at the first opportunity.

That opportunity arose almost immediately. Soon after the Badasht conference Quddús had been imprisoned in the town of Sárí at the instigation of local priests. On hearing of this, the Báb sent a message to Mullá Husayn telling him to lend assistance to Quddús. Mullá Husayn, together with a small group of Bábís made his way to the place where Quddús was imprisoned. On arriving at the nearby town of Bárfurúsh they were set upon by a wild mob which had been told that the Bábís were mischief-makers and destroyers of religion. Appeals to reason were in vain. At last, after several Bábís were killed by the mob, Mullá Husayn ordered the group to defend itself and in the ensuing skirmish the mob was put to rout. The Bábís then retired a short distance from the town to the shrine of Shaykh Tabarsí where they erected a fort so that they could more easily defend themselves.

The fort was attacked several times but each attack was vigorously repulsed. Soon afterwards Quddús was set free and he joined his comrades in the fort. Meanwhile the court heard of these events and in November 1848 an army of some twelve thousand soldiers was sent to besiege the Bábí fort. The Bábís kept their peace and reasoned with the army commander but to no avail. With many other Bábís, Bahá'u'lláh tried to get through to the fort to lend His assistance but He was caught by soldiers, imprisoned and beaten. The army was poorly led and its half-hearted attacks were smashed by the small band of inexperienced but inspired Bábís who defended the fort. The siege went on month after month with conditions gradually becoming more and more desperate. During one of the many clashes in that period the heroic Mullá Ḥusayn lost his life. At last in May 1849 the commander of the army, a brother of the Sháh, wishing to terminate a costly enterprise, decided to achieve his objective by treachery. He offered an amnesty which he swore on the Qur'án to uphold. Without illusion as to the general's intent the Bábís accepted the offer. Then after they had emerged from the fort the soldiers set upon them and hacked them to pieces. Quddús was taken to Bárfurúsh, his hometown, where he was brutally tortured and then paraded through the streets before his torn body was finally rent to pieces. It is recorded that a hundred and seventy three Bábís, including nine Letters of the Living, lost their lives at Shaykh Ṭabarsí and in the subsequent massacre.

The heroic defence of Fort Ṭabarsí against overwhelming odds excited the admiration of many and Mírzá Taqí Khán realized that the Cause of the Báb, far from having been crushed was likely to grow even stronger. He plotted with several leading clergy in the capital to counter this effect by staging a public trial of seven prominent persons, merchants, professionals, and members of leading families who had become Bábís. The charges would be heresy and treason. However, his hope that the Bábís, threatened with torture and death, would publicly recant and so lower the Faith's prestige was not realized. Not one of the seven recanted despite heavy pressure and all went to their execution with joyful spirit. One of the seven was that uncle of the Báb who had raised Him and who had recognized His station soon after the Báb made His claim.

The clergy and government were by now thoroughly alarmed by the spiritual strength of the Bábís. Not once did they try to understand it; all they could do was to react with hysterical savagery. Within a few months persecutions of Bábís broke out all over the country. In Yazd and then in Nayríz the local Bábí communities were attacked by mobs led by Muslim clergy. Once again the Bábís valiantly defended themselves. The governor of the province, later assisted by the central government, marshalled an army which was ultimately five thousand strong to crush them. As at Ṭabarsí, the high morale of the Bábís enabled them to resist all the efforts of the hate ridden clergy and their corrupt military allies to subdue them by force. The military commander was obliged to offer peace and like his dishonourable colleague at Ṭabarsí he imediately broke it as soon as the Bábís had laid down their arms. All the men who had taken part in the Bábí defence, including Vaḥíd, the former court scholar, were brutally murdered and their women and children were forced to look upon their severed heads.

Soon afterwards a community of some three thousand Bábís in the city of Zanján (west Persia) was put under siege by the army. Under the skilled and heroic leadership of Ḥujjat, another distinguished priest of Islám who had recognized the Báb, the Bábís defended themselves with immense courage in the face of numbers far superior to their own. Incredibly, they held our for about nine months until January 1851, and once again it was only through the most cowardly methods that the defence was finally broken. Bahá'í historians estimate that nearly two thousand Bábís lost their lives in this siege, including the lion-hearted Ḥujjat.

Mízrá Taqí Khán sought to show that these incidents proved that the Báb was a rebel as well as an heretic and used them to justify his next step which he believed would offer the final solution. Orders were issued for the Báb to be moved to Tabríz. The Báb who had been heartbroken to hear of what had been happening to His followers, knew what was intended and as a symbolic act arranged for His Writings, pencase, seals and rings to be taken to Bahá'u'lláh. Amongst His papers was a scroll on which He had penned about five hundred verses, all consisting of derivatives from the word "Bahá".

When the Báb arrived in Tabríz the governor was ordered to have Him executed. Outraged at such injustice, the governor refused to comply and Mízrá Taqí Khán was obliged to have his own brother make the necessary arrangements. Tense crowds watched, perhaps understanding the significance of what was happening, as the Báb was conveyed to the barracks in the centre of the city where he was to be executed. A young man ran from the crowd and begged to be allowed to die with the Báb.

On July 9, 1850, the day after His arrival the chief law officer in the city quickly had the city's religious leaders approve the death sentence on the Báb. Meanwhile the Báb engaged in conversation with His secretary. At midday He was interrupted and was taken out of his cell and secured along with His young follower to a nearby pillar in the barrack square. Then an Armenian regiment under the command of a Christian, Sám Khán, was drawn up, the order was given and seven hundred and fifty muskets fired on the Báb and His young follower. When the smoke had cleared the large crowd watching was astounded to see that the bullets had only cut the ropes; the young Bábí was standing unharmed, whilst the Báb Himself could not be seen. The Báb was shortly found back in His cell continuing the previously interrupted conversation with His secretary. Orders were given for Him to be tied up again but Sám Khán refused to take any more part in the proceedings and marched his men away. A second regiment was brought up and this time when the smoke cleared after the firing it was found that hundreds of bullets had found their mark.* It was noted, however, that the faces of both the Báb and His young follower remained untouched and serene. That evening the bodies were removed under guard to the edge of a moat outside the gate of the city. Two nights later two Bábís managed to slip past the guard and rescue the bodies. Subsequently, under instruction from Bahá'u'lláh, they were transported to a secret hiding place in Tihrán. Fifty nine years later these remains were taken to Palestine and they now rest in the Shrine of the Báb in Haifa.

So ended the first chapter in the history of the new religion. The first trumpet blast had sounded. Thousands

---

* The same year two hundred and fifty members of the second regiment lost their lives in an earthquake. Three years later the rest of the regiment (some five hundred men) was shot down in mass execution for mutiny.

full of hope had committed themselves without reserve to the new Cause. Then a shortsighted, reactionary and savage government and clergy, fearful that the Cause would threaten their position, did all in their power to destroy it, not hesitating to stoop to the lowest and most cowardly acts of violence and treachery. The parallels with the events surrounding the life of Jesus are most striking. As in His case, the world at large knew little of what had happened until years after. Even in the middle of the nineteenth century there was little contact between Persia and the West. Nevertheless, something of the sublimity of the Báb's life and teaching, and of the heroism of His followers in the face of the most brutal persecution eventually did trickle out of Persia. Several Europeans who lived or travelled in Persia in the latter half of the nineteenth century wrote about the Báb including A.L.M. Nicolas, the Comte de Gobineau, Lord Curzon who was later Viceroy of India, and E.G. Browne, who was a professor of oriental studies at Cambridge.* For a time in the last decades of the century plays were staged in central and eastern Europe which told something of the life of the Báb. However, the real significance of these happenings was not appreciated and soon they were forgotten.

B — Bahá'u'lláh

When the persecutions of the Bábís finally subsided those who remained were for a time in disarray and, like the early Christians after the death of Jesus, very despondent. The Báb's Writings had not been collected together, many were lost and most Bábís had only a limited knowledge of His teachings. Of the leading figures of the Faith, Bahá'u'lláh alone remained alive and free because the government

---

* A major part of the Comte de Gobineau's 'Les Religions et les Philosophes dans l'Asia Centrale' (Paris 1865) was devoted to an account of the Báb. The writings of A. L. M. Nicolas included 'Siyyid Ali Mohammad dit le Báb (Paris 1905) and a translation of the Bayan. Considerable reference to the Bábís is the found in Lord Curzon's 'Persia and the Persian Question' (London, 1892). E. G. Browne wrote a number of books on Persia, the Bábís and the Bahá'ís which will be referred to later in this chapter. Other Europeans who wrote about the Báb included Clément Huart ('La Religion du Báb, Paris, 1889); and Baron Victor Rosen and A. G. Toumanski, both of whom published manuscripts and commentaries in Russia.

could find no evidence to link Him directly with what they called the Bábí 'uprising'. The Prime Minister had the greatest respect for Bahá'u'lláh's abilities and feared that if left alone He would soon revive the spirit of the Bábís. Hoping to forestall such a possibility he offered Him a government position. When the offer was not accepted the Prime Minister told Bahá'u'lláh He should leave the country. This He did in June 1851, taking up residence in Karbilá. Here Bahá'u'lláh taught as before and gave renewed confidence to the local Bábí communities.

Early in 1852 the Sháh's mother managed to engineer the overthrow of Mízrá Taqí Khán in revenge for his attempts to reduce the nepotism of the royal family. The former Prime Minister was banished from court and ordered to stay at this home in Fín. However, the Sháh's mother was not content with mere banishment and a short time later Mírzá Taqí Khán, this most cruel and treacherous persecutor of the Bábís was himself treacherously put to death in the public baths by a royal agent.

The new government was headed by Mírzá Áqá Khán-i-Núri who was an acquaintance of Bahá'u'lláh and a native of the same district. Almost immediately the new Grand Vazír, who had been the one minister to oppose Mízrá Taqí Khán's scheme to kill the Báb, wrote to Bahá'u'lláh in a conciliatory manner and requested Him to return to Ṭihrán. Subsequently Bahá'u'lláh returned to Persia and was a guest of the Prime Minister's brother. On August 15, 1852, soon after His arrival in Persia two young Bábís distraught at the execution of the Báb waylaid the Sháh when he was taking a morning ride. This assassination attempt, which was a complete failure was so badly planned that the shot used in the pistols was inadequate for the purpose. Though only slightly wounded, the Sháh was badly shaken, as was his entourage, and one would-be assassin was put to death on the spot. The other was executed shortly afterwards. This was not enough for the Sháh's mother. She demanded that, in revenge, the most heavy retribution should be carried out against the Bábí community.

As soon as Bahá'u'lláh heard of the assassination attempt He set out to meet the imperial party, despite strong protestations from His host and other friends who feared for His life. Their fears were fully justified. He was seized by soldiers and was forced to march barefooted and bareheaded in the summer heat from the outskirts of Ṭihrán to the old city, a distance of many miles. On the way He was constantly stoned and beaten by angry mobs. At the end of His journey He was flung into a dungeon known as the Síyáh-Chál, or the Black Pit. The Black Pit, which was formerly a cistern for supplying a public bath with water, was filthy and its air foul in the extreme. Nearly a hundred and fifty persons including some of the worst criminals in the country were crammed into this narrow space. Prisoners in the Black Pit were barely given enough food and water to keep them alive. Bahá'u'lláh was put in stocks and a heavy chain was placed around His neck. The latter was so heavy that He bore its mark for the rest of His life. Despite these conditions Bahá'u'lláh daily led the Bábís in loud chanting of prayers.

The demands for revenge made by the Sháh's mother and others cowed the moderates at court into silence. A persecution of Bábís all over the country began which was to be far more terrible than anything the community had had so far to endure. Most of the Bábís imprisoned in the Black Pit with Bahá'u'lláh were taken out one by one to be executed. Houses of Bábís in Ṭihrán were marked for attack, just as were those of Jews in Germany some eighty years later. Members of the government were forced to take part personally in executions to demonstrate their loyalty to the monarchy. Other places where pogroms were particularly savage were Nayríz, Yazd and Shíráz. Before the terror was over thousands of Bábís had lost their lives, and countless others had been beaten, tortured, robbed and otherwise mistreated. Amongst those who lost their lives was Ṭáhirih who had been under arrest since the conference of Badasht. As she was taken to her place of execution it is recorded that she said:

"You may kill me as soon as you like, but you cannot stop the emancipation of women."[1]

In these most terrible physical conditions when daily He saw His companions being led away to die and He Himself was under the constant threat of death, Bahá'u'lláh had as in a dream an intimation of the burden and the glory that was to be His: that He indeed was the one whom the Báb had referred to as "He whom God small make manifest". He later described His feelings at this time as follows:

"I was but a man like others, asleep upon My couch, when lo, the breezes of the All-Glorious were wafted over Me, and taught me the knowledge of all that hath been. This thing is not from Me, but from One Who is Almighty and All-knowing . . . . His all-compelling summons hath reached Me, and caused Me to speak His praise amidst all people."[2]

As the months passed by the forces of moderation began to reassert themselves. The Russian minister, Prince Dolgorouki, used his considerable influence at court to persuade the Sháh that enough was enough, and that the bloodbath should be brought to an end. He was particularly insistent in his defence of Bahá'u'lláh, Whom he knew and he stoutly spoke up for His character and maintained His innocence of having had anything to do with the assassination attempt. His case was strengthened when a Bábí prisoner named Aẓím confessed to having planned the assassination attempt and confirmed that Bahá'u'lláh and all other Bábís knew nothing of his activity. At long last in late December after four months of terrible imprisonment the government reluctantly agreed to release Bahá'u'lláh. The Prime Minister agreed also to Bahá'u'lláh's demand that attacks on Bábís be stopped but informed Him that He and His family were to be banished from the country.

In January 1853 in the dead of winter, Bahá'u'lláh still weak and in ill health after His ordeal,* was escorted across the mountains into 'Iráq with His wife, Navváb, and other members of His family. When the party arrived in Baghdád

---

[1] God Passes By, p. 75 (USA).

[2] God Passes By, p. 102 (USA).

* In addition to other privations in the dungeon Bahá'u'lláh's food had been poisoned on one occasion.

on April 8, 1853, Bahá'u'lláh was still very sick. The family was also almost destitute for during the terror Bahá'u'lláh's house in Núr had been ransacked and destroyed and when they arrived in Baghdád they possessed only a small sum of money which Navváb had obtained by selling her garments and jewels.

Gradually Bahá'u'lláh recovered and by the end of the year He had begun to restore some of the community's lost confidence. Within a short while the community was badly hurt by dissension. Bahá'u'lláh's younger half brother, Mírzá Yaḥyá was persuaded by a schemer named Siyyid Muḥammad-i-Iṣfáhání that he was being slighted and he became openly antagonistic toward Bahá'u'lláh. Heartbroken to be opposed in His work for the Faith by His own half-brother, Bahá'u'lláh quietly withdrew from Baghdád in April 1854, feeling that this was the only course open to avoid further dispute. He left instructions that His family should treat Mízrá Yahyá with all kindness and consideration.

For the next two years Bahá'u'lláh assumed the name of Darvish Muḥammad and lived like a hermit in prayer and meditation in the rugged mountains of northern 'Iráq, an area which borders Persia and which is mostly inhabited by Kurdish tribesmen. Over a period of time local inhabitants came to respect the strange Darvísh for His exceptional kindliness and knowledge and a scholarly religious group, the Khálidíyyih Order, invited Him to stay with them in the town of Sulaymáníyyih. There His reputation grew even more because of His clear and reasonable answers to their questions concerning religious matters, and because of the beauty and quality of his poetry.

News of the distinguished Darvísh in Sulaymáníyyih reached Baghdád and the Bábís whose morale had reached a very low level, guessed that it was Bahá'u'lláh. They immediately made an urgent and desparate appeal to Him to return to Baghdád. The strongest plea of all came from 'Abdu'l-Bahá, Bahá'u'lláh's twelve year old son.

On March 19, 1856, Bahá'u'lláh returned to Baghdád and was greeted with joy by the Bábí community. So began a period of seven years of relative serenity in Bahá'u'lláh's life. Under His guidance the Bábí community rose from a low point to the very highest ethical standards. Bahá'u'lláh inspired them to try to live by standards of absolute

"godliness, kindliness, humility and piety . . . honesty and truthfulness, chastity and fidelity . . . justice, toleration, sociability, amity and concord . . . self sacrifice and detachment . . . patience, steadfastness and resignation to the will of God." Shoghi Effendi.[1]

He laid particular emphasis on dissociation from all forms of politics and from secret societies. He stressed that there must be strict obedience to established authority, there must be no sedition or backbiting, nor must there be retaliation in case of disputes. Above all a Bábí must be nonviolent and loving in every aspect of his life.

At this time Bahá'u'lláh, His family and friends lived in considerable material poverty as a result of the persecutions they had endured, but this only seemed to add to the serenity of the community. The presence of Bahá'u'lláh and the high ethical standards and joyful spirit of the community attracted many from far and wide. Muslim visitors included those of the Sunní persuasion as well as Shí'ihs. Colonel Burrows Kemball, the British Consul-General offered Bahá'u'lláh British protection if He should ever need it and even the Governor of the city paid his respects.

It was during the Baghdád period that Bahá'u'lláh composed some of the most weighty and significant of His writings. Walking beside the Tigris in 1858 He set forth to His secretary verses which were later collected together as the *Hidden Words*. Each of these verses which is in the form of an address from God to man, goes to the very essence of some aspect of the human condition. The second verse of this book seems to sound the anthem of the world civlization to come:

"The best beloved of all things in My sight is Justice; turn not away therefrom if thou desirest Me, and neglect it not that I may confide in thee. By its aid thou shalt see with thine own

[1] God Passes By, p. 132 (USA).

195

eyes and not through the eyes of others, and shalt know of thine own knowledge and not through the knowledge of thy neighbour. Ponder this in thy heart; how it behoveth thee to be. Verily justice is My gift to thee and the sign of My loving kindness. Set it then before thine eyes."[1]

Another composition written in response to the question of a Ṣúfí scholar was the *Seven Valleys* which describes the spiritual progress of man as he passes through the "valleys" or stages of "Search", "Love", "Knowledge", "Unity", "Contentment", and "Wonderment", to reach the ultimate state of true fulfilment: the valley of "True Poverty and Absolute Nothingness".

Perhaps the most important work of Bahá'u'lláh at this time was the *Kitáb-i-Íqán* or *Book of Certitude*. The two hundred pages of this book were dictated in the course of two days and two nights in 1862 as an answer to some questions asked by one of the uncles of the Báb. In it Bahá'u'lláh affirms that there is a personal God but that He is unknowable and inaccessible to man save through what is reflected in the lives and words of His Messengers or Educators. Though there were differences of detail in Their teachings because of the particular needs of the times when They lived, the Educators were united in Their teachings of the great universal principles of life. He put the new Revelation in the context of the past and the future and said that it would embrace and unite all religions and lead eventually to the unity of man. The vast sweep of these themes was accompanied by detailed analysis of many generally misunderstood passages in the Bible and in the Qur'án. A spiritual and deeper meaning is shown pertaining to such concepts as "The Return", "The Resurrection", "The Seal of the Prophets", and the "Day of Judgment".

The love, respect and honour with which Bahá'u'lláh was treated by nearly all in Baghdád alarmed a number of the more fanatical Shí'ih priests in the city. At first they planned to challenge Bahá'u'lláh to a public debate hoping to show Him up as a heretic. However, when the challenge

[1] Hidden Words (Arabic), No. 2 (UK).

was accepted they drew back fearing that it would be they who would be humiliated. They turned to the Persian Consul-General* who was sympathetic with their viewpoint and he sent alarming reports to the Sháh about the revival of the Bábí community in Baghdád. Disturbed by these reports, the Persian Government after some negotiation persuaded the Sulṭán of the Ottoman Empire to have Bahá'u'lláh removed to a place less close to the Persian border. Soon afterwards 'Álí Páshá, the Sulṭán's Prime Minister, invited Bahá'u'lláh to proceed to Constantinople.

On April 22 1863, Bahá'u'lláh entered into the Najíbíyyih Garden (subsequently known as the Garden of Riḍván — the Garden of Paradise) on the outskirts of Baghdád and spent twelve days there bidding farewell to the community and other friends. It was then that the great event took place for which the Bábís had waited so long and for which they had suffered so much. To the joy of His listeners Bahá'u'lláh made His claim to be the Universal Manifestation of God for this Age. This announcement came almost exactly nineteen years after that of the Báb, just as the Báb himself had foretold. It is interesting to recall that some four months earlier on the other side of the globe President Lincoln had issued the great Emancipation Proclamation by which all slaves in the United States were declared free, a major event in the dismantling of the old social system. Two years before that Tsar Alexander II had signed the Emancipation Edict which legally abolished serfdom in Russia. For Bahá'ís, Bahá'u'lláh's Proclamation is the other side of the picture: the foundation stone of new world civilization. This is why this event, and not, say, the birthday of Bahá'u'lláh is celebrated in the Bahá'í calendar as the most important commemorative occasion in the year.

On May 3, 1863, Bahá'u'lláh set out for Constantinople accompanied by His family and twenty-six followers. The journey took some three-and-a-half months to complete. In

---

* Persia had a resident minister in Baghdád, then under Turkish rule, to represent the local Persian population and to supervise Persian pilgrims who visited the Shí'ih shrines in the nearby city of Karbilá.

the Turkish capital Bahá'u'lláh refused to indulge the Turkish politicians at court by giving presents or making social calls on those with influence. For four months the goverment kept Bahá'u'lláh waiting, then, prejudiced by the Persian ambassador, it was announced that Bahá'u'lláh was to be banished to Adrianople. On receipt of the notice of banishment Bahá'u'lláh sent a letter to the Sulṭán admonishing him for the corruption of the Turkish Government, an admonition which is not surprising considering that the regime at that time was as rotten and oppresive as any in the world not excluding the one in Persia. The journey to Adrianople took twelve days and occurred in December 1863 in the midst of one of the most severe winters for many years.

The five years which Bahá'u'lláh spent in Adrianople were to be the most painful. Soon after their arrival Siyyid Muḥammad, who had managed also to get to Adrianople, persuaded Mírzá Yaḥyá to denounce Bahá'u'lláh's claim. Nevertheless Bahá'u'lláh continued to show the greatest consideration for His half-brother and tried to effect a reconciliation. This was to no avail. Matters grew worse and culminated in several attempts on Bahá'u'lláh's life. One attempt by poisoning very nearly succeeded. The poison so damaged Bahá'u'lláh's body that He was left with a shaking hand until the end of His life. To allay the dispute Bahá'u'lláh withdrew from all save his Family for a period of two months, but to no avail. Though there were no further attempts on His life, the disruption in the community continued and Siyyid Muḥammad and Mírzá Yaḥyá in addition began denouncing Bahá'u'lláh to the Turkish authorities. The shaky state of the Ottoman Empire tended to make the government nervous and ready to listen to even the most absurd charges. In August 1868, the Bahá'ís were abruptly ordered to leave Adrianople. They were taken to Gallipoli where the party was split in two: Bahá'u'lláh and the major part of the group were put on ship for the ancient fortress city of 'Akká in Palestine, whilst a much smaller group consisting of Mírzá Yaḥyá, a few supporters and some

Bahá'ís was dispatched to Cyprus.* The Turks, to serve their own purpose, put Siyyid Muḥammad and two or three other opponents of Bahá'u'lláh on the ship for 'Akká.

Bahá'u'lláh's party arrived in 'Akká on August 31, 1868. They were immediately confined in the city barracks and orders were given that they were to be kept in strict isolation. At this time 'Akká was the prison city of the Ottoman Empire, a forbidding and extremely unhealthy place from which few who were imprisoned there ever emerged alive. Within a short time most of the party fell sick and three died. These conditions continued for some two years until during one of the periodic emergencies to which the empire was prone it was decided that the barracks were needed for troops and the Bahá'ís were moved out and were put under house arrest elsewhere within the city walls. Just before the move there was a tragic event in the family: on June 23, 1870 whilst in meditatioin, Bahá'u'lláh's second son, Mírzá Mihdí, surnamed the Purest Branch, fell through a skylight and was fatally injured. He was twenty-two years old. Later the same year another terrible blow fell on Bahá'u'lláh. On being released from the barracks Siyyid Muḥammad began to spy on Bahá'í visitors from Persia who had taken grave risks to come to 'Akká to hear word of Bahá'u'lláh; then he would denounce them to the authorities. One day seven Bahá'ís, driven beyond endurance by numerous acts of treachery and completely forgetting the most basic of Bahá'í teachings, set upon Siyyid Muḥammad and two accomplices and cut them down. Bahá'u'lláh cried out against this horrible deed:

"My captivity can bring on Me no shame. Nay, by My life, it conferreth on Me glory. That which can make Me ashamed is the conduct of such of My followers as profess to love Me, yet in fact follow the Evil One."[1]

* This is to be the last mention of Mírzá Yaḥyá in this account. His few supporters rapidly dwindled in numbers and later two or three became involved in a PanIslamic Movement which sought to unite the Muslim countries under the Sulṭán-Caliph and which was responsible for the assassination of the Sháh in 1896. Mírzá Yaḥyá died in 1912 and was given a Muslim funeral.

[1] God Passes By, p. 190 (USA).

Bahá'u'lláh was arrested and interrogated and 'Abdu'l-Bahá was put in chains. They were released when it became evident that the Bahá'ís as a whole had had nothing whatsoever to do with the crime, and that in fact they decried it more than anyone.

It was in the last year in Adrianople and in the first years in 'Akká that Bahá'u'lláh made public His claim to be the Universal Manifestation for this Age. As one of the most important objectives of Bahá'u'lláh's mission was the establishment of universal peace it was appropriate that He should speak first to those who wielded political power. The instruments He used for His Proclamation were a series of letters to the chief rulers of the world which are known collectively as the "Tablets to the Kings". Those which were written in Adrianople included one which was addressed to all rulers, ecclesiastical leaders and philosophers in which He announced the coming of a World Order. He called on them to unite, to reduce armaments, to look after the poor, and He warned them of the consequences of ignoring His advice. Another letter was sent to Napoleon III, Emperor of France, 1852-1870. In it he was advised to demonstrate in action as well as words his much publicized concern for the oppressed. A letter to the Sulṭán warned him that if he did not govern with more equity the empire would be overthrown. Yet another was addressed to Náṣiri'd-Dín Sháh in which Bahá'u'lláh said that He prayed for him to rule justly. He stressed that the Bahá'í teachings were of benefit to all mankind and that in particular they included a condemnation of all forms of violence.

This last letter was not immediately sent. Some two years later a seventeen-year-old Bahá'í named Badí' carried it to the Sháh. Walking overland, it took him four months to accomplish his mission. For his pains he was viciously tortured and put to death. Since the terror of the early 1850s the Bahá'ís in Persia were unable to live openly as a community and were constantly subject to spasmodic and ferocious attacks of this sort. The history of the time is full of accounts of Bahá'ís heroically maintaining their Faith despite all that the clergy and corrupt officials might inflict on them.

During His incarceration in the prison of 'Akká, Bahá'u'lláh wrote to Napoleon III for a second time; to Victoria, Queen of England 1837-1901; to Alexander II, Tsar of Russia 1855-1881; to William I, Emperor of Germany 1871-1888; to Franz Joseph I, Emperor of Austro-Hungary 1848-1916; to Pius IX who was Pope from 1846-1878; and to the governments of America. He announced His claim and said that if they did not immediately accept Him, at least they should be reconciled amongst themselves, establish a Lesser Peace, and protect rather than overburden their subjects. Napoleon III had treated Bahá'u'lláh's first letter with contempt. The second letter warned him that he would lose his throne if he persisted in such arrogance. It was delivered only a short time before the outbreak of the Franco-Prussian War of 1870 in which the Second Empire of the Bonapartes was overthrown. In His letter to Queen Victoria, Bahá'u'lláh gave praise for the representative system of government in Britain and for the efforts of her government to abolish slavery. He said that the only lasting remedy for the world's ills was the union of all peoples in one common Faith. He warned William I that "the banks of the Rhine would run with gore" and there would be "lamentations in Berlin" if the Empire acted with excessive pride. He told Pius IX not to emulate the Pharises at the time of Jesus, and to leave his palaces and other riches. In addition to the letters to the kings, Bahá'u'lláh also addressed passages to Jewish, Muslim, Zoroastrian, Christian and Bábí communities in which He prophesised that this new Faith would unite all religions.

The next major work of Bahá'u'lláh was the *Kitàb-i-Aqdas (Book of Laws)* which was composed in 1873 and which Shoghi Effendi epitomized as the "Charter of the future world civilization".[1] In it Bahá'u'lláh described the functions of His Successor and of the Universal House of

[1] God Passes By, p. 214 (USA).

Justice. He said that there would not be another great Teacher from God for at least one thousand years. Shoghi Effendi summarized the laws given in this book as follows:

"He ... prescribes the obligatory prayers; designates the time and period of fasting; prohibits congregational prayer except for the dead ... formulates the law of inheritance; ordains the institution of the Mashriqu'l-Adhkár; establishes the Nineteen Day Feasts, the Bahá'í festivals and the Intercalary Days; abolishes the institution of priesthood; prohibits slavery, asceticism, mendicancy, monasticism, penance, the use of pulpits and the kissing of hands; prescribes monogamy; condemns cruelty to animals, idleness and sloth, backbiting and calumny; censures divorce; interdicts gambling; the use of opium, wine and other intoxicating drinks ... stresses the importance of marriage and lays down its essential conditions; imposes the obligation of engaging in some trade or profession, exalting such occupation to the rank of worship; emphasizes the necessity of providing the means for the education of children; and lays upon every person the duty of writing a testament and of strict obedience to one's government.

"Apart from these provisions Bahá'u'lláh exhorts His followers to consort with amity and concord and without discrimination with the adherents of all religions; warns them to guard against fanaticism, sedition, pride, dispute, and contention; inculcates upon them immaculate cleanliness, strict truthfulness, spotless chastity, trustworthiness, hospitality, fidelity, courtesy, forbearance, justice and fairness; counsels them to be 'even as the fingers of one hand and limbs of one body'.[1]

This book was supplemented by a whole series of letters addressed to His followers which, amongst other principles emphasized the oneness of the human race, the need for one world government, the necessity of consultation in government, the importance of agriculture in the world economy, and the significant part which could be played in establishing a just society by a reformed press.

As the years went by the restrictions on the Bahá'ís in

[1] God Passes By, p. 214 (USA).

'Akká were gradually relaxed by governors who came to have the highest regard for Bahá'u'lláh and 'Abdu'l-Bahá despite an initial hostility. About 1877 Bahá'u'lláh was allowed to live outside 'Akká and a small house some four miles away known as Mazra'ih, was rented for Him by 'Abdu'l-Bahá. For the first time in nine years He was able to see the countryside which since His youth He had loved so much. Two years later 'Abdu'l-Bahá secured for His use the mansion of Bahjí where He lived for the rest of His life. In 1890, the distinguished Orientalist, Professor E. G. Browne, of Cambridge University who had taken great interest in the Bábí Faith came to Bahjí to meet Bahá'u'lláh. He was the only westerner to leave a record of his impressions of Bahá'u'lláh:

"The face of Him on Whom I gazed I can never forget, though I cannot describe it. Those piercing eyes seemed to read one's very soul; power and authority sat on that ample brow; while the deep lines on the forehead and face implied on age which the jet black hair and beard flowing down in indistinguishable luxuriance almost to the waist seemed to belie. No need to ask in Whose presence I stood, as I bowed myself before One Who is the object of a devotion and love which kings might envy and emperors sigh for in vain.[1]**

In His last years Bahá'u'lláh made several visits to Mount Carmel which stands above Haifa, and there He appointed the site for the tomb of the Báb. He also wrote two more very important documents. The first was a letter addressed to one of the most savage and relentless persecutors of Bahá'ís in the city of Iṣfáhán. This *Epistle to the Son of the Wolf* was in effect a summary of the teachings of the Báb and Bahá'u'lláh. Forgiveness and hope were offered to even the most cruel and hate-ridden if only they could bring themselves to ask for it. The second was the *Book of the Covenant* in which the Bahá'í community was told that

---

[1] Bahá'u'lláh and the New Era, p. 37 (UK).

* The views of the Bahá'í Faith held by Edward Granville Browne (1862-1924) fluctuated violently during the course of his life. Though very much impressed as indicated by the above passage, he had reservations which derived, first from being taken in by some crude forgeries put out by allies of Mízrá Yaḥyá, and secondly, because later he felt that the Bahá'ís should have committed themselves to the new liberal constitution movement in Persia — thereby missing the much greater vision of a new civilization which is at the core of the Bahá'í Faith.

when Bahá'u'lláh died His eldest Son, 'Abdu'l-Bahá (called the Centre of the Covenant) was to succeed Him as Head of the Faith (this had been mentioned in His Book of Laws, written in 1873), with sole right to act as Interpreter of His Writings. He added that the property given to the Bahá'ís in 'Akká belonged to the Faith and not to His family. As mentioned in Chapter Six, Bahá'ís see this document and the *Will and Testament* of 'Abdu'l-Bahá as the foundations for the continuation of authority and legitimacy within the Bahá'í Faith and so as the rock on which will be built the future world government.

And so the life of Bahá'u'lláh drew to a close. Early in May 1892 having contracted a slight fever He grew progressively weaker. He died at dawn on the twenty ninth day of that month. He was seventy-five years old. The community was grief-stricken and Nabíl-A'zam, historian of the Bahá'í Faith, unable to bear the loss walked into the sea never to return.

C — 'Abdu'l-Bahá

At the time of His Father's demise 'Abdu'l-Bahá was 48 years old. He had been born on May 23, 1844, on the very night of the Báb's Declaration. As a child He had met many of the great Bábí heroes and had witnessed the fierce persecutions to which they had been subjected, including His Father's imprisonment in the Síyáh-Chál. He was a strong and vibrant young man and He loved to spend His free time on horseback. He was also deeply spiritual and long before Bahá'u'lláh made His announcement to His followers 'Abdu'l-Bahá had come to recognize, from His own intuition, the great station of His Father.

As time passed and especially after the journey to Adrianople, 'Abdu'l-Bahá gradually assumed the burden of administering to the needs of the community and He generally protected His Father from day to day concerns. After banishment to 'Akká He established contacts with many non-Bahá'ís in the area including several of religious and public distinction. One was Midhat Páshá, a former

Prime Minister of the Ottoman Empire who in 1876 had temporarily persuaded the Sulṭán to grant a liberal constitution. Beside conducting a voluminous correspondence 'Abdu'l-Bahá also wrote at this time a short history of the Bahá'í Faith entitled *A Traveller's Narrative* which was later translated and published (1891) in the West by E. G. Browne. Earlier in 1875 He addressed a message entitled *The Secret of Divine Civilization* to the people of Persia, in which He advised reform as essential for the achievement of a truly just social order.

In all relationships 'Abdu'l-Bahá was infinitely considerate and kind and He was deeply loved even by those who were initially hostile to the Bahá'í community, including many of the government officials in 'Akká. Bahá'u'lláh said that 'Abdu'l-Bahá lived the perfect Bahá'í life and that He was a model for all to follow — the perfect Exemplar. During His Father's lifetime. He had been known as 'Abbás Effendi or as the 'Master' but after 1892 He took the title 'Abdu'l-Bahá which means *Servant* of the Glory so that the Bahá'ís would know that His station was not that of the Báb or Bahá'u'lláh.

One of the greatest wishes of both Báb and Bahá'u'lláh was to see the Faith spread to the West. When Bahá'u'lláh died it was still essentially confined to the East; Persia, India, Burma, South Russia, the Ottoman Empire, Egypt and Súdán. 'Abdu'l-Bahá was to make it His life's work to fulfil the wishes of the Báb and Bahá'u'lláh and soon after His Father's death He prepared His first plans. Late in 1892 Ibráhím <u>Kh</u>ayru'lláh, a Bahá'í doctor of Christian Lebanese background, travelled to the United States and began to give talks on the new Faith. The refreshing relevance and rationality of the teachings attracted many and within a few years there were thriving Bahá'í communities in Chicago, Kenosha, New York, Montreal and California. Bahá'í Writings were translated into English, a Bahá'í summer school was established in New Hampshire, and in the first years of the new country plans were drawn up for a Bahá'í house of worship to be built at Wilmette, Illinois. In 1898 a small party of the new Bahá'ís travelled from North America to visit 'Abdu'l-Bahá in 'Akká, and on their way back contacts were established in Europe. In the following years small communities began to spring up in England, France and Germany and then later in Australia, Japan, and Hawaii.

In Persia, meanwhile, the community was subjected to further abuse following the assassination of Náṣiri'd-Dín Sháh in 1896 by a panislamic political group. As is the practice in many countries, innocent but defenceless minorities are the first to be blamed whenever there is trouble. During the course of this outburst of violence many Bahá'ís were killed. In the ensuing years the Bahá'ís were attacked by goverment officials and clergy and also by supposedly liberal supporters of a new constitution who were indignant that Bahá'ís declined to enter the political arena and actively support their cause. Nevertheless, as the influence of the clergy gradually waned during the early years of the twentieth century and especially after the establishment of the new constitution in 1906, there was some respite for the Bahá'ís and for the first time they were able to act openly, albeit cautiously, and to start their own schools. As a result the community expanded rapidly. A signal of hope for better times was the beginning in 1902 of work on the first Bahá'í house of worship in the world in 'Ishqábád just across the frontier in the South Russia.* This project was completed in 1920.

The Faith, in the early years of 'Abdu'l-Bahá's ministry, was subject to even more severe trials than the persecution in Persia. All religious and political movements, including those that are progressive, are afflicted at some stage by the fiercest dissent within their own ranks with the frequent consequence that the original objective is lost sight of and the movement breaks up into warring factions. The Bahá'í Faith has also had its share of dissidents who have tried to undermine its central authority. However, because of the stress on unity in Bahá'í teachings as expressed in precise

---

* The Bahá'ís had been able to live much more openly in Russia than in Persia. In 1889 a Bahá'í had been murdered by a group of Persian Muslim fanatics, but much to their surprise the Russian Government immediately arrested them and put them on trial. They were found guilty and would have been executed if the Bahá'ís had not pleaded for mercy on their behalf.

terms in the Covenants of Bahá'u'lláh and 'Abdu'l-Bahá, the breaks which have occurred in the Bahá'í Faith have been confined to very small numbers whose cause would wither into insignficance within a short time whilst the Bahá'í community would increase in strength and vigour, purified by this most severe of tests.

The first to rebel against 'Abdu'l-Bahá was His own half-brother Mírzá Muḥammad 'Alí, who was uncontrollably jealous and would not accept 'Abdu'l-Bahá's position as head of the Faith. Later Ibráhím Khayru'lláh, who had taken the Faith to the United States, his ego inflated with success, demanded that 'Abdu'l-Bahá recognize him as co-head of the Faith. 'Abdu'l-Bahá extended the utmost love and patience to these rebels but they did not respond and in the end they left the Faith. These happenings caused the deepest sadness in the heart of 'Abdu'l-Bahá and it was always made clear that Covenant-breakers would be welcomed back into the fold of the Faith if their pride would let them. He insisted, too, that Bahá'ís recognize the important part Ibráhím Khayru'lláh had played in taking the Faith to the West before he became a Covenant-breaker. The lesson of these events and of those of a similar nature which have occurred since 'Abdu'l-Bahá's time is that no man can ever be sure of his own loyalty, no matter what his achievements, and that all must be ever on their guard against the call of ego and selfishness. The danger is greatest for those who are in prominence, and this is one reason why universal participation and the construction of a form of government which does not rely on individual leadership is so significant for the future welfare of mankind.

Full of spite and jealousy Mírzá Muḥammad 'Alí and his allies surreptiously hinted to the Turkish authorities that 'Abdu'l-Bahá was planning a revolt. As evidence they pointed to the tomb which 'Abdu'l-Bahá was having built to receive the remains of the Báb and which they said was to be a fortress. In these years the Turkish Government, incompetent and repressive as ever, was fearful that an Arab rebellion might break out at any time and it was therefore more than usually disposed to take seriously such ridiculous stories. In 1901 orders were sent from Constantinople that the relaxation of restrictions on the movement of 'Abdu'l-Bahá were to be rescinded and henceforth He was to be kept under house arrest. In 1904, a commission was sent to look into the charges that had been made. Questioned in court 'Abdu'l-Bahá was easily able to demonstrate the absurdity of such accusations.

Undisturbed by these alarms, 'Abdu'l-Bahá continued his work with the poor and sick of 'Akká whom he visited every Friday, and, except for a period when He felt they might be in danger, He continued to receive streams of visitors from all over the world. One of these was Laura Barney who, having received His prior permission, had a record made of a series of talks she had with Him, a record which was later published under the title *Some Answered Questions*. In this book Bahá'í teachings, which had hitherto been mainly related to an Islamic audience, were presented for readers of a Christian or humanist background. The informal talks as recorded were typical of 'Abdu'l-Bahá's method of teaching: straightforward, logical, full of common sense and spiced with a gentle dash of humour. During this period 'Abdu'l-Bahá also set down His *Will and Testament* in which He said that the unity of the Bahá'í world would be preserved after His death if the same obedience and loyalty given to Him was given to the succeeding authorities: the Guardian and the Universal House of Justice. The problems which had afflicted both Christianity and Islám with regard to succession must be avoided. He also gave more detailed guidance on the establishment of the future Bahá'í system of administration, mentioning specifically for the first time the need for *National* Houses of Justice as well as Houses of Justice at the world and local levels.

The troubles of the Sultán's government continued to increase and in an atmosphere of suspicion and intrigue orders were given for a further investigation of 'Abdu'l-Bahá. In late 1907 a second Commission was sent from Constantinople. The Commission was so clearly hostile that many Bahá'ís abroad fearing for 'Abdu'l-Bahá's life, begged

Him to flee to the West. These fears were not exaggerated: the Sultán had a well-earned reputation for brutality as had been only recently demonstrated in the cold-blooded murder of tens of thousands of Armenian subjects. 'Abdu'l-Bahá, however, refused to move. After a short stay the Commission was recalled to Constantinople. Before it could complete its report, news was received of an attempt on the life of the Sultán. In the disturbances of the next few months 'Abdu'l-Bahá was forgotten by the government and no action had been taken before it was forced to change its whole policy as a result of the successful Young Turk rebellion of 1908. The new regime proved initially far more liberal than its predecessor and one consequence was that 'Abdu'l-Bahá was set free. For the first time since the days in Baghdád, 45 years earlier, He was free of government restrictions. At last He could fulfil His dream and travel to the West. However, He was then some sixty-four years old and His health was not good after so many years of confinement and hardship. It was ill-health which forced Him to abandon His first planned trip to the West in 1910, when He had only got as far as Egypt.

By the summer of 1911, however, His health had greatly improved and in August He was able to set sail from Egypt for England. He spent the month of September in London. There for the first time in His life He delivered several public addresses, including one at the City Temple. His reputation having travelled before Him, He was soon called upon by many visitors from all classes and walks of life. Among His visitors were Annie Besant, Mrs. Pankhurst, the leader of the Suffragette movement, Professor Geddes, advocate of sweeping economic and social reform, and William T. Stead, the great progressive journalist. Besides seeing the famous, 'Abdu'l-Bahá went to the East End of London, and also travelled briefly to Bristol. He then crossed the Channel and stayed in Paris for about nine weeks. Again there was a busy round of meetings in open houses, and public addresses to a wide variety of audiences. Many of these addresses were recorded and have been brought together in a book entitled *Paris Talks*. The themes of the talks were summarized by Shoghi Effendi as follows:

"The independent search after truth, unfettered by superstition or tradition; the oneness of the entire human race, the pivotal principle and fundamental doctrine of the Faith; the basic unity of all religions; the condemnation of all forms of prejudice, whether religious, racial, class or national; the harmony which must exist between religion and science; the equality of men and women, the two wings on which the bird of human kind is able to soar; the introduction of compulsory education; the adoption of a universal auxiliary language; the abolition of the extremes of wealth and poverty; the institution of a world tribunal for the adjudication of disputes between nations; the exaltation of work, performed in the spirit of service, to the rank of worship; the glorification of justice as the ruling principle in human society, and of religion as a bulwark for the protection of all peoples and nations; and the establishement of a permanent and universal peace as the supreme goal of mankind."[1]

Many stories are told of how in His work 'Abdu'l-Bahá was very direct, but in a loving way so that offence could not be taken, concerning the way society treated the poor, religious bigotry, and the evils of extreme nationalism which, He warned, would soon bring in its wake great devastation. He always showed the utmost concern for those who were sick or who were not of much consequence in society, and on the other hand He had a way, pointed but not cruel, of deflating the pompous and arrogant.

Though the reception of 'Abdu'l-Bahá on this trip was almost totally friendly and warm, there were a few carping voices. In England some narrow-minded clergymen tried to maintain that the Faith was an uninspired eclecticism. Perhaps they had not heard of the thousands who died for the Faith when they called it uninspired. As for the charge of eclecticism, they never did say from whence the Bahá'ís were supposed to have derived such fundamental philosophical principles as progressive revelation and the Bahá'í Administrative Order.

[1] God Passes By, p. 281 (USA).

This first of His journeys came to an end in December when He returned to Egypt. In March 1912, He set out on His second journey to the West, this time going first to the United States. Sailing via Naples on the S.S. *Cedric* He reached New York on April 11. Between April and August He stayed mostly in New York from whence He made extended trips to the surrounding regions going as far South as Washington D.C., as far West as Chicago and as far North as New Hampshire. In September He travelled to the West Coast. He stayed in California for most of October and returned to New York in November. All told, it is recorded that in the eight months of His stay in the United States and Canada, 'Abdu'l-Bahá visited thirty-nine towns and cities and delivered more than one hundred and forty public addresses — an amazing feat for a man of His age, and for an Easterner with no formal schooling Who had spent the greater part of His life in prison.

As with His trip to Europe the previous year, He met and received men, women and children of all backgrounds. He spoke at numerous universities, including Columbia, Howard, New York and Palo Alto, and at many churches of all denominations, as well as at Jewish synagogues. He addressed the Fourth Annual Meeting of the National Association for the Advancement of Coloured Peoples (NAACP), a meeting of socialists in Montreal, scientific associations and such groups as the Rationalists and the Theosophists. Many of His talks were directly related to current social problems such as the unjust economic and social system in the United States, and the unrest amongst the poor which was an inevitable consequence. He repeated His warnings that the hatred engendered by extreme nationalism would soon set the world at war on a scale never before seen. He spoke very strongly on racial injustice which at that time was certainly not a popular issue, and He foretold that unless minority groups of the United States, including the black people, were treated as equals and as brothers, there would be great hardship and bloodshed.

His words were always supported by His deeds. For

instance, on one occasion at an official reception in
Washington He observed when the guests sat down to
dinner that a negro Bahá'í had not been given a place and
had stayed outside. 'Abdu'l-Bahá refused to eat until His
friend had been brought into the room and given a place of
honour at His side. On another occasion He publicly
married two Bahá'ís, one black, one white — virtually an
unheard of union at that time. He often went to the poor
areas of a city, such as the Bowery in New York, and he was
continuously inviting children from the street to come and
visit Him, which they often did.

'Abdu'l-Bahá left the United States on December 5 on a
ship bound for England. Landing at Liverpool, He paid
short visits to Oxford, Edinburgh, Bristol and London
before departing for the Continent in January 1913. There
He stayed first in Paris. He later journeyed to Stuttgart,
Geneva, Budapest and Vienna. His journey to the West
ended with a final visit to Paris. In the summer He boarded
ship for Egypt where He stayed a few months before finally
returning to 'Akká in December 1913. He had been away on
His world travels for more than three years.

In less than a year the terrible conflict which 'Abdu'l-
Bahá had foretold broke out in Europe. The Ottoman
Empire, allied with the Central Powers against Russia and
the other Slav peoples, was drawn into the maelstrom. As
in previous times of crisis, the Ottoman Government went
in constant fear of rebellion from its subject peoples,
including the Arabs of Syria, 'Iráq, Palestine and Arabia.
Thanks to the promptings of Mírzá Muḥammad 'Alí and His
fellow Covenant-breakers, Jamál Páshá, the Turkish
commander-in-chief, suspected that 'Abdu'l-Bahá might
become the leader of an Arab revolt, and in consequence for
a time there was a danger that He would be imprisoned or
even executed.* However, as there was absolutely no

*Jamál Páshá had been one of the leaders of the Young Turk rebellion in 1909. When on
one occasion he accused 'Adu'l-Bahá to His face of being a *religious* mischiefmaker, 'Abdu'l-
Bahá smilingly replied that perhaps at one time he, Jamál Páshá, might have been described
as a *political* mischiefmaker. He was on of the triumvirate with Enver Páshá and Tal'at Páshá
who ruled the Ottoman Empire during the war. As Governor of Syria he treated Arabs and
Armenians alike with great barbarity. His cruelty was not forgotten after the war and in 1922
he was assassinated by an Armenian nationalist.

evidence to support these allegations no action was taken. 'Abdu'l-Bahá was left free to organize the growing of food and its distribution to the poor of 'Akká, whose normal supplies had been taken by the Turkish army. The Bahá'í community under 'Abdu'l-Bahá's direction also organized free medical services for the poor of the city.

During the war, 'Abdu'l-Bahá maintained contact with friends in the West mainly by means of steady correspondence. Of particular importance were a series of letters sent to the American community known collectively as the *Tablets of the Divine Plan* in which He told them that they could most quickly bring about a new civilization based on a permanent peace if they spread out systematically all around the world. These letters were later to be the basis for the plans of Shoghi Effendi and the Universal House of Justice for the creation of a world network of communities and administration.

In 1917 the tide of war began to turn decisively against the Turks. The British advancing from their bases in Egypt, acting in concert with the long-feared Arab rebels, took Jerusalem in December. In their hour of defeat the Turks had lashed out in revenge against anyone who offended them. It was said that Jamál Páshá had sworn to crucify 'Abdu'l-Bahá before he surrendered Haifa. Alarmed, English Bahá'ís petitioned their government to take all measures they could to ensure His safety. Accordingly, the Foreign Secretary, Lord Balfour, sent special orders to that effect to General Allenby, the Commander of the Allied troops in Palestine. When later (September 1918) British troops reached 'Akká they immediately made for the residence of 'Abdu'l-Bahá to provide protection against the Turks.

The new British Government of Palestine had the highest respect for 'Abdu'l-Bahá and they treated Him with the utmost reverence. General Allenby and the High Commissioner, Lord Samuel, called on Him several times. In recognition of His humanitarian activities during the war He was asked to accept a knighthood.

Though now well on into His seventies and not strong

after the hardships of the war, 'Abdu'l-Bahá continued His work as determinedly as ever. In 1919 He wrote to those involved, praising the establishment of the League of Nations which He described as a step in the right direction, though far more would have to be done to strengthen such a world authority if there were to be a continuing peace.

In late 1921 feeling increasingly tired from His labours 'Abdu'l-Bahá told His friends that His days were coming to an end. Some eight weeks later, on November 28, He died quietly. Condolences to His family and the Bahá'í community came from all over the world. The cable of condolence sent on behalf of the British Government was signed by Winston Churchill, who was then Secretary for the Colonies. Forgetting for a while community tensions, some ten thousand persons of all backgrounds, including Christian, Muslim and Jewish, came together to pay homage to 'Abdu'l-Bahá as He took His last earthly journey. The coming together that day was a beautiful symbol of what would ultimately spring from the life work of 'Abdu'l-Bahá.

D — Shoghi Effendi

In His *Will and Testament* 'Abdu'l-Bahá said that in the future the Faith should be guided by the twin institutions of a Universal House of Justice and a Guardianship. The Guardian would have the authority to interpret the Bahá'í Writings and would be a permanent member and head of the Universal House of Justice. The Guardianship would stay within the family of Bahá'u'lláh. However, there was to be no automatic succession. Each Guardian would have to nominate His successor in his own lifetime and he could only nominate one who was of the most exemplary character.

"*He that is appointed must manifest in himself detachment from all worldly things, must be the essence of purity, must show in himself the fear of God, knowledge, wisdom and learning.*"[1]

[1] *Will and Testament* of 'Abdu'l-Bahá, p. 12 (UK).

'Abdu'l-Bahá appointed as the first Guardian and as His own successor, His eldest grandson, Shoghi Effendi Rabbani, who was then twenty-four years old and a student at Oxford. The death of 'Abdu'l-Bahá came as a great shock to Shoghi Effendi who had been very close to his Grandfather since early childhood. The shock was compounded by news of his appointment as Guardian for he understood very clearly how great would be the responsibility of that office. Up until this time his only ambition had been to serve the Faith by translating Bahá'í works into the English language.

To the sadness at the loss of his Grandfather and the burden of office was added the painful experience of difficulties with several members of his family who at first tried to interfere with his work and then later went their own way without regard to the interest of the Faith. In these trials, which lasted many years, the Guardian had the unshakable support of Bahíyyih Khánum, the sister of 'Abdu'l-Bahá, until her death in 1932, and later of his wife, Rúḥíyyih Khánum whom he married in 1937.

To ease the stress caused by these difficulties the Guardian would try to leave Haifa each year for a few months and go to the mountains of central Europe where he could exercise and be alone in the wilds of nature. It was typical of the Guardian that on these treks into the mountains he would live in the greatest simplicity, stopping at only the humblest of inns and always travelling third class by train.

The Guardian's first major task was to lay the foundations of a working Administrative Order throughout the world along the lines laid down by Bahá'u'lláh and 'Abdu'l-Bahá. Only when this was done could there be elected a Universal House of Justice. Though during 'Abdu'l-Bahá's time there were rudimentary Bahá'í forms of government in several local communities, it was the Guardian who surely, step by step, knitted these communities into a regular and world-wide system. In the twenties and early thirties, under the supervision of the Guardian National Spiritual Assemblies were first elected in the British Isles, Germany, India, Egypt, the United States and Canada, Persia and Australia.

In this work the Guardian received much assistance from the American community. The American Bahá'ís, for instance, drew up a model Assembly constitution, established specialized committees to administer different aspects of Bahá'í work, developed procedures for incorporation of Assemblies so that they could hold property, and pioneered in the task of obtaining official recognition of Bahá'í holy days, marriage, divorce, and burial. These were humdrum activities but typical of the Bahá'í concept that a lasting transformation in men's affairs will only come from life-long committal and from building a new society step by step from the foundations up. The Guardian was in continuous contact with every community by mail and through visitors to Haifa, giving encouragement, praise and advice and creating in all a sense of belonging to an intimate world family. He told the communities to remember that no matter how small were their numbers at that time and how numerous the tests, their work was of the utmost significance for the future of mankind. He contrasted the love and fellowship which was being channelled to fruitful ends by the embryonic administrative organs of the Bahá'í community with the evident failure of traditional institutions to deal with the problems of the world, and he noted especially the decline of the established churches, quoting the dramatic happenings in Russia, Turkey and Persia, where modern secular governments were trying to clear the stifling atmosphere of religious superstition and obscurantism.

In these years there was a considerable increase in the amount of information on the Faith available in the West. In 1922 the first comprehensive book on the Bahá'í Faith written by J.E. Esslemont, a Scottish medical doctor was published. By 1970 this book had been translated into fifty-eight languages. The Guardian himself translated into English many of the Writings of Bahá'u'lláh and 'Abdu'l-Bahá, as well as a detailed account by Nabíl-í-A'zam of the early history of the Cause. Much of this translation work was done by the Guardian during his sojourns in the Alps. Information on the Faith was also carried around the world by Bahá'ís who travelled from country to country or who settled in new areas. The most distinguished of the travelling teachers was a woman journalist named Martha Root who, during the twenty year period between the World Wars, visited just about every part of the world, talking with high and low alike. Through her many wellknown figures came to know and respect the Bahá'í Faith, including Queen Marie of Romania, who later became a Bahá'í despite much opposition from her family. Queen Marie was a granddaughter of Queen Victoria, the one monarch who had shown any response to Bahá'u'lláh's letters to the Kings.

As the main outline of the Bahá'í Administrative Order started to take shape the Guardian began plans for a world centre in Haifa.* Over a period of time he gradually bought land around the site of the Shrine of the Báb and elsewhere in the vicinity on which the future buildings of the Universal House of Justice and its associated services would be erected. He also made a small but significant gesture to indicate the new phase in the development of the Faith. Throughout His life, 'Abdu'l-Bahá had attended Friday prayers at the mosque to refute in a visible manner the charge of atheism levelled against the Bahá'ís. Now that the Faith was firmly established as an independent religion it was no longer considered appropriate for its head to be seen showing special ties with another religion and the Guardian did not continue 'Abdu'l-Bahá's practice.

During the interwar period Bahá'ís continued to be harried and attacked in several countries. In *Persia* the new nationalist and western orientated regime of Reza Sháh Pahlavi enforced a greater degree of law and order than had pertained for years, and of particular significance from the point of view of the Bahá'ís curbed the worst excesses of a reactionary priesthood. Bahá'ís who were sympathetic with some of the reforms of the new Sháh, notably the improved position of women, won some acceptance of their claim to be an independent religion and therefore not subject to Muslim

---

*'Abdu'l-Bahá said that Haifa-Akká would be the metropolis of the future world civilization Bahá'u'lláh and the New Era, p. 228 (UK).

religious courts. However, their position remained far from secure and they continued to undergo various forms of persecution. In 1926 there was a particularly savage outbreak of violence against them in the village of Jahrum in south Persia in which eight Bahá'ís lost their lives. Twelve others were killed elsewhere in Persia that year. In 'Iráq the House of Bahá'u'lláh in Baghdád was taken by force from the Bahá'ís. The case was taken to the highest courts in the country and ultimately to the League of Nations. However, despite verdicts favourable to the Bahá'í Faith, the buildings were never restored to the Bahá'ís because of the weakness of the League and the government's fear of antagonizing the Muslim clergy. In *Egypt* the clergy, in an attempt to deprive some Bahá'ís of their normal civil rights, inadvertently tripped over its own argument and by mistake admitted that the Bahá'ís belonged to a separate religion (as distinct from a Muslim heresy). As a result the Bahá'ís were later able to obtain from the courts recognition of the Bahá'í marriage and the right to have their own burial grounds. In *Turkey* the Government of Ataturk, busy imposing social reforms in the face of strong resistance from the Muslim clergy, tended to be highly highly suspicious of any religious group, and because of the near vicinity of Soviet Russia, was additionally suspicious of anything that sounded even vaguely communistic. It was in these circumstances that a group of Bahá'ís in the city of Smyrna were arrested and thrown into prison. This particular story had a happy ending. The calm and dignified way in which the Bahá'ís presented their teachings in court created a most favourable impression and instructions were given for their release. In *Russia* the new Soviet Government, pursuing a relatively tolerant policy toward minority racial and religious groups during Lenin's lifetime, left the Bahá'ís alone. However, by 1929, through no fault of the Bahá'ís the situation had changed. Associated with the drive toward collectivization in the countryside was an increase in government interference and supervision in all aspects of life. Restrictions were placed on Bahá'í meetings, assemblies were dissolved and property confiscated.'* Later the restrictions became persecution and as this reached its peak in the late 1930s Bahá'ís were seized and imprisoned or sent into exile. It was of no avail that Bahá'ís had nothing whatsoever to do with politics. In *Germany* when the National Socialists came to power in 1933 it was inevitable that the Bahá'í Faith would be outlawed almost immediately as in its philosophy of life it stood at the furthest possible point away from that of the new rulers.

By 1937 the Guardian was satisfied that the Bahá'í Administrative Order was firmly established and he felt able to turn his attention to 'Abdu'l-Bahá's instructions for taking the Bahá'í Faith to all corners of the earth. Several national teaching plans were adopted, including a Seven-Year Plan for the United States and Canada. The latter had as its goals the establishment of Bahá'í communities in every state of the United States and in every republic of Latin America. In a letter to the American Bahá'í Community written in December 1938, subsequently published under the title of *The Advent of Divine Justice*, the Guardian impressed upon his readers how much the future of the world depended upon their success. He urged them to spread out and to teach by the example of their own character as well as by word of mouth. In teaching they should merge into their new surroundings, support themselves, contribute to the welfare of the community in which they lived, and pay particular attention to the poor, the Negro and the Indian. In the Bahá'í community there should be discrimination, not against but, in favour of the minority. He pointed out that such peoples, because of their harsh experiences, would understand the significance of the Faith more quickly than others. Teaching was the most effective way of adding depth to life.

Despite the ravages and difficulties caused by the Second World War, all the goals of the Seven Year Plan had been achieved by 1944. In that year to mark the first centenary

---

* Including the first Mashriqu'l-Adhkár of the Bahá'í Faith which had been built in 'Ishqábád. Years later this building was levelled by Soviet authorities after it had been badly damaged by an earthquake in 1948.

of the Faith there was published a complete history of the Faith written by the Guardian — complete, that is, except for any reference to his own tremendous labours in the preceeding twenty years.

In 1946 a second series of plans were launched, including a second Seven Year Plan for the American community which this time was mainly directed toward war-torn Europe. By 1953 the goal of establishing communities in ten more European Countries was achieved. During this period the Mashriqu'l-Adhkár at Wilmette was finally completed as was the Shrine of the Báb in Haifa. Both buildings whose costs were met by the personal sacrifice of tens of thousands of Bahá'ís, many very poor, have become great silent teachers of the reality of life — as anyone will testify who has experienced the spirit of serenity which pervades the sky-filled House of Worship at Wilmette or who has seen that golden dome glistening in the sun on Mount Carmel — a bright light at the centre of the world. In 1951, as the second Seven Year Plan came to a conclusion the Guardian selected a nine-member International Bahá'í Council to represent the Bahá'í world community in dealings with the Israeli Government and to help complete the Shrine of the Báb. This was one more step toward the creation of the Universal House of Justice. The same year he appointed twelve outstanding Bahá'ís to be Hands of the Cause of God to help with the spiritual development of the world community. This number was raised to nineteen the following year.

The Bahá'í community was now ready for a major expansion into all corners of the earth. In 1953 the Guardian set in motion a Ten Year Crusade, the main goal of which was to establish a Bahá'í community in every country of the world. The crusade was an outstanding success. In Africa, India, and Latin America people of all classes, ages and cultures began to come into the Faith in their thousands, an experience the Bahá'ís had not had since the early days in Persia. These triumphs were proof of what both 'Abdu'l-Bahá and the Guardian had said concerning the insight of the oppressed and the poor. A beginning was made on the construction of three more houses of worship, one in Sydney, Australia (completed in 1961); a second in Kampala, Uganda (completed in 1962); and a third in Frankfurt, Germany (completed in 1964). All were nine-sided and domed as prescribed by 'Abdu'l-Bahá, but each design was adapted to local styles and materials, a permanent symbol of the theme of unity in diversity.

The happiness of the Bahá'í world at these successes was marred in 1955 by a particularly vicious outbreak of persecution in Írán (Persia). The Government, unsure of itself after the turbulent activities of extreme nationalists in the early 1950s, attempted to strengthen its right-wing support by ingratiating itself with clergy. A well-organized campaign to stir up public hostility against the defenceless Bahá'í community was put in motion. Priests were allowed to broadcast hate-filled diatribes on the radio, and as the campaign moved into topgear the Government banned the Faith, occupied its buildings throughout the country and published pictures showing the destruction of the national Bahá'í centre in Ṭihrán. All Bahá'ís in public service were dismissed from their posts. Police stood aside as bands roved the country attacking Bahá'ís and looting their property. In the worst known incident seven Bahá'ís were hacked to pieces by a mob in the village of Hurmuzak.

The response of the world Bahá'í community led by the Guardian was immediate and vigorous. Cables requesting an end to the persecution were sent to the Sháh from all over the world. Strongly worded appeals were made to the United Nations and to President Eisenhower. It was apparent that the government was startled by the outcry and it gradually took steps to calm down the situation which it had created.

In November 1957, some four years after the beginning of the Ten-Year Plan, the Guardian, prematurely exhausted by thirty-six years of the most wearying work and by continued betrayal by some members of his family, died suddenly in London after an attack of Asian flu. In October, perhaps sensing that his life was drawing to a close the Guardian had, in his last message to the Bahá'í world before he died, raised the number of Hands to twenty-seven. In that message he referred to them as the "Chief Stewards of Bahá'u'lláh's embryonic World Commonwealth".[1] Bahá'ís from all over the world came to attend the funeral of their beloved Guardian. He was buried in a secluded glade of the Great Northern Cemetery in London. On his grave was erected a pillar surmounted by an eagle of victory, wings outspread over the globe, symbol of the hope of Man.

E — *The Universal House Justice*

Soon after the funeral of the Guardian, the Hands of the Cause of God gathered in Haifa and determined from his papers that he had not nominated a successor because there was no one eligible according to the terms of the Will and Testament of 'Abdu'l-Bahá. In 1960 the Community was to face a trial similar to those of the past in times of transition. One of the Hands of the Cause, who was by this time very old, persuaded himself that he should be the second Guardian. The others treated him with great love but when he not only persisted with his claim but actively tried to build up support for it amongst the Bahá'í community and so cause dissension, the worst act a Bahá'í can commit, the Hands had no choice but to expel him from the Faith. The episode served to confirm what had been shown in the past: that the Faith could not be split by even the most prominent of its adherents. Such people have fallen away from the Faith leaving the community itself stronger and more resolved than ever to accomplish its great mission.

The Hands of the Cause decided that it was their duty to continue the Ten-Year Plan and to make arrangements for the election of the first Universal House of Justice. During the next six years the Faith went from success to success and by 1963 had achieved all the goals established ten years before. In April of that year the members of no less than fifty-six National and Regional Spiritual Assemblies met in Haifa to elect the Universal House of Justice. An embryonic world government was thus born — a truly momentous

[1] Messages to the Bahá'í World, p. 127 (USA).

event in the world's history, appreciated as yet by only a tiny minority of the world's population. A week later six thousand Bahá'ís from all over the world came together in London for the first Bahá'í World Congress, held on the hundredth anniversary of Bahá'u'lláh's declaration of His mission. This also was an epoch-making event, for this was not the usual meeting of statesmen or experts or the privileged rich; this was the first real meeting of all the peoples of the world; poor, rich, educated, illiterate, brown, white, yellow, black — mankind in all its richness and diversity.

It is sad to have to record that along with these glorious events there continued to be persecutions of Bahá'ís in many parts of the world during the sixties, most notably in 'Iráq, Egypt, and Morocco. These cowardly attacks, which were totally unprovoked, were by-products of political struggles which had no connection at all with the Bahá'í communities in those countries.

Within a year of taking office the Universal House of Justice had drawn up a new Nine-Year Plan to follow the Ten-Year Crusade. The Plan called for a multitude of new goals for a growing and more sophisticated community. The goals included one to raise up a total of fifty-two new National Spiritual Assemblies, one to increase the number of publishing trusts from eight to twelve and another to build two more Mashriqu'l-Adhkárs, one in Panama, a great crossroad of the world, and one in Tihrán. Following in the footsteps of the Guardian, the Universal House of Justice kept in constant communication with every community in the world. A constant theme of letters has been the declining state of the established order and the tremendous responsibility which rests on the shoulders of every Bahá'í to do all in his power to help build up the New World Order.

In 1967, to celebrate the hundreth anniversary of Bahá'u'lláh's letters to the rulers of the world, a major project was launched to have a copy of this proclamation put into the hands of as many persons as possible holding public office, and at both national and local levels. The campaign was opened with six inter-continental conferences in

Panama City, Chicago, Sydney, Kampala, Frankfurt and New Delhi, which were linked together by radio-telephone — once again a highly symbolic first occasion in the history of man.

The following year members of eighty-one National Spiritual Assemblies met to elect the second Universal House of Justice. Since that election perhaps the greatest triumphs of the Faith have been in North America and Vietnam. In the United States large numbers of the poor rural Negroes of the South and also of college and high-school youth who can see little of value in the conventional society around them, have enrolled in the Faith. In Canada a large number of new Bahá'ís are Indians. In Vietnam at the time of writing there are over a hundred thousand newly enrolled Bahá'ís of whom a considerable number are Montagnards.

In 1973 the Nine Year Plan came to a successful conclusion with the election of the third Universal House of Justice by members of a hundred and thirteen National Spiritual Assemblies.

The following year, the Universal House of Justice launched a Five Year Plan which had three main objectives: preservation and consolidation of past successes; further expansion; and development of the distinctive character of Bahá'í life, particularly in local communities. Special emphasis was placed on the Local Spiritual Assembly and on the education of children. The Plan called for the establishment of 16 additional National Spiritual Assemblies. Other important goals included the construction in Haifa of a permanent seat for the Universal House of Justice and the start of work on two new Houses of Worship, one in India and one in the Pacific. It is interesting that the start of the former, which symbolically is shaped like a lotus flower, has coincided with a vast growth in the size of the Indian Bahá'í community which is now one of the largest and strongest national communities in the world. Bahá'ís, both individually and collectively, continued to provide services to the wider community, e.g. a radio service in Ecuador, an agricultural training school in India, help with a U.N. scheme to bring pure water to villages in Kenya, research in the fields of education and health in North America, substantive contributions to work of various commissions at the United Nations on the environment, population, improving the status of women, combatting the spreading use of drugs for non-medicinal purposes, etc.

As the Five Year Plan came to a close and preparations were made for a subsequent Seven Year Plan, the community came under the most dire physical threat since the earliest days. In February 1979, a new government took power in Iran which was dominated by the Muslim clergy, many of whom were determined to use the opportunity to try and obliterate the Bahá'ís. Within a short while the Bahá'í National Centre in Ṭihrán was occupied by revolutionaries and all files, membership lists and seals were seized. This was followed by confiscation of other Bahá'í properties including a well-known charitable hospital and two companies in which many Bahá'ís had placed all their savings. Bahá'í cemeteries were desecrated, and the House of the Báb in Shiraz was taken over and destroyed. The new constitution which recognized rights for Muslims, Christians, Jews and Zoroastians specifically omitted any protection for Bahá'ís.* Bahá'ís were dismissed from government service** and Bahá'ís in retirement had their pensions terminated. Bahá'í marriages even of 50 years were declared null and void and labelled prostitution. Newly-born babies were refused birth certificates. School authorities systematically began to refuse registration of Bahá'í children and the Ministry of Education decreed that Bahá'ís were banned from universities both as students and as teachers. There were instances of Bahá'í children being pressured by their teachers to denounce their parents and Faith, and of Bahá'í girls being kidnapped and forced into

---

* In August 1983, the Attorney General issued an edict saying that Bahá'í institutions and membership in them are criminal. In a 1985 court case in which a muslim defendent was found guilty of negligent driving and of killing a Bahá'í pedestrian, the court ruled that no compensation should be paid to the victim's family because he was a "member of the misguided and misleading Bahá'í Community and is considered an unprotected infidel".

** It is estimated that some 10,000 Bahá'ís have lost their jobs since 1979.

marriage with Muslims. Much private property of individuals was destroyed including 300 homes in Shiraz. It is estimated that some 10,000 Bahá'ís are now homeless. Revolutionary guards are able to enter Bahá'í homes without warrants and to take hostages if they do not find the person for whom they are seeking. Consular officials all over the world were instructed to collect the names of all Iranian Bahá'ís living abroad and to revoke their passports with a view to forcing them to return to Iran.

This systematic campaign to disable the Iranian Bahá'í community by administrative means and violent intimidation has been accompanied by a growing number of killings. In 1979 about 20 Bahá'ís lost their lives in various incidents involving the clergy or government officials. During 1980 some 20 Bahá'ís are known to have been executed in various parts of Iran, including seven in Yazd on September 8 (five of the latter, including one who was 85 years old, were members of the Local Spiritual Assembly). In August of that year all nine members of the National Spiritual Assembly and two other Bahá'ís with them were arrested in Ṭihrán and have not been heard of since. Amongst the most notorious events of that time were the murder in the village of Nuk in K͟hurasan of an old Bahá'í couple who were drenched in kerosene and burned to death by a gang of 15 masked men (November 23, 1980) and the assassination of the internationally respected Bahá'í physician, Professor Hakim of Ṭihrán University, who was gunned down in his office on January 12, 1981. In 1981 the elimination of "prominent" Bahá'ís became more systematic. In April and May five Bahá'ís were executed in Shiraz after being found "guilty of being Bahá'ís" — the first time this charge was made so openly. In June, seven

* Torture of Bahá'ís in prison has become routine. In May 1984 the Universal House of Justice made the following statement about some incidents at that time:
"For a period of months they have been subjected to floggings of all parts of the body, particularly the legs and feet, sometimes up to 400 strokes by wire cables have been administered to one prisoner, then he or she has been made to walk. Finding this impossible, the unfortunate prisoner has been forced to crawl on hands and knees back to a dark cell. In Mashad and Yazd, Bahá'í prisoners are regularly whipped on the head and face with thick plastic tubes. Similar procedures are used to a lesser degree in other prisons. A number of these victims of torture have lost their sight and hearing, others their mental competence. The bodies of four prisoners subjected to such treatment were seen before being buried in unknown graves".

Bahá'ís were executed in Ṭihrán and seven in Hamadan. The bodies of six of the latter showed clear signs of torture: burns, broken backs, legs, shoulders, hands and fingers.* In July, nine were executed in Tabriz and in September another five in Darrun, near Isfahan. In several instances families of those executed were required to pay for the bullets. The year came to a horrific climax with the secret execution in December and early January of 15 Bahá'ís in Ṭihrán, including eight members of the second National Spiritual Assembly to be arrested and six members of the Local Spiritual Assembly of Tihrán. Equally horrific was the mass execution in Shiraz in June 1983 of seven men and ten women, including several teenagers.* Since then arrests and executions of Bahá'ís have continued. In December 1987 it was reported that since the beginning of 1979 over 200 Bahá'ís have lost their lives at the hands of Islamic Courts or clergy-led mobs, and that several hundred more still languish in prison.

This cold blooded campaign to destroy the Bahá'í community in Iran which consists of over 300,000 men, women and children has resulted in an unprecedented coverage of the Bahá'í Faith in the world's media which has reported the persecution with overwhelming sympathy for the Bahá'ís. The United Nations General Assembly in December, 1985 expressed deep concern about the situation of the Bahá'ís in Iran, as has the U.N. Human Rights Commission in each of five consecutive years (1982-1986).** Similar concerns have been expressed by the European Parliament, Amnesty International, the Congress of the United States and the governments of Canada, West Germany, Australia and the United Kingdom as well as individual statesmen from a large number of other countries and all have appealed to the Iranian Government to end the persecution immediately. One of the earliest

* The story of one of the teenagers has been made into a video-musical called "Mona with the Children" and shown on television around the world.

** The Iranian authorities have denied permission for an official of the U.N. Human Rights Commission to visit Iran to investigate the situation, and their representative at the U.N. has stated that his government will not abide by the U.N. Delcaration on Human Rights if it is contrary to its view of Islamic law.

reports by a non-Bahá'í body was issued in September 1979 by the Federation of Protestant Churches in Switzerland which pointed out that the persecution even at that stage was comprehensive and consisted of harassment on four specific levels: administrative, financial, personal and social.

The Iranian authorities have reacted by either denying that there is any persecution of Bahá'ís or that they have been persecuted as a political rather than a religious group.* In this connection they have charged the Bahá'ís with being supporters of the Shah's regime, members of the Shah's secret police, SAVAK, and agents of western imperialism and Zionism.** They have also charged the Bahá'ís with prostitution and being "corrupters of the earth." The Bahá'ís have vehemently denied all these charges. They refer to the Bahá'í principles of abstention from politics and loyalty to government which are strictly adhered to, and point out that when the Shah required everyone to join his Rastakhiz party in 1975, the Bahá'ís did not do so. They add that high officials in the Shah's governments who were widely believed to be Bahá'ís were nothing of the sort, and that the Bahá'í community was often persecuted by SAVAK which worked in cooperation with Muslim fanatics. The connection with the West is nothing more sinister than the fact that the Bahá'í Faith has modern teachings and many adherents in western as well as eastern countries. There is no connection with Zionism and only with Israel because the Bahá'í World Centre is located in Haifa. This is due to the fact that Bahá'u'lláh was exiled to that part of the Turkish empire, as it then was, and died there in 1892. Any

* A typical example occurred in connection with the secret execution of 15 Bahá'ís in Ṭihrán in December 1981 and January 1982 mentioned above. On January 5, 1982 the Chief Justice of Iran called a press conference to deny reports of the executions. However, when the press countered with documentary evidence, he made a second statement on January 7, in which he admitted there had been executions but that the victims were spies for foreign countries. In his statement he said, "There was not any question of religious discrimination in this matter, and a Muslim would also have been executed on the same charge." A few days later the Ṭihrán press reported that one of the Bahá'ís arrested had been set free because he had renounced the Faith and converted to Islam. Thus the second statement of the Chief Justice as well as the first was shown to be false.

** The latter charges are similar to charges in the nineteenth century that the Bahá'ís were either agents of Russia or England.

objective observer would regard the charges of moral turpitude as totally absurd, in the light of the high standards of the Bahá'í community as compared with the standards of much of the non-Bahá'í world including those who are the persecutors of the Faith.

The real reason for the persecution is that the clergy recognize, first, that the Bahá'í Faith is a threat to their privileged position in society because it has teachings which are attractive to all peoples, and, second, that they are unable to rebut the logic of the teachings in fair open discussion. They think the answer is violence, forgetting that history shows that religions flourish when persecuted. They are torn between a desire not to let the rest of the world know what is going on because clearly it would reflect badly on them, and an equally strong wish to terrorise Iranians by letting them know what will happen to them if they should become Bahá'ís or even have sympathy for them. They seek to justify their bloody activities to fellow Muslims by asserting that any religion founded subsequent to Islam must be heretical because Muḥammad was the "Seal of the Prophets"* and to other Iranians by asserting that Bahá'ís are traitors and agents of the Shah.

The Iranian Bahá'ís have shown immense heroism in the face of their ruthless persecutions. Stories abound. One is of the second National Spiritual Assembly elected after the 1979 Revolution which identified itself to the government and demanded to know what had happened to the first National Spiritual Assembly which was arrested in August 1980. Another concerns the Bahá'ís of Hamadan who openly carried the bodies of the members of their Local Spiritual Assembly through the city and showed the citizens the marks of torture, and then gave a funeral oration describing the main teachings of the Faith. Another was of the eleven-year old girl from Yazd whose school essay

---

* Islamic leaders seem to be ambiguous as to what is meant by this title. On the one hand it is implied that Muḥammad is the last of God's Messengers. On the other hand there is still the expectation of the coming of the Qá'im or the Mihdi. The Bahá'í view is that the title means that Muḥammad was the last of the Messengers of God to prophecy the coming of the "new Jerusalem" and that the next Messengers (the Báb and Bahá'u'lláh) would lay the foundation of that new world.

was of her experiences in the summer holidays when her
father was arrested and executed. Yet another was of the
eight-year old girl from Shiraz who distributed sweets at
her school after the execution of her father. Above all is the
steadfast way the hundreds have refused to renounce their
Faith in order to save themselves from imprisonment and
death.

The Bahá'í world community, far from being crushed by
the persecution, has redoubled its efforts to build a new
world, inspired by the heroism of the Iranian Bahá'ís and
encouraged by the tremendous upsurge of sympathy and
interest of the rest of humanity. During the Seven Year Plan
(1979-86), the number of National Spiritual Assemblies
increased by 23, the number of local Spiritual Assemblies
by 9,230, and the number of tribes represented in the
community by 300.

As the community grew it became practical to become
more involved in general world affairs. In 1983 the
Universal House of Justice established a new office of social
and economic development to promote and coordinate the
activities of the community in this field. By the end of the
Plan there were nearly 800 development projects being
sponsored by the community, mostly in the fields of
education, health and agriculture. They included several for
the establishment of new radio stations for rural areas
which provide important local news services, weather
forecasts, advice on agricultural and health practices and
which foster local culture such as music, local language,
folk stories, etc. Another development of great significance
was the issue, in late 1985, in connection with the U.N.
International Year of Peace, of "The Promise of World
Peace", a statement of the Universal House of Justice,
setting forth the Bahá'í view on how world peace can be
achieved. The Promise of World Peace, which is addressed to
"The Peoples of the World" may be divided into a preamble
and four sections. The preamble states that peace is within
our grasp and is inevitable; the only question is whether it
follows "unimaginable horrors" or comes now from "an act
of consultative will". All nations say that they want peace

but they are paralysed by the prevailing view that humans are "incorrigibly selfish and aggressive", and therefore incapable of building a peaceful social system. This view is a distortion of the evidence concerning the human spirit. Furthermore, we should not be discouraged by present tumults which are but a sign of man coming of age, when peace will be achieved and civilization will flourish. The first of the four sections points out that man is distinguished by the human spirit which has both created civilization and has searched, under the guidance of religion, for the ultimate reality of existence. Religion has been such powerful influence in human affairs (in such areas as law and morality) that it cannot be ignored when we consider the issue of peace. This truth has been obscured by arguments issued in the name of religion which are contrary to the actual utterance of the Founders of the great religions, all of whom taught that "we should treat others as we ourselves would wish to be treated". Confused, men have turned to hedonistic substitute religions but these have failed to fulfil their promises of material prosperity for all and so affected the spirit of men that they have sunk into apathy and hopelessness. We should ponder whether such systems should be swept aside. The second section says that peace requires more than disarmament; we must remove the root causes of war, including racism, the inordinate disparity between rich and poor, unbridled nationalism, religious strife, the subjugation of women, the absence of universal education and the absence of proper means of communication, such as a universal auxiliary language. Peace requires a high level of commitment by nations and acceptance of certain fundamental principles as the basis of action. The third section states that the first fundamental principle is the oneness of mankind, which should be universally proclaimed and taught in all schools. In the Bahá'í view, this principle necessarily calls for a world government. Such a government would broaden rather than undermine "existing foundations of society" and would uphold "sane and intelligent patriotism". This vision of a new order, based on the world-wide law of Bahá'u'lláh "repudiates excessive centralisation on one hand, and disclaims all attempts at conformity on the other. Its watchword is unity in diversity . . .[1] To implement such a measure, there is a need for a world assembly which will consult on the peace and draw up a binding treaty which will clearly fix frontiers, establish principles underlying relations between governments, set strict limits on national armaments, and provide for collective security. The Universal House of Justice appeals to national leaders, the United Nations, and the peoples of the world to convoke such assembly. The final section states that a permanent peace is essential but the ultimate vision is of a unification of all peoples in one universal family. There are many signs of a beginning of such unification: an international civil service, countless international congresses, international projects for youth and children, and the ecumenical movement. The worldwide Bahá'í community, united in diversity and steadfast in the face of persecution, is a proof of what can be achieved. Bahá'ís join with all peace-seekers in this great enterprise and are confident that "These fruitless strifes, these ruinous wars shall pass away and the Most Great Peace shall come."

By September 1986, "The Promise of World Peace" had been presented to the leaders of the 154 independent nations and 32 dependent territories; the complete text of the statement had been translated into 62 languages. By April 1987, in the United Kingdom alone, some 75,000 copies had been distributed to prominent citizens, leaders of thought, civic dignitaries and the general public. In a related field, many outside bodies gave the U.S. Bahá'í Community credit for its work in helping persuade the U.S. Senate to finally ratify the U.N. Genocide Convention in February 1986 after decades of hesitation. At the time of writing, a new Six Year Plan (1986-92) is in process. The last year of the Plan will be the hundreth anniversary of the passing of Bahá'u'lláh and only eight years away from the end of the twentieth century. It develops several of the new

[1] Gudiance for Today and Tomorrow, p. 173 (UK)

themes of the Seven Year Plan, including social and economic development and "greater involvement of the Faith in the life of human society". A distinguishing aspect of the new plan has been a much greater involvement than hitherto of local communities in the setting of their own goals within the total framework, a sign of the growing maturity of the Bahá'í world.

In the relatively short time since the momentous announcement in 1844 by the Báb in S̲h̲íráz, the Bahá'í Faith has spread to all parts of the earth and has won adherents amongst all races and classes of men.

It has undergone the most fierce trials both from within and without, and has emerged all the stronger and brighter from them, like tempered steel. At the present time more men and women the world over, from all backgrounds but especially from the poor, the oppressed and the young, are joining this world family at a faster rate perhaps than at any time since the very earliest days of its history. And these new Bahá'ís are not just the nominal converts so familiar in the old order of life, but men and women full of fire, joy and vigour because they have found that which they have hoped for all their lives. These friends know they are swimming with the tide of history. They have no delusions about the perilous state of the world, in fact they are prepared to face this reality more directly than most. But they are not afraid, for they know the just society can and shall be built . . . and they have the privilege of helping in this most glorious task.

CHAPTER IX

ON BEING A BAHÁ'Í

AS RELIGION is a matter which concerns our deepest feelings there is perhaps still something missing in a description of the Bahá'í Faith confined to an account of its teachings and its history. There is a need also to have some statement of what it means to be a Bahá'í. What is special about the experience?

Bahá'ís are from a multitude of backgrounds and clearly their feelings about being Bahá'ís will differ though there will be a great deal in common too. The best that the writer can do is to recount his own experience. This may be of some value to the reader because like so many others in present-day society the writer, before becoming a Bahá'í, held an agnostic or humanist view of life and believed that society could be only improved through radical political reform.

First, being a Bahá'í has meant starting to think afresh about all the most important questions in life. It is fundamental to Bahá'í life to learn to think independently and to question all ideas most rigorously to see if they ring true. It is particularly important to recognize how much we are shaped, willy-nilly, by the currently-accepted notions of the society in which we live, and be able to step back and try to see them in a detached and objective fashion. It is salutary, for instance, to reflect upon how radically accepted ideas have changed in only the last one hundred years and then to think of what changes might take place in, say, the next one hundred years. On another plane, it is interesting to think about how differently things seem to rational and educated men in such places as Peking, Algiers and Washington.

Secondly, the writer has found that being a Bahá'í has brought serenity to the mind and hope for the future. The exercise in rethinking the fundamental questions which we face, demonstrated for the writer that the classical arguments proving the "non-existence" of God were unsatisfactory because the terms of reference were too narrow. It has seemed to him that their general acceptance has had less to do with their intellectual soundness than with an emotional reaction against religion because it had become associated with hypocrisy and superstition, and seemed totally irrelevant to the needs of our time. Deeper reflection inspired by Bahá'í Writings convinced the writer that in reality both science and religion are in harmony in giving overwhelming evidence of an "Unknowable Essence" Who through His Educators has demonstrated through all recorded time His great love for all mankind.

The modern mind, split between that deep sense in all of us of something beyond our comprehension governing the universe, and the suppressing influence of a narrow secularism, begins to heal. The wound of confusion mends still more as the significance of the theme of Progressive Revelation is understood. All thinking men of religion must have faced the question of how it is possible, say, as a Christian, to reject Buddha and Muḥammad — as one is bound to do according to the churches — when, in all honesty, it has to be recognized that Their teachings have many similarities to those of Jesus and are obviously just. Bahá'u'lláh's theme of the spiritual evolution of man under the guidance of successive Educators, each bringing teachings adapted to the needs and capacities of the society of His day, for the first time makes sense of history and resolves this most fundamental question.

The theme is even more profound than this, for it shows that there is hope for the future of man: he is not condemned to useless self-obliteration. It shows that the logical next step in the spiritual evolution of man is the establishment of a just and peaceful society on a world scale — the dream of all men down the ages. An objective analysis of the condition of man today goes beyond the surface confusion and decline of existing institutions to the fact that not only is such a world society now technically feasible for the first time in history, but that it offers the only lasting solution to those major issues of our time which were mentioned in the first chapter. What the Bahá'í Faith brings: a deep sense of the brotherhood of all mankind, a sense of service as the real source of happiness, a government of unity and universal participation which can give form and direction to these feelings, will mean an end to the threat of war, an end to the unjust and greedy misuse of the world's resources and an end to the sense of despair which afflicts the minds of millions of men and women today to a greater or lesser degree.

As these concepts permeated the consciousness of the writer, his perspectives seemed to widen and deepen. There was no longer that horrifying feeling of alienation and loneliness in a hostile and meaningless universe. On the contrary, we see that no matter how humble we may be in the eyes of conventional society we all belong to, and have an essential part in, the scheme of things. Anxiety about the unknown, that tremendous waste of energy, is replaced by a free-flowing and joyous development of our human potential.

This leads on to the third aspect of what it is to be a Bahá'í, and that is that life acquires real purpose. The promised new world civilization is not some highly finished Utopia to be handed down from heaven at some distant time in the future. If it is to be achieved, it must be built by man himself following the blueprint given in the Bahá'í Writings. The sooner the foundations are firmly laid down, the sooner that Great Peace will come. This means total commitment by every single Bahá'í. There is no passing the buck to politician or priest. We have to do the work. To be a Bahá'í today is to have the greatest and most glorious challenge of all time.

The sense of joy which this challenge gives must be similar to that felt by the early Christians as they demonstrated by their lives how much greater was man's potential. This might be what the American philosopher Josiah Royce (1855-1916) meant when he wrote in *Philosophy of Loyalty* that man reaches maturity when he finds a cause to which he can devote himself and in which he can lose himself.

With such a challenge, personal morality acquires meaning and it becomes clear that to strive to reach to the highest standards of the Bahá'í code is highly rational and a practical guide for making the most of life. Bahá'í morality is not an imposition or burden, and neither has it anything to do with the accepted idea of sin or with extreme guilt complexes about worldly enjoyments. It is to follow the golden rule of all the great religions: moderation, detachment, and concern for the welfare of others. It is the basis for self-respect, real freedom and spiritual growth and happiness. It is also an essential element in the building of a new society. A Bahá'í knows that it would be unrealistic, not to say hypocritical to talk of creating a new civilization if in his personal life he were to be dishonest, untrustworthy, lazy and careless of the body and mind of himself, his family and others. The highest standards of morality will undoubtedly be the hallmark of the New Race of Men:

> *"These things shall be: a loftier race*
> *Than e'er the world hath known shall rise*
> *With flame of freedom in their souls,*
> *And light of knowledge in their eyes.*
> *They shall be gentle, brave and strong*
> *To spill no drop of blood, but dare*
> *All that may plant man's lordship firm*
> *on earth, and fire, and sea, and air. . . ."**
>
> J. A. Symonds (1940-1893).

It is this part of the Bahá'í way of life which first attracts many of the young, disillusioned with both the mindless authoritarianism of the old morality and the cruel swindle of present day "liberal" permissiveness.

The great challenge of the Bahá'í Faith also means everyday, personal commitment to the practice of a completely new form of government. Only a purified system of administration can hope to provide the channel for the achievement of the goals of a just society. This is a truly exciting experience. Gradually a new Bahá'í learns the art of universal participation, of thinking and speaking about the welfare of all, of forgetting the ego, of listening to, and encouraging the development of, the thoughts of all in the

---

* From a *'Vista'* by J. A. Symonds (1840-1893). This was later adopted as a hymn by the League of Nations.

community, the art of consultation, orderly decision making, of spiritual unity once a decision is made, of truly democratic and objective methods of election. With relief he finds that here there is no trace of those dreary characteristics of conventional politics: the in-fighting for personal and sectional interests, childish parliamentary games, meaningless debates, corruption and violence, authoritarianism, the sheer narrowness of purpose and consequential incompetence. The beauty of it all is that it works. As a Bahá'í lives in a community and he sees the day-by-day growth in maturity in understanding of Bahá'í concepts, he has that exhilarating feeling that he is taking part in the creation of the strongest of foundations for a new system of world government.

And as the Bahá'í travels, he begins to see that the Administrative Order is in essence very simple and adaptable to all conditions, ranging from the most primitive to the most sophisticated and that it grows in strength in step with the spiritual development of the individuals who make up a community. Unlike many contemporary movements the Bahá'í Faith is not a Western system to be imposed on the rest of the world regardless of local culture, neither is it some mysterious Oriental idea — any more than Christianity. It is universal in application and appeal. It is radical because it goes to the very root of the needs of men and society and because it works — it actually can and does give people a unifying means of putting into practice their ideals.

Another aspect of building a new Bahá'í society is that you are a member of a huge world family. Wherever you travel, whatever your background, you know that you will receive a warm welcome by the local Bahá'í community and that you will be loved for your own sake. In this family you can be your own true self. The old barriers of race, culture, class, education and generation which have always divided men in fear and hatred are gone. A Bahá'í does not have to play a part or wear a mask. Natural feelings of love and concern for others can be expressed without fear of rebuff or accusation of pretentiousness. For instance, an illiterate tribesman can and does talk freely and intimately with a college professor with no feeling of artificiality or difference on either side. They are both members of the same family which is united in purpose and knows where it is going. Differences of background are a source of joy and enrichment, not discord. To a Bahá'í, the greater the diversity of culture in his community, the greater its education and growth.* This feeling, it should be stressed, should certainly not be confused in any way with that still strong Western "liberal" trait of patronizing "quaint natives" and their "colourful" customs and art.

There is no competition of personalities in this family. All strive for the same end and if one achieves great things it is an inspiration and a point of pride for all. Neither is the family flawed with self-righteousness. When, as can happen, Bahá'ís fall and do not reach the highest standards of personal conduct there is no question of guilt or recriminations. Friendly helping hands are offered and the community presses on together, looking not to the past, but always the future.

As a Bahá'í comes to know the world community to which he belongs, he begins to appreciate its rock-like strength and constancy. He realizes that the Faith is not one of those movements which bursts into the news one day and has disappeared by the next day. No less than twenty thousand have given their lives rather than deny this Faith, and around the world today thousands more are making the greatest sacrifices to forward its success. This family is united and inspired in the pursuit of the greatest of goals. To anyone who believes in the brotherhood of man this practical, living, everyday demonstration of brotherly unity surely means more than ten thousand political manifestoes. All a Bahá'í can say to those whose last argument against the Faith is that such idealism could never work in practice is: "Come and see for yourself!"

This family is not, however, an inward looking community caring little for the thoughts and ideas of others. On the contrary, to be a Bahá'í is consciously to adopt an open and

* See Appendices II-III for some information on the diversity of the Bahá'í community.

239

friendly stance toward people of all persuasions. Though most independent in speaking about the cruelty and superficiality of present-day society and institutions, a Bahá'í will, when consorting with others, also lay emphasis on what they hold in common, and what is good and praiseworthy in the others' practices and beliefs. When a Bahá'í talks with Christians, Muslims, Buddhists, or Jews, he will not dwell on the man-made differences between their religions, but rather on the deep respect and love which he has for the Founders of each religion and Their teachings. A Bahá'í in discussion with members of various Christian denominations might, for instance, draw attention to universal thinking of the Catholic Church, the broad-mindedness of the Unitarians, the social conscience of the Quakers, or the strong faith of the Baptists. Members of such social movements as those for the equality of women, civil rights and liberties, the United Nations, a world language and a balanced ecology soon find, when talking to Bahá'ís, that their broad objectives are also the objectives of the Bahá'í Faith. Though from a Bahá'í point of view, the whole process of politics is archaic and essentially negative in the long run, a Bahá'í recognizes that there are many facets of the various political philosophies which do have within them the seeds of potential good. For instance, a Bahá'í has the greatest sympathy with the radical and the socialist in their desire to eliminate social, political and economic injustice, with the liberal who defends freedom of thought and expression, and with the conservative with his strong conviction of the importance of social continuity and stability.

By emphasizing the nobler aspects of other religious, social and political organizations to their adherents, it is hoped to encourage them to make their organizations more enlightened and also to come to see that the Faith is the logical development of their viewpoint and promises the fulfilment of all that they hope for. Those who are engaged in planning for social projects are recognizing more and more that change in one area often has important repercussions in many other areas, and that the most efficient and effective way to make improvements is to think in terms of the whole: in short, to plan comprehensively. Bahá'ís are conscious that though there is clearly much that is progressive and fruitful in many organizations and movements, they all have objectives which by the measure of world standards are narrow in concept. These objectives can be ultimately achieved only if they are put in a broader perspective, if they are brought together in one unified and fully comprehensive plan for the whole world. It is believed that this is done by the Bahá'í Faith.

APPENDIX I

STATISTICS ON THE BAHÁ'Í WORLD COMMUNITY*

A. Growth Over Fifty Years

Number of:	1933[1]	1944[1]	1953	1963	1973	1986
National Spiritual Assemblies	9	8	12	56	113	148
Local Spiritual Assemblies	300	500	611	3,551	17,037	32,854
Localities where Bahá'ís reside [2]	800	1,900	2,425	11,071	69,541	116,707
Independent nations open to Faith					141	166
	46	77	128	250		
Significant territories and islands open to Faith					194	48[3]

[1] Approximate figures only.
[2] Includes communities with Local Spiritual Assemblies.
[3] The figure is lower in 1986 because the term has been revised to approximate current geographical and political divisions. Previously the term covered divisions based on cultural, geographic and demographic factors.

* The Bahá'í Community puts emphasis in its statistics on functioning communities and on diversity and dispersal as indicated in the following tables rather than on numbers of adherents. Perhaps the most comprehensive attempt by non-Bahá'í sources to estimate the number of adherents to the Bahá'í Faith is that given in "The World Christian Encyclopaedia", Oxford University Press, 1982. This publication lists estimates of numbers of Bahá'ís in each of some 200 nations and significant territories and islands, with a worldwide total of 3.8 million (page 6). It must be stressed that this is certainly not an official Bahá'í figure, and it is clear that many of the figures for individual countries are not accurate; nevertheless it is perhaps interesting to the reader as a very rough indicator of the size of the Bahá'í community. Confirmation that the figure was roughly correct in aggregate was given in a 1986 slide show on the Seven Year Plan issued from Haifa which mentioned that the number of Bahá'ís in the world had increased from 3.5 million to 4.5 million between 1979 and 1986.

GROWTH OVER 50 YEARS

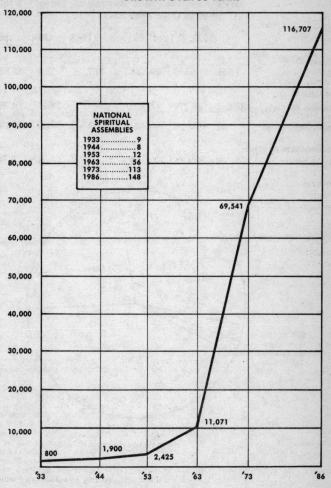

NATIONAL
SPIRITUAL
ASSEMBLIES
1933.............9
1944.............8
1953............12
1963............56
1973...........113
1986...........148

116,707

69,541

11,071

800

1,900

2,425

'33 '44 '53 '63 '73 '86

APPENDIX I—Continued

B. Bahá'í Community in 1986 by Continent

	Africa	Americas	Asia	Australasia	Europe	Total
National Spiritual Assemblies	43	41	26	17	21	148
Local Spiritual Assemblies	7,258	6,500	17,524	857	715	32,854
Localities where Bahá'ís reside[1]	35,657	26,570	48,730	2,902	2,848	116,707*
Independent nations	51	35	36	11	33	166
Significant territories and islands	6	16	3	13	4	48

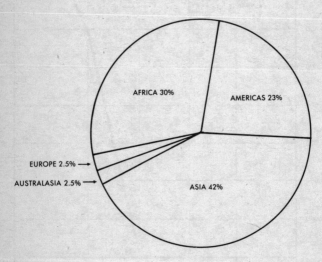

AFRICA 30%

AMERICAS 23%

EUROPE 2.5% →

AUSTRALASIA 2.5% →

ASIA 42%

*DISTRIBUTION

[1] Approximate figures only.

244

APPENDIX II

MINORITY GROUPS AND TRIBES REPRESENTED IN THE BAHÁ'Í COMMUNITY
(1,975 in 1982)

AFRICA

Tribe or Minority	*Country or Area of Origin*
1. Abo ("Aba")	Cameroons
2. "Abua" (Bua?)	Nigeria
3. "Achaorua"	North Africa
4. "Achrarda" ("Cherarda")	North Africa
5. Acholi (Gan, Shuli)	Sudan; Tanzania; Uganda
6. Adangme (Adangbe, Dangwe)	Ghana
7. ADANGME: Ada	Ghana
8. ADANGME: Krobo	Ghana
9. ADANGME: Shai	Benin; Ghana
10. Adare ("*Adere*")	Ethiopia
11. Adja (Sawoeh, Sahoué)	Benin; Togo
12. "Afari"	Ghana
13. Afewa	Nigeria
14. Afrikaaners	South Africa
15. "Agame"	Ethiopia
16. "Agbor"	Nigeria
17. "Agila"	Nigeria
18. "Ahafo (Khafo)"	Ghana
19. Ahanta(n)	Ghana; Ivory Coast
20. "Ahizi"	Ivory Coast
21. Ait Ba Amrane	North Africa
22. Ait Baha	North Africa
23. Ait Moussa-ou-Ali	North Africa
24. Ait Om El Bakht (Ait Oum-El Bekhta)	North Africa
25. Ait Ou Azzouz	North Africa
26. Ait Ouirra	North Africa
27. Ait Saoun	North Africa
28. Ait Sokhmane (Sakhman)	North Africa
29. Aizo (Whydah)	Benin
30. Ajukru (Adjoukrou)	Ivory Coast
31. "Akhmalcha"	North Africa
32. "Akpafu"	Ghana
33. Akposo ("Akposso")	Togo
34. "Aku"	Cameroons: Gambia; Guinea Bissau
35. "Alhoceima"	North Africa
36. Ali	Central African Republic
37. Alur	Uganda
38. Ambo (Kambonsenga)	Zambia
39. Ambo (Ovambo)	South West Africa/Namibia
40. AMBO (OVAMBO): u-Kualuthi	South West Africa/Namibia
41. AMBO (OVAMBO): u-Kuambi	South West Africa/Namibia

42.	AMBO (OVAMBO): u-Kuanyama	South West Africa/Namibia
43.	AMBO (OVAMBO): o-Mbalantu	South West Africa/Namibia
44.	AMBO (OVAMBO): omu-Mbandja	South West Africa/Namibia
45.	AMBO (OVAMBO): Ndonga (Ondonga)	South West Africa/Namibia
46.	AMBO (OVAMBO): "Onkolonkathi"	South West Africa/Namibia
47.	Anhara	Ethiopia
48.	"Anécho"	Benin; Togo
49.	Angas	Nigeria
50.	Antaisaka	Madagascar
51.	Antambahoaka	Madagascar
52.	Antankarana	Madagascar
53.	Antanosy	Madagascar
54.	Anteifasy	Madagascar
55.	Anteimoro	Madagascar
56.	Anuak	Ethiopia
57.	Anum	Ghana
58.	"Aowin"	Ghana
59.	"Arab-ou-Sais (Sayess)"	North Africa
60.	ARABS: Shuwa	Nigeria
61.	Arago ("Alango"; "*Alago*")	Nigeria
62.	"Arhamna"	North Africa
63.	Aro ("*Arochukwa*", "*Arochoku*")	Nigeria
64.	"Arusha (Marusha)"	Tanganyika
65.	Arussi	Ethiopia
66.	Atakpamé (Ana)	Togo
67.	Aten (Ngell)	Nigeria
68.	"Atingong"	Cameroons
69.	Aushi (Ushi; Waushi)	Zambia
70.	Avatime	Ghana
71.	"Awanchi" ("Awnchi", "Kendem")	Cameroons
72.	"Awutu" ("Afutu"; "Efutu")	Ghana
73.	Azande (*Zande*, Nyam-Nyam)	Central African Rep.; Sudan
74.	"Babaji"	Cameroons
75.	"Babbe" (Bade?)	Nigeria
76.	"Babonte"	Cameroons
77.	"Babilis" (ba-Bira? Bebele?)	Cameroons
78.	"Baburawa" (Pabir?)	Nigeria
79.	Babwa ("*Babua*")	Congo
80.	Bachama ("*Bahama*")	Nigeria
81.	"Badjong"	Cameroons
82.	"Bafek"	Cameroons
83.	"Bagindo"	Congo
84.	Bagirmi ("*Baguirmiens*")	Chad
85.	"Baguiri" ("Baguiro")	Central African Republic
86.	Bajun (Bagiuni)	Somalia
87.	Baka (Abaca)	Sudan
88.	"Bakanigui" (ba-Kanike? Koniagui?)	Gabon
89.	"Bakkoya"	North Africa
90.	"Bakwere" ("Bakweri")	Cameroons; Nigeria
91.	Balante	Guinea Bissau
92.	"Balee"	Nigeria
93.	Bali (Chamba)	Cameroons

94.	"Balinyoga"	Nigeria
95.	Balom	Cameroons
96.	"Balong" (Balung?)	Cameroons
97.	Bamba (*Obamba*)	Gabon
98.	"Bambalang"	Cameroons
99.	Bambara (Banmana)	Upper West Africa
100.	"Bameng" ("Bawang"?)	Cameroons
101.	"Bamessing"	Cameroons
102.	Bamiléké (Bamiliki)	Cameroons; Chad
103.	"Bamoun"	Cameroons
104.	"Bamounkembu"	Cameroons
105.	"Bananda"	Nigeria
106.	Banda	Central African Rep.; Ghana
107.	BANDA: "Djotto"	Central African Republic
108.	BANDA: "Gbi"	Central African Republic
109.	BANDA: "Gbuendi"	Central African Republic
110.	BANDA: Langba	Central African Republic
111.	BANDA: Langwasi ("Langbassi")	Central African Republic
112.	BANDA: "Linda"	Central African Republic
113.	BANDA: "Mbres"	Central African Republic
114.	BANDA: "Morouba"	Central African Republic
115.	BANDA: "Ndocpo" (Dakpa?)	Central African Republic
116.	BANDA: "N'Goubou-Banda" (Gobu? Ngbougou?)	Central African Republic
117.	BANDA: "Pagoua" ("Kpagoua"; Pangwa?)	Central African Republic
118.	BANDA: "Togbo"	Central African Republic
119.	BANDA: "Yacpa" (Yakpa)	Central African Republic
120.	BANDA: "Vora" ("Vara-Banda")	Central African Republic
121.	Banen (Banyin, Ndiki, Penin)	Cameroons
122.	Bangandu ("Bagandou")	Central African Republic
123.	ba-Bangi	Cameroons
124.	Bangwa	Cameroons
125.	"Bangwinji"	Nigeria
126.	Bani Akil	Sudan
127.	"Banyo" ("Banya"; ba-Nya?)	Cameroons
128.	Banyun (*Bainouk,* Bainungko)	Gambia; Sénégal; Sierra Leone
129.	Banziri	Central African Republic
130.	"Baoumbou"	Gabon
131.	Bara (Ibara)	Madagascar
132.	"Bara" (Dari?)	Chad
133.	"Baraka"	Chad
134.	"Bareka (Baroka)" (ba-Rega?)	Cameroons; Congo
135.	Bargu (*Bariba*)	Benin; Togo
136.	Bari	Sudan
137.	"Bartorchu"	Cameroons
138.	"Baseki" (Seke?)	Cameroons
139.	Bashi	Congo
140.	"Basila"	Zaire
141.	Bassa (*Basa*)	Cameroons; Central African Republic
142.	Bassa	Nigeria
143.	Bassa-Komu (-Kwomu)	Nigeria

144.	"Bassar" (Basari?)	Togo
145.	"Bassari"	Ghana; Nigeria
146.	Bata	Nigeria
147.	"Batchimba" (Simba?)	Congo
148.	"Batomo"	Cameroons
149.	"Batschenga" (ba-Changi?)	Cameroons
150.	"Batut" (Batu?)	Nigeria
151.	Baule (*Bowiri* (*Bowli*))	Ghana
152.	Baya (Gbaya)	Cameroons; Central African Republic
153.	BAYA: "Bokaré"	Central African Republic
154.	BAYA: "Kara"	Central African Republic
155.	BAYA: "Ngbaka-Mandja" (Ngbaka-Manza)	Central African Republic
156.	"Baya-Kaka"	Central African Republic
157.	"Bazela"	Zaire
158.	"Bazi"	Cameroons
159.	i-Bea (Bujeba, Mabea)	Cameroons; Equatorial Guinea
160.	"Beama" (Amap?)	Cameroons
161.	Beba	Cameroons
162.	"Beisja" ("Beissa")	Chad
163.	BEJA: Haddendowa ("Hedendowi")	Sudan
164.	ba-Bemba (wa-Wemba)	Malawi; Tanzania; South Africa; Zaire; Zambia
165.	BEMBA: ba-Lomotwa	Zaire
166.	wa-Bembe (Vabembe, Balembe)	Tanzania, Zaire
167.	wa-Bena	Tanganyika
168.	"Bende"	Cameroons
169.	"Beni Ahmed" ("Beni Hamad"?)	North Africa
170.	"Beni ("Oulad") Aros" (Aulad Hronss?)	North Africa
171.	"Beni Boufrah (Boug(h)afar, Bou Yafer)	North Africa
172.	"Beni Chigg(u)ar (Chikar, Shigguer)"	North Africa
173.	"Beni El Mansour"	North Africa
174.	"Beni Gorfet"	North Africa
175.	"Beni Hassan(e)"	North Africa
176.	"Beni Ittaft (Itteft, Yattaft)"	North Africa
177.	"Beni Maadane"	North Africa
178.	"Beni Mesguilda"	North Africa
179.	"Beni Msaouar (Mezouar)"	North Africa
180.	"Beni Ouakil (Oukil)"	North Africa
181.	"Beni Oualid"	North Africa
182.	"Beni Ouariaghel (Wariaghel)"	North Africa
183.	"Beni Ouelchak (Ouichek, Washik)"	North Africa
184.	"Beni Sidal (Sidel, Sedjel)"	North Africa
185.	"Beni Touzen (Touzine)"	North Africa
186.	"Beni Yazgha (Yazrha)"	North Africa
187.	"Beni Ziat"	North Africa
188.	"Benyada"	Cameroons
189.	BERABER: Ndhir (*Beni Mtir*)	North Africa
190.	BERABER: Zemur ("Beni Zammour")	North Africa
191.	Berber	Morocco; Tunisia
192.	Beriberi	Benin; Niger
193.	"Beti" (Beté? Betié?)	Cameroons; Chad
194.	"Betieku"	Cameroons

195.	Betsileo	Madagascar
196.	Betsimisaraka	Madagascar
197.	"Bette-Bendi"	Nigeria
198.	Bhaca (Baka, Baca)	Transkei
199.	"Biase"	Nigeria
200.	"Bidjir" ("Bidjr")	Chad
201.	"Bigunde" (Gundi?)	Cameroons
202.	"Bikélé"	Cameroons
203.	Birom ("Berom")	Nigeria
204.	"Birrizi"	Nigeria
205.	"ba-Birwa"	Botswana
206.	ba-Bisa (a-Wisa, Muiza; "Biza")	Tanzania; Zambia
207.	"Biwandi"	Cameroons
208.	Bobo	Upper Volta
209.	BOBO: Bua (Bobofing)	Upper Volta
210.	BOBO: "Bwabo"	Upper Volta
211.	Bofi ("Boffi")	Central African Republic
212.	Bogoto ("Baya-Bogoto")	Central African Republic
213.	"Bohara" ("Bohora")	Tanzania
214.	"Boje" (Baji? Buji?)	Nigeria
215.	Boki (Nki)	Cameroons; Nigeria
216.	"Boko"	Benin
217.	"Bolemba"	Central African Republic
218.	"Bolga"	Nigeria
219.	Boloki (ba-Ngala, ba-Mangala)	Zaire
220.	"Bom"	Chad
221.	wa-Bondei (wa-Shensi)	Tanganyika
222.	Bondjo (bandjo, Mbondjo)	Cameroons
223.	"Bournou(ans)"	Chad
224.	Brong (Abron)	Ghana; Nigeria
225.	"Brosa"	Ghana
226.	Bubi ("Bobi")	Eq. Guinea; Nigeria
227.	"Buderi"	Sudan
228.	Buem	Ghana
229.	Bujawa (Buji)	Nigeria
230.	Bura	Nigeria
231.	Buraka ("Bouraka")	Central African Republic
232.	Burun	Nigeria
233.	Busansi	Upper Volta
234.	BUSHMEN (ba-SARWA): //Gana (Kana)	Botswana
235.	BUSHMEN (ba-SARWA): /Gwi (!Kwi)	Botswana
236.	BUSHMEN (ba-SARWA): ‡Hoa	Botswana
237.	BUSHMEN (ba-SARWA): Naron	Botswana
238.	BUSHMEN (ba-SARWA): Shua	Botswana
239.	BUSHMEN (ba-SARWA): Tsase	Botswana
240.	BUSHMEN (ba-SARWA): !xo	Botswana
241.	"Butou" (Butu?)	Chad
242.	Buye ("Babuyu")	Congo
243.	Bwaka (Mbaka)	Central African Republic
244.	wa-Bwari ("Babwari")	Burundi
245.	"Byamo"	Cameroons
246.	"Cape Malay"	Southern Africa

247.	Chag(g)a	Tanzania
248.	Chakossi (Tchakossi)	Ghana; Togo
249.	"Challa" (Bokkos, Daffo-Batura, Shagawa)	Nigeria
250.	Chamba	Nigeria
251.	ama-Chara	Nigeria
252.	"Cherepong (Kyerepong, Ocere)"	Ghana
253.	a-Chewa (Cewa, "Shewa")	Malawi; Swaziland; Tanzania
254.	Chiga (*Kiga*)	Uganda
255.	a-Chikunda	Zambia
256.	Chisenga (Chishinga)	Zambia
257.	Chokwe (Atsokwe, Chokune, "Tshokwe")	Zaire; Zambia
258.	ba-Chopi	Swaziland; Mozambique
259.	ba-CHOPI: "Inhambane"	Swaziland
260.	"Chounber"	Cameroons
261.	"Coloured" ("Cape Colored")	Southern Africa
262.	Comorian (Ngazija)	Comoro Islands; Tanzania
263.	Creole (Criole)	West Africa
264.	Dafi[ng]	Upper Volta
265.	Dagaba	Ghana
266.	Dagari (*Dagarti*)	Ghana
267.	Dagomba	Ghana; Nigeria
268.	Dagu ("*Dajo*")	Chad
269.	Daka (Madaka)	Nigeria
270.	Dakakari ("Lela")	Nigeria
271.	Dakpa	Central African Republic
272.	Damara	South West Africa/Namibia
273.	Dan (*Gio*)	Liberia
274.	"Daoui Mani'a"	North Africa
275.	Daya ("Daye")	Chad
276.	Delim ("Oulad D'lim")	North Africa
277.	Dendi (Dandi)	Benin; Central African Republic; Niger
278.	Dialonke (*Yalunka*)	Sierra Leone
279.	"Dikome" ("Dikume")	Cameroons
280.	Dinka ("Denka", Denkawi, Jang)	Sudan; Tunisia
281.	Diola (Jola)	Gambia; Sénégal; Upper Volta
282.	DIOLA (JOLA): "Bassene"	Sénégal
283.	DIOLA (JOLA): Casa (Cassa; Kasa)	Gambia
284.	DIOLA (JOLA): "Gouna"	Sénégal
285.	DIOLA (JOLA): Karone ("Karoni")	Gambia
286.	DIOLA (JOLA): "Sabadje"	Sénégal
287.	DIOLA (JOLA): "Tabacounda Diediely"	Sénégal
288.	"Dipenda Balue" (ba-Lue?)	Cameroons
289.	"Djali" ("Jali")	Chad; Sudan
290.	wa-Doe	Tanzania
291.	Dogon (*Kado*)	Chad
292.	"Dongolawi"	Sudan
293.	DRAWA: Mesgita ("*Mezquiten*")	North Africa
294.	"Dschang" (Fondang? Dinka? Chang?)	Cameroons
295.	Duala (Douala)	Cameroons
296.	Duga ("Douga")	Chad
297.	Dukkala	North Africa
298.	Dukkawa (Dukawa)	Nigeria
299.	Duru	Cameroons

300.	a-Duma (Aduma; Adouma)	Gabon
301.	Dyerma (Djerma, Germa, Zarma)	Benin; Niger; Nigeria
302.	"Eassankom"	Cameroons
303.	"Ebira" (Ebrie? ba-Bira?)	Nigeria
304.	Edo (Bini)	Nigeria
305.	EDO, NORTHERN: Etsako	Nigeria
306.	EDO: Ishan (Esan)	Nigeria
307.	EDO: Isoko, Central	Nigeria
308.	EDO: "Oghara"	Nigeria
309.	EDO: Urhobo:	Cameroons; Eq. Guinea; Nigeria
310.	"Eggon" ("Egoni", "Egun")	Nigeria
311.	EKOI: Assumbo-Ambele	Cameroons
312.	EKOI: Ejagham (Ekwe; Ekoi)	Cameroons; Nigeria
313.	EKOI: Etung	Nigeria
314.	EKOI: Keaka ("Keayka")	Cameroons
315.	EKOI: Manta ("Takamanda")	Cameroons
316.	EKOI: Nkumm (Nkem)	Nigeria
317.	EKOI: Obang	Cameroons
318.	Ekpeye (Ekpe)	Nigeria
319.	"El Ajmas"	North Africa
320.	"El 'Aounat"	North Africa
321.	"El Fahs" (GHARBYA: Fahsya?)	North Africa
322.	"El Hajeb"	North Africa
323.	"Elandi" ("Elende")	Cameroons
324.	"Eleme"	Nigeria
325.	Embu	Central & East Africa
326.	"Engenni (Egene)"	Nigeria
327.	"Eugono"	Cameroons
328.	Ewé	Benin; Ghana; Togo
329.	EWE: "Anlo"	Ghana
330.	"Fabanka"	West Africa
331.	Fang (Mpangwe, Pahuin)	Cameroons. Eq. Guinea; Gabon
332.	FANG: Bene ("Bane")	Cameroons
333.	FANG: Bulu (Boulou)	Cameroons; Chad
334.	FANG: Eton (Toni)	Cameroons; Chad
335.	FANG: Yaunde (Ewondo)	Cameroons; Central African Republic; Nigeria
336.	"Farkhanah"	North Africa
337.	"Fetwaka" ("Ftcuaka") (Fezwata?)	North Africa
338.	ba-Fia (Bafia, etc.)	Cameroons
339.	"Fichtala"	North Africa
340.	Filala (*Tafilalet*)	North Africa
341.	Fingo (ama-Mfengue)	North Africa
342.	FIOME: Burunge (*Burungi*, Mbulunge)	Tanzania
343.	FIOME: Iraqw (wa-Mbulu)	Tanzania
344.	FIOME: Wasi (Alawa)	Tanzania
345.	wa-Fipa	Tanzania
346.	ba-Fo (Bafaw, Bafon)	Cameroons
347.	Fon	Benin; Togo
348.	"Forleke"	Cameroons
349.	Fulbe (Fula, Fulani, Peulh)	West Africa
350.	FULBE: Laube (Lorobeh)	Gambia

351.	wa-Fulero	Congo
352.	ba-Fut(i)	Cameroons
353.	Gä	Ghana
354.	Gaberi (Ngabre, "*Gabri*")	Chad
355.	Ganda	Tanzania
356.	ba-Ganda (Waganda)	Uganda
357.	Gane (*Banana*)	Cameroons; Chad
358.	"Gara"	Nigeria
359.	"Gardea"	Cameroons
360.	"Gawza" (Gwaza? Guzawa?)	Nigeria
361.	Gbande (Bandi)	Liberia
362.	"Gbanou" (Banu?)	Central African Republic
363.	Gbari (*Gwari*)	Nigeria
364.	"a-Gbo (Agbo)"	Nigeria
365.	"Ghagyi"	Nigeria
366.	Gharbya (Garbia, "Algharbea")	North Africa
367.	GHARBYA: Beni Malik (Malek)	North Africa
368.	GHARBYA: K̲h̲lot(t)	North Africa
369.	Ghaznaya	North Africa
370.	Ghomara (*Rhomara*)	North Africa
371.	"Giseka" (Seke?)	Cameroons
372.	mun-Gisu (Gishu, Masaba)	Tanzania; Uganda
373.	Glavuda (Glavda)	Nigeria
374.	Godye ("*Godie*")	West Africa (Ivory Coast)
375.	wa-Gogo	Tanzania
376.	Gola	Liberia
377.	wa-Goma ("Gome")	Tanzania
378.	Gonja (Ngbanya)	Ghana
379.	"Gorgani"	Somalia
380.	Gourma (Grumeh, "Gourmantche")	Benin; Ghana; Togo; Upper Volta
381.	Gowa	Zambia
382.	Grusi ("Gourounssi"; Grunshi)	Ghana; Upper Volta
383.	GRUSI: Awuna (Aculo, "Anloa")	Ghana; Togo
384.	GRUSI: Builsa (Kanjaga)	Ghana
385.	GRUSI: Isala (Sissala)	Ghana
386.	GRUSI: Kasena (Sena, Kasem, Kassim)	Ghana; Upper Volta
387.	GRUSI: Nunuma ("Nouna")	Upper Volta
388.	GRUSI: "Nébola/Lélé"	Upper Volta
389.	GRUSI: Vagala ("Vagla")	Ghana
390.	Guan (Guang?)	Ghana
391.	Gudo (Gude, Mude, "Muba")	Nigeria
392.	"Gujji (Guji)"	Ethiopia
393.	Gula ("Ghoula)	Central African Republic
394.	Gulai ("*Gulaye*")	Chad
395.	"Guluka" ("Guruka")	Tanzania
396.	Gusii (Kisii, Kosove)	Kenya; Tanzania
397.	"Guzang"	Cameroons
398.	Gwandara	Nigeria
399.	Gwere	Uganda
400.	"Gzennaia" (Zenaga?)	North Africa
401.	mu-Ha (Abaha; mu-Waha)	Mozambique; Tanzania
402.	"Hadjarai"	Chad

252

403.	"Hallela"	Ethiopia
404.	mu-"Hangaza"	Tanzania
405.	"Harbawa"	North Africa
406.	Hausa	North Africa; West Africa
407.	wa-Haya (ba-Siba; Ziba; "mu-Zita")	Tanzania
408.	"Hayaina" ("Lahyaina, Lahyayna")	North Africa
409.	wa-Hehe	Tanzania
410.	"ba-Henba"	Zaire
411.	ova-Herero	Southern Africa
412.	"Hina"	Tanzania
413.	Hlubi	Southern Africa
414.	Holoholo	Central & East Africa
415.	Hombo (*Bangobango*)	Burundi
416.	HOTTENTOT: Grigriqua	South Africa
417.	HOTTENTOT: Nama(qua) ("Khoi-Khoin")	South West Africa/Namibia
418.	"Houara" (Hawawir? Wara?)	North Africa
419.	IBIBIO: "Abakaliki"	Nigeria
420.	IBIBIO: "Abakpa"	Nigeria
421.	IBIBIO: "Ahoada"	Nigeria
422.	IBIBIO: Anang (Western)	Nigeria
423.	IBIBIO: Calabar	Nigeria
424.	IBIBIO: Delta (Andoni-Ibeno; "Obolo")	Nigeria
425.	IBIBIO: Efik	Cameroons; Nigeria
426.	IBIBIO: Eket (Southern)	Cameroons; Nigeria
427.	IBIBIO: Ibibio (Eastern)	Cameroons; Nigeria
428.	IBIBIO: "Ibekwe"	Nigeria
429.	IBIBIO: "Marrigge"	Nigeria
430.	IBIBIO: "Opobo" ("Opopo")	Nigeria
431.	IBIBIO: Oron	Nigeria
432.	Ibo (Igbo)	Cameroons; Nigeria; Togo
433.	IBO: "Amai"	Nigeria
434.	IBO: "Anafia"	Nigeria
435.	IBO: Afikpo	Nigeria
436.	IBO: "Etche"	Nigeria
437.	IBO: "Ika" (Western)	Nigeria
438.	IBO: "Ogbah"	Nigeria
439.	IBO: "Ohuhu"	Nigeria
440.	IBO: Oratta-Ikwerri (*Ikwere*)	Cameroons
441.	IBO: Owerri (Southern)	Cameroons
442.	IBO: "Ukwani" (Kwale, "Ekwale")	Nigeria
443.	"Idda ou Gnadif"	North Africa
444.	Idoma(h)	Nigeria
445.	Igala (Igara)	Nigeria
446.	Igbira	Nigeria
447.	Igede (Egede)	Nigeria
448.	Ijaw (Ijo; Nembe)	Nigeria
449.	IJAW: "Okrika"	Nigeria
450.	Ikizu	Tanzania
451.	Ikoma	Tanzania
452.	ba-Ila (Mashukolumbwe)	Zambia
453.	Iramba (Ranba; "Munyiramba")	Tanzania
454.	Irigwe (Aregwe, "Miango")	Nigeria

455.	"Isenye, Issenya" (Kenya?)	Tanzania
456.	Issungo, ("*Issongo*", "*Mbati*")	Central African Republic
457.	ISSUNGO: "Bouaka"	Central African Republic
458.	ISSUNGO: "Boulemba"	Central African Republic
459.	"Isu" (Subu (Isuwu)?)	Cameroons
460.	Itsekiri (Jekri)	Nigeria
461.	Iwa (Awiwa; Waiwa)	Zambia
462.	"Iyassa"	Cameroons
463.	Jaba	Nigeria
464.	"Jaikiwa" (Dzhika?)	Tanzania
465.	Jarawa	Nigeria
466.	"Janjo (Jenjo)"	Nigeria
467.	Jera ("Jara")	Nigeria
468.	wa-Jita	Tanganyika
469.	"Ju'ala Shindi"	Sudan
470.	Jukun (Korofawa, "*Jakun*")	Nigeria
471.	Jur (Dyur, Gur, Jo-Luo, Lwo)	Sudan
472.	Kaba ("Sara Kaba")	Central African Rep., Chad
473.	Kabalai ("Kabalaye")	Chad
474.	Kabure (*Kabre*, Cabrai, "Kabye")	Ghana; Togo
475.	Kadara	Nigeria
476.	Kafficho (Kaffa, Kefa)	Ethiopia
477.	Kagoma (Agoma, *Kaboro*)	Nigeria
478.	Kagoro	Nigeria
479.	Kaje	Nigeria
480.	[ba]-Kaka (Kadei)	Cameroons
481.	"Kakar"	Nigeria
482.	Kakwa	Sudan
483.	Kalabari	Nigeria
484.	ba-Kalanga (Malawian)	Southern Africa
485.	"Kamatan" (Kamantan?)	Nigeria
486.	wa-Kamba (Akamba)	Kenya; Tanzania
487.	Kambata	Ethiopia
488.	wa-Kami	Tanzania
489.	Kanembu	Chad
490.	"Kaningkon"	Nigeria
491.	Kan(o)uri	Chad; Niger; Nigeria
492.	Kaonde	South & West Africa; Zambia
493.	"Karaboro"	Upper Volta
494.	Karamojong	Uganda
495.	Kare (Karré, Tali)	Central African Republic
496.	"Kasai"	Zaire (in Zambia)
497.	Katab	Nigeria
498.	"Kateli"	Cameroons
499.	Kavango	South West Africa/Namibia
500.	"Kayauma" (NIKA: Kauma?)	Zambia
501.	"Kebdana(h)"	North Africa
502.	"Kele" ("Kela") (a-Kalai?)	French Equatorial Africa; Togo
503.	"Kenyi"	Central & East Africa
504.	"Kéra" (Kerre?)	Chad
505.	ba-Kerewe (Wakerewe, mu-Kelewe)	Tanzania

506.	ba-Kete	Zaire
507.	"Kétonnou (Setonnou)"	Benin
508.	Keyu (*Elgeyu*)	Kenya
509.	ba-Kgalagadi	Botswana
510.	"Khaha"	Cameroons
511.	Khutu ("ba-Kutu", Wakuti)	Tanzania
512.	Kikuyu	Kenya; Tanzania
513.	Kilba	Nigeria
514.	"Kilindi"	Tanzania
515.	Kin	Chad
516.	Kimbu ("Kimbo")	Tanzania
517.	Kinga ("Mkinga")	Tanzania
518.	Kipsigis (Lumbwa)	Kenya
519.	"Kirari"	Zaire
520.	"Kisandu"	Zambia
521.	Kis(s)i (*G(h)izi*)	Sierra Leone
522.	ba-Koba (*ba-Yei*, Yeye)	Botswana
523.	"Kofyar" (Kofa?)	Nigeria
524.	Kohumono (*Bahumono*)	Nigeria
525.	ba-Koko (Betjek, Mwelle (*Mvele*))	Cameroons
526.	i-Kom (Bekom)	Cameroons; Nigeria
527.	Koma	Cameroons
528.	"Kombe" (Ndowe)	Cameroons; Equatorial Guinea
529.	Kongo	Zaire
530.	KONGO: "ba-Lari" (Laadi?)	Central African Republic
531.	KONGO: Mbamba (Mubamba)	Zambia
532.	KONGO: Monokutuba	Zaire
533.	KONGO: Sundi (Basundi)	Central Africa
534.	ba-Konjo	Uganda; Zaire
535.	Konkomba ("Konkoma")	Ghana
536.	Kono	Sierra Leone
537.	"Konnono" (Konongo?)	Zambia
538.	Kony (Elgonyi)	Kenya
539.	Koranko	Sierra Leone
540.	Koro (*Megili*)	Nigeria
541.	ba-Kossi (Bakosi, Nkossi)	Cameroons
542.	Kotokoli	Ghana; Togo
543.	"Kouga" (Kuka?)	Chad
544.	Kpelle (Guerze)	Liberia
545.	Krachi	Ghana
546.	KRU: Dei ("Dey")	Liberia
547.	KRU: Grebo (Glebo)	Liberia
548.	KRU: Krahn (Kran, Krahan)	Liberia
549.	KRU: Kru (Krao)	Liberia
550.	KRU: Sapo (Sapa)	Liberia
551.	KRU: "Tinepo"	Liberia
552.	"Ksar Essouk"	North Africa
553.	ba-Kuba (Bushongo, Tukubba)	Zaire
554.	Kubu ("Koubou")	Chad
555.	wa-Kuguru ("Guru")	Tanzania
556.	"Kuki" (Kukwe?)	Tanzania
557.	Kuku	Central & East Africa

558.	ba-Kulya ("Kulia"; "Kurya"; Tende; "Mtende")	Tanzania
559.	Kumam ("Kuman")	Central & East Africa
560.	Kunama (Kunema)	Ethiopia (Eritrea)
561.	ba-Kundu	Cameroons
562.	Kurama	Nigeria
563.	Kusasi (Kussasi, "Kusaal")	Ghana
564.	ba-Kusu	Tanzania
565.	"Kuturmi"	Nigeria
566.	Kwanda (Kwandi)	Zambia
567.	"Kwangwa"	Zambia
568.	Kwaya	Tanzania
569.	wa-Kwere	Tanzania
570.	"Laamong"	Nigeria
571.	"Laba"	Central & East Africa
572.	Lakka (Tolakka, "Laka")	Cameroons; Chad; Nigeria
573.	ba-Lala (Bukanda)	Zambia
574.	Lam(b)a	Togo
575.	ba-Lamba (wa-Lamba)	Zambia
576.	Lambya ("Lambia")	Tanzania
577.	"Landia"	Zambia
578.	Lango	Sudan
579.	Lango	Uganda
580.	"Laraich"	North Africa
581.	"Larteh"	Ghana
582.	Lebu (Lebou)	Sénégal
583.	Lele	Chad
584.	Lemba (*Malimba*)	Cameroons
585.	ba-Lenje (Benimukuni)	Zambia
586.	Lessel (Essel, *"Essele"*)	Cameroons
587.	Leya	Zambia
588.	Likpe(le)	Ghana
589.	Limba	Sierra Leone
590.	"Limba (Lima)"	Zambia
591.	"Littos" (Leto?)	Central African Republic
592.	"Lizon"	Nigeria
593.	Lobi	Upper Volta
594.	Lokele	Zaire
595.	Loko	Sierra Leone
596.	Longuda (Nungula, "Nungura")	Nigeria
597.	"Losso" (Lossa?)	Togo
598.	Lotuko (Latuka)	Sudan
599.	"Loubbachta"	North Africa
600.	Lovale (Luvale; Kaluwale)	Zambia
601.	Lozi (ba-Rozi; Barotse)	Tanzania; Zambia
602.	ba-Luba	Zambia; Zaire
603.	Luchazi	Zambia
604.	Luena (Kaluena)	Zaire
605.	Lugbara	Uganda; Zaire
606.	wa-Luguru	Tanzania
607.	aba-Luhya (Bantu Kavirondo)	Tanzania
608.	aba-LUHYA: Bukusu	Tanzania

609.	aba-LUHYA: Kabras (Nyala; "Kabarasi")	Tanzania
610.	aba-LUHYA: Kakamega (Idakho)	Tanzania
611.	aba-LUHYA: Khayo	Central & East Africa
612.	aba-LUHYA: Kisa	Central & East Africa
613.	aba-LUHYA: Marachi	Central & East Africa; Tanzania
614.	aba-LUHYA: Maragoli ("Lagoli")	Central & East Africa; Tanzania
615.	aba-LUHYA: Nyole	Central & East Africa; Tanzania
616.	aba-LUHYA: Samia	Central & East Africa; Tanzania
617.	aba-LUHYA: Tachoni	Central & East Africa
618.	aba-LUHYA: Tiriki	Tanzania
619.	aba-LUHYA: Tsotso	Central & East Africa
620.	aba-LUHYA: Vugusu (*Kitosh*)	Central & East Africa
621.	Lulua	Zaire
622.	ba-Lunda (Arund)	Zaire, Zambia
623.	mu-Lundi (Mulundi)	Tanzania
624.	Lundu (Barondo, Balondo)	Cameroons
625.	a-Lungu (wa-Lungu; "Mlungu")	Tanzania; Zambia
626.	ja-Luo (Nilotic Kavirondo; Nyifwa)	Kenya; Tanzania
627.	"Luwano" (ba-Wongo?)	Zambia
628.	Mada	Nigeria
629.	Madi	Sudan; Uganda
630.	Mahi ("Manhi")	Benin (in Togo)
631.	Maka (Makie)	Cameroons
632.	wa-Makonde	Tanzania
633.	MAKUA: a-Lomwe (Nguru)	Malawi
634.	MAKUA: Makua	Tanzania
635.	"Makunduchi"	Tanzania
636.	Malagasy (Malagache)	Madagascar
637.	Malila (Penya)	Tanzania
638.	Malinke (Mandingo, Mandinka)	Gambia; Sénégal
639.	MALINKE: Jahanke	Gambia
640.	MALINKE: "Mandinka More"	Gambia
641.	a-Mambwe	Tanzania; Zambia
642.	Mamprusi (Maniprussi)	Ghana
643.	Mandi (Lemande, "Lemunde")	Cameroons
644.	Mandjia (Mandja)	Central African Rep., Chad
645.	Mandyak (Manjak, Manjago)	Gambia; Guinea Bissau; Sénégal
646.	"Mango" (Manga?)	Chad
647.	"Manguissa"	Cameroons
648.	"Manja" (Maji?)	Ethiopia
649.	"Mano"	Liberia
650.	Mankanya (Mankagne)	Guinea Bissau
651.	"Manyema"	Tanzania
652.	"Manyoro" (Manyere)	Ghana
653.	Marba(h)	Chad
654.	Margi	Nigeria
655.	Marka	Upper Volta
656.	Masa	Chad
657.	MASA: "Baiga"	Chad
658.	MASA: "Doba" (Hoho?)	Chad
659.	MASA: "Mouloui"	Chad
660.	MASA:"Mousougoum" (Musgu? Musugoi?)	Chad

661.	Masai ("Kwavi")	Kenya; Tanganyika
662.	"kwa-Mashi"	Zambia
663.	"Mashingoli"	Somalia
664.	"Masmouda" ("Mesmouda")	North Africa
665.	Matakam	Nigeria
666.	Matengo	Tanzania
667.	"Matumbi"	Tanzania
668.	"Mauyuh" (ba-Ngu? Mao (Mau)?)	Cameroons
669.	"Mba-Ana-Soka"	Nigeria
670.	Mbai ("*Mbaye*")	Central African Rep.; Chad
671.	MBAI: "Mbaye-Dora"	Cameroons; Chad
672.	"Mbalmayo"	Cameroons
673.	"Mbam" (Mbum?)	Cameroons
674.	"Mbana" (Bana?)	Nigeria
675.	"Mbatu" (Mbato? KONGO: ba-Mbata?)	Cameroons
676.	"Mbedzi"	Swaziland
677.	Mbembe	Nigeria
678.	bo-Mbesa (Mombesa; *Mbeza*)	Zambia
679.	Mbimu ("Mbimou")	Central African Republic
680.	Mbo	Cameroons
681.	"M'bogoro" (FULBE: Bororo?)	Central African Republic
682.	"Mbonda"	Cameroons
683.	"M'Bondegue"	Central African Republic
684.	Mbonge (*M'Bonge*, Barombi)	Cameroons
685.	"Mbosi" (Boshi (Mboshi)?)	Congo
686.	"Mbote" (Mbuti?)	Tanzania
687.	Mbowe (Mamboe)	Zambia
688.	wa-Mbugu ("Bugu")	Tanzania
689.	Mbuin (Gwin)	Upper Volta
690.	bi-Mbundu (Ovimbundu; Mbali; ma-Mbari)	Zambia
691.	ki-Mbundu (shi-Mbundu)	Angola; S.W. Africa/Namibia
692.	wa-Mbunga (Bunga)	Tanzania
693.	"Mbwela (Mbwak)"	North Africa
694.	"M'dakra"	North Africa
695.	"Mekende"	Cameroons
696.	"Memo" ("meno") (ba-Mena?)	Cameroons
697.	Mende	Sierra Leone
698.	"Menjenger"	Ethiopia
699.	Menka	Cameroons
700.	"Menoua"	Cameroons
701.	MERINA: Hova	Madagascar
702.	"Mernissa"	North Africa
703.	Meru	Tanzania
704.	Meru (Mweru)	Kenya
705.	"Messoujah" ("Mezzouya", "Mzouda")	North Africa
706.	Meta ("Metta")	Cameroons
707.	Metalsa	North Africa
708.	"Mezime" ("Medjime")	Cameroons
709.	"ba-Mfuamba	Zaire
710.	Mfumte (*Kaka*)	Nigeria
711.	"Miéne"	Gabon
712.	bo-Mitaba	Congo (in Central African Rep.)

713.	"Mkuiga" (Kwegu?)	Tanzania
714.	"Mlanda"	Swaziland
715.	"Mlazi"	Tanzania
716.	"Mlude" ("Mludi")	Tanzania
717.	"Mndwere" ("Mndwewe")	Tanzania
718.	"Mnyakipsa"	Tanzania
719.	Moba ("Bimawba, Bimoba")	Ghana; Togo
720.	"Mobou"	Chad
721.	"Mocolé" (Mukulehe?)	Benin
722.	"Modani"	Cameroons
723.	"Mogande"	Cameroons; Equatorial Guinea
724.	"Moghamo"	Cameroons
725.	"Monamenan" ("Moremanam")	Cameroons
726.	Mondjembo ("Monjombo")	Central African Republic
727.	Mono ("Bomono")	Cameroons
728.	"Mopou Kassarye"	Chad
729.	Moré (Maure, Moors)	Mauritania
730.	"Morro"	Zaire (in Central African Rep.)
731.	MORU: Avukaya	Sudan
732.	MORU: Moru Misa (Moru, Moro)	Sudan
733.	Mossi (Moshi(e)	Ghana; Ivory Coast; Upper Volta
734.	"Mposiwa"	Tanzania
735.	"Mshukwa"	Tanzania
736.	"Msimbwe"	Tanzania
737.	Mubi	Nigeria
738.	"Mubr"	South West Africa/Namibia
739.	"Muchiku"	Zambia
740.	"Mufugwe"	Zambia
741.	"Mugomo"	Zambia
742.	"Mukangwa"	Tanzania
743.	"Mukaza" (BIDEYAT: Nakaza?)	Tanzania
744.	"Mukolo"	Zambia
745.	"Mumapwe"	Tanzania
746.	"Mumhonga" (Unga (ba-HONGA)?)	Tanzania
747.	Mundang	Chad
748.	"Mundani"	Cameroons
749.	"Muokani"	Cameroons
750.	"Mupun"	Nigeria
751.	"Murum" ("*Mouroum*")	Chad
752.	"Musgu" ("*Mousgoum*")	Cameroons
753.	Mussoi (Musei; "*Mouseille*")	Chad
754.	"Mutandu"	Zambia
755.	"Mutanga"	Zambia
756.	"Mutawala"	Zambia
757.	"Mvog-Ada"	Chad
758.	"Mvog-Kam"	Cameroons
759.	"Mwachueze" ("Muachusa", "Muacusa")	Tanzania; Zambia
760.	"Mwaehuen"	Tanzania
761.	Mwanga	Zambia
762.	"Mwemka"	Tanzania
763.	mu-Mwere (wa-Muera)	Tanzania
764.	Mzab ("Amzab")	North Africa

765.	"Namjoma"	Tanzania
766.	Nandi	Kenya
767.	Nangire (Nandjiri, Nangtchere)	Chad
768.	Nankanse (Gurense)	Ghana; Upper Volta
769.	Nata	Tanzania
770.	"Nawda"	Togo
771.	Ndali	Tanzania
772.	Ndamba (Gangi)	Tanzania
773.	ama-Ndebele (Matabele)	South Africa; Swaziland; Zambia
774.	Ndebele, Transvaal	Lesotho. South Africa
775.	Ndembu ("Ndembo-Lunda")	Zaire
776.	Ndembu (Ndembo)	Zambia
777.	Ndengereko	Tanzania
778.	Ndob ("Ndop")	Cameroons
779.	"Ndoka"	Central African Republic
780.	"Ndokwa"	Nigeria
781.	Ngala	Cameroons
782.	Ngama	Central African Rep.; Chad
783.	Nganda	Tanzania
784.	"N'gangan"	Togo
785.	ba-Ngangte (Ngoteng)	Cameroons
786.	Ngbandi	Zaire (in Central African Republic)
787.	Ngemba	Nigeria
788.	wa-Mgindo ("Mngindo")	Tanzania
789.	"Ngoe"	Cameroons
790.	Ngolo ("Ngolle")	Cameroons
791.	Ngolo	South & West Africa
792.	wa-Ngonde (Konde)	Central & East Africa
793.	ba-Ngongo (*Wangongo*)	Tanzania
794.	Ngoni (Machonde, Mafiti, Magwangara, Mazitu, Watutu)	Tanzania
795.	a-Ngoni (Agoni. Mangoni; Wangoni)	Malawi; Tanzania; Zambia
796.	a-NGONI: Gomani (chi-Gomoni)	Zambia
797.	"Ngulu"	Tanzania
798.	Ngumba (Mvumba)	Cameroons
799.	Ngumbu (Ngumbo)	Zambia
800.	"Ngungar"	Chad
801.	NGUNI, SOUTH: Pondo (Mpondo)	Lesotho; Transkei
802.	NGUNI, SOUTH: Tembu (Bathepu; Thembu)	Lesotho; Transkei
803.	NGUNI, SOUTH: ama-Xosa (Xhosa, Kaffir)	Southern Africa
804.	XOSA: ama-Gcaleka	Transkei
805.	XOSA: Pondomise	Transkei
806.	XOSA: Xesibe	Transkei
807.	Nguruimi (wa-Ngoroine)	Tanzania
808.	"Nguu"	Tanzania
809.	"Nhyembe"	Swaziland
810.	Nielim ("Niellim")	Chad
811.	Nika (wa-Nyika; Mijikenda):	Tanzania; Zambia
812.	NIKA: mu-Chonyi	Central & East Africa
813.	NIKA: wa-Digo	Kenya; Tanzania

814.	NIKA:	Giryama (Giriama)	Kenya; Tanzania
815.	NIKA:	Kambe	Central & East Africa
816.	NIKA:	Rabai	Tanzania
817.	NIKA:	Segeju ("Seguju")	Tanzania
818.	Ninzam		Nigeria
819.	ba-Njambi ("Bandjabi")		Gabon
820.	Njawi (Banjabi, Banzabi)		Gabon
821.	"omu-Njemba"		South West Africa/Namibia
822.	"Nkada (Nkafa?)		Nigeria
823.	"Nkam" (Kam?)		Cameroons
824.	"Nkambe"		Cameroons
825.	"Nko"		Nigeria
826.	ma-Nkoya		Zambia
827.	"Nkwen"		Cameroons
828.	"Non(n)i" (Non(e)?)		Cameroons
829.	Nsaw (ba-Nso)		Cameroons; Equatorial Guinea
830.	Nsenga (Senga)		South Africa; Swaziland; Zambia
831.	Nsungli (Dzungle, Njungene)		Cameroons
832.	"Ntakwo" (Tabwa?)		Cameroons
833.	"Ntipachort"		Nigeria
834.	"Ntwan"		Cameroons
835.	Nubians		Chad
836.	NUBIANS, NORTHERN: Halfa		Sudan
837.	Nuer		Ethiopia; Sudan
838.	Nungu (*Rindre*)		Nigeria
839.	Nupe		Nigeria
840.	"Nvoguiengue"		Cameroons
841.	Nweh		Cameroons
842.	Nyakusa (Sokile)		Tanzania
843.	"Nyambo"		Central & East Africa
844.	Nyamawanga (Ainamwanga, na-Mwanga)		Tanzania; Zambia
845.	ba-Nyamwezi		Tanzania; Zambia
846.	ba-Nyang (Anyang)		Cameroons
847.	ba-Nyangi		Cameroons; Nigeria
848.	a-Nyanja		Malawi; Swaziland; Zambia
849.	a-Nyasa (Wanyassa)		Swaziland; Tanzania; Zambia
850.	"Nyege (Nyenge)"		Cameroons
851.	Nyiha (ba-Nyika)		Tanzania
852.	Nyong ("Njong")		Cameroons
853.	"Nyore" (Nyole? Nyoro?)		Tanzania
854.	ba-Nyoro		Uganda
855.	ba-NYORO: ba-Nyankole (Munyankole, "Nkole")		Uganda; Zambia
856.	"Nyounga"		Cameroons
857.	Nzakara		Central African Republic
858.	Nzimu (Nzema, Nzima)		Ghana; Ivory Coast
859.	"Obala"		Cameroons
860.	"Obogya"		Ivory Coast
861.	"Obubra"		Nigeria
862.	"Obudu"		Nigeria
863.	"Ogive" (?Ogi? Uggi?)		Cameroons
864.	"Ogoja"		Cameroons; Nigeria

865.	"Ogoni"	Nigeria
866.	"Ohaji"	Cameroons
867.	"Oko"	Nigeria
868.	"Okobo"	Nigeria
869.	"Okonala"	Cameroons
870.	"Okuni"	Cameroons
871.	"Olu"	Cameroons
872.	"Omagawa"	Nigeria
873.	"Omoku"	Nigeria
874.	Oromo (*Galla*)	Ethiopia
875.	"Oshie"	Cameroons
876.	"Oshobori"	Nigeria
877.	"Osoney"	Cameroons
878.	"Otoloa"	Cameroons
879.	"Ouadda"	Central African Republic
880.	"Oulad 'Aguil (Hquel)"	North Africa
881.	"Oulad Arous (Houz)"	North Africa
882.	"Oulad Haddou (Dahhou)"	North Africa
883.	"Oulad Issa (Aissa)"	North Africa
884.	"Oulad Khal(l)ouf"	North Africa
885.	"Oulad Moussa"	North Africa
886.	Oulad Nasser (O. Ncir; O. Asr (Nsir))	North Africa
887.	"Oulad Said"	North Africa
888.	"Pana"	Cameroons; Central African Republic
889.	Pangwa	Tanzania
890.	wa-Pare (Asu)	Tanzania
891.	"Péda"	Togo
892.	ba-Pedi	South Africa; Swaziland
893.	"Pen"	Chad
894.	ba-Pende	Zaire
895.	Pépél	Guinea Bissau
896.	Pilapila ("*Pila*")	Benin
897.	Pimbwe	Tanzania
898.	wa-Pogoro ("Mpogoro"; "mu-Kogoro")	Tanzania
899.	wa-Pokomo	Central & East Africa
900.	Popo (*Ge*(n); *Mina*)	Benin; Togo
901.	Popoi	Central & East Africa
902.	Puno ("BaPounou")	Gabon
903.	"Pygmies"	Cameroons; Central African Rep.
904.	PYGMIES: Atsoua	Congo
905.	PYGMIES: Bambote	Zaire
906.	PYGMIES: Rundi ba-Twa	Burundi
907.	PYGMIES: Ruanda ba-Twa	Rwanda
908.	"Qzanaya" (Zenaga?)	North Africa
909.	"Rahhala"	North Africa
910.	i-Rangi (Langi, wa-Rangi)	Tanzania
911.	wa-Rega	Zaire
912.	Rehamna ("R'hamna")	North Africa
913.	Rehoboth Basters	South-west Africa/Namibia
914.	"Rharb"	North Africa
915.	"Ribinia" (Ribanawa?)	Nigeria
916.	"Rito"	Chad

917.	ba-Ron (Boram)	Nigeria
918.	"Rounga" (o-Rungu?)	Central African Republic
919.	banya-Ruanda ("Nyaruanda")	Burundi; Rwanda; Tanzania; Uganda; Zaire
920.	RUANDA: ba-Hutu	Rwanda
921.	RUANDA: ba-Tutsi (Watusi)	Rwanda
922.	ba-Rundi	Burundi; Tanzania
923.	ba-RUNDI: ba-Hutu	Burundi
924.	ba-RUNDI: ba-Tutsi (Watusi)	Burundi: Tanzania
925.	Runga ("Rongo")	Chad
926.	"Rungu" (Rungwa?)	Tanzania
927.	"Sabanga"	Central African Republic
928.	"Sable" (Subu?)	Cameroons
929.	wa-Safwa	Tanzania
930.	Safwi (Sefwi; Sefni; Sahwi)	Ghana; Ivory Coast
931.	wa-Sagara (Sagala)	Tanzania
932.	"Sahafatra"	Madagascar
933.	Sakalava	Madagascar
934.	SAKALAVA: Vezo	Madagascar
935.	"Sala"	Cameroons
936.	ba-Sala	Zaire; Zambia
937.	"Samba"	Central & East Africa
938.	Samo[gho]	Upper Volta
939.	Sand(a)we (wa-Sandaui)	Tanzania
940.	ba-Sanga	Cameroons; Ghana
941.	ba-Sanga	Zaire
942.	Sango (Sahanga, Sangho)	Central African Republic
943.	Sangu (Rori)	Tanzania
944.	Sara	Cameroons; Central African Republic; Chad
945.	SARA: "Benoyé"	Chad
946.	SARA: "Daba" ("Douba")	Chad
947.	SARA: Gambaye ("Ngambaye")	Cameroons; Central African Republic; Chad
948.	SARA: "Madjingaye"	Chad
949.	SARA: "Nar"	Chad
950.	SARA: "Sar"	Chad
951.	Sebei	Central & East Africa
952.	"Sebta" (Sebha?)	North Africa
953.	"Sefrou"	North Africa
954.	"Sémérois"	Benin
955.	a-Sena (wa-Sena)	Malawi
956.	a-Senga	Zambia
957.	Senhaja	North Africa
958.	Senufo ("Senoufo", Siena)	Upper Volta
959.	Serer(e) ("Serrere")	Cameroons; Gambia; Guinea; Liberia; Sénégal
960.	"Seto" (Leto?)	Benin
961.	Shaikia ("Shaighi)	Sudan
962.	"Shambaa" ("Sambaa")	Tanzania
963.	"Sharaghah"	North Africa
964.	"Shashani" ("Shanshi")	Somalia

965.	wa-Shashi ("Shashe")	Tanzania
966.	Shawiya (*Chaouia*)	North Africa
967.	"Shehu" (Saho Shiho)?)	Ethiopia
968.	Sherbro	Sierra Leone
969.	Shilluk	Sudan
970.	ma-Shona	Swaziland; Zambia; Zimbabwe
971.	SHONA: "Danda" ("Dande")	South & West Africa
972.	SHONA: mu-Kalanga ("Karanga"; Kalinda?)	Tanzania; Zambia
973.	SHONA: Kolekole (Korekore)	Zambia
974.	SHONA: va-Ndau (Njao)	South & West Africa
975.	SHONA: ma-Nyika (Manyika)	Zimbabwe
976.	SHONA: ma-Tawara ("Mtawara")	South & West Africa
977.	SHONA: Zezuru	South & West Africa; Zambia
978.	"Shongon"	Nigeria
979.	Sidamo	Ethiopia
980.	Sikh (religious minority)	Malawi
981.	Simbiti	Tanzania
982.	"Sizaki" ("Siziki")	Tanzania
983.	So ("*Sso*")	Cameroons
984.	"Soba" (Suba?)	Benin
985.	Soga	Tanzania
986.	"Soli"	Zambia
987.	Somba ("Soumba")	Benin
988.	SOMBA: Berba	Benin
989.	SOMBA: Ditiamarin	Benin
990.	SOMBA: Natimba ("Countimba")	Benin
991.	SOMBA: Niendé (Gniande)	Benin
992.	SOMBA: Yoabou	Benin
993.	Songe (Bassonge, "Basonge")	Zaire (in Burundi)
994.	Songhai (Sonrai)	Ivory Coast; Niger
995.	Soninke (Sarakole, Serahuli)	Central African Republic; Gambia; Sénégal
996.	Sonjo	Tanzania
997.	ba-Sossi ("Basosi")	Cameroons
998.	ba-Sotho (Basuto)	Lesotho; Southern Africa
999.	"Souma"	Central Africal Republic
1000.	Sragna ("S'rar̲ha")	North Africa
1001.	Suba (Soba)	Tanzania
1002.	"Subi" (Subia?)	Tanzania
1003.	ba-Sukuma (Wassukuma, "Sokuma")	Tanzania
1004.	Sumbwa	Tanzania
1005.	Sura	Nigeria
1006.	Susu (Soso)	Guinea (in Gambia): Sierra Leone
1007.	Swahili (Shirazi)	Eastern & South-eastern Africa
1008.	SWAHILI: Bajun(i) ("Bayuni")	Tanzania
1009.	SWAHILI: "Kimvita"	Kenya
1010.	SWAHILI: "Kinhwana"	Tanzania
1011.	SWAHILI: Rufiji ("Mrufiji")	Tanzania
1012.	"Swaka"	South & West Africa; Zambia
1013.	ama-Swazi	Lesotho; South Africa; Swaziland, Transke
1014.	ba-Tabwa (wai-Tabwa; i-Tawa; ba-Tambwa)	Tanzania; Zambia
1015.	Tadla ("Takla")	North Africa

1016.	"Taferist"	North Africa
1017.	"Takun" (JUKUN: Takum?)	Nigeria
1018.	"Tal"	Nigeria
1019.	Tallensi	Ghana
1020.	"Tamaman" ("Timsama")	North Africa
1021.	an-Tanala	Madagascar
1022.	Tanga, Northern (Batanga; "Ngolo-Batanga")	Cameroons
1023.	Tanga, Southern (Batanga)	Equatorial Guinea
1024.	Tangale	Nigeria
1025.	Tarok	Nigeria
1026.	"Taroudant"	North Africa
1027.	Teita (wa-Taita)	Tanzania
1028.	ba-Téké	Gabon
1029.	"Telouet"	North Africa
1030.	Temne (Temmeny)	Cameroons; Gambia; Sierra Leone
1031.	ba-Teso (Iteso, Kedi)	Sudan; Uganda
1032.	THONGA: Hlengwe	South & West Africa
1033.	THONGA: ba-Ronga	Mozambique; South Africa; Swaziland
1034.	THONGA: "Shangaan" ("Chagana")	Mozambique; South Africa; Swaziland
1035.	THONGA: ba-Thonga (Tonga)	Mozambique; South Africa; Swaziland; Zambia
1036.	THONGA: "Tsonga"	Swaziland
1037.	THONGA: ba-Tswa ("Batsua")	South & West Africa
1038.	"Tiéfo"	Upper Volta
1039.	Tienga (*Kenga*)	Chad
1040.	TIGRE: Billen (Bilen)	Ethiopia
1041.	Tikar ("*Tikari*")	Cameroons
1042.	Tiv	Cameroons; Nigeria
1043.	"Toboca"	Sudan
1044.	ba-Toka (Matoka)	Zambia
1045.	Toma (Loma; Buzi)	Liberia
1046.	Tonga (a-Tonga)	Malawi
1047.	Tonga (ba-Tonka)	Zambia
1048.	Tongwe	Tanzania
1049.	"Tori" ("Torri/Seto")	Benin
1050.	"Toro"	Central & East Africa
1051.	"Touhra"	North Africa
1052.	"Toussian" (Tusya-Win)	Upper Volta
1053.	Tsimihety	Madagascar
1054.	ba-Tswana (Bechuana)	Southern Africa
1055.	TSWANA: "bo-Hongo (Mohongo)"	Bophuthatswana
1056.	TSWANA: Hurutshe (ba-Khurutshe)	Lesotho
1057.	TSWANA: ba-Kgatla (Bahkhala, Bakhatla, Baklatla)	Bophuthatswana; Botswana
1058.	TSWANA: ba-Kwena (mo-Kwena; Wena)	Bophuthatswana; Botswana
1059.	TSWANA: "ba-Lete"	Botswana
1060.	TSWANA: ba-Ngwaketse	Botswana
1061.	TSWANA: bo-Ngwata (Mongwata: bama-Ngwato)	Bophuthatswana; Botswana
1062.	TSWANA: ba-Rolong	Bophuthatswana; Botswana
1063.	TSWANA: ba-Tawana	Botswana

1064.	TSWANA: ba-Tlharo (Batlokwa, Botlhako)	Bophuthatswana; Botswana
1065.	Tuareg	North East Africa; Niger
1066.	Tuburi ("*Tupuri*")	Cameroons; Chad
1067.	"Tugbang"	Cameroons
1068.	Tukulor (Toucouleur, Torado)	Gambia; Mauritania; Sénégal
1069.	TUKULOR: "Barikala"	Mauritania
1070.	Tumak ("Toumak")	Chad
1071.	ba-TUMBUKA (TUMBUKU): wa-Henga	Tanzania
1072.	ba-TUMBUKA (TUMBUKU): wa-Kamanga	Tanzania
1073.	ba-TUMBUKA (TUMBUKU): "Nkhonde"	Malawi
1074.	ba-TUMBUKA (TUMBUKU): Sisya (Siska)	Zambia
1075.	ba-TUMBUKA (TUMBUKU): Tumbuka	Malawi; South Africa; Zambia
1076.	Turkana	Kenya; etc.
1077.	nya-Turu ("Lima")	Tanzania
1078.	Twi (Akan)	Ghana; Nigeria; Togo
1079.	TWI: Akwamu	Ghana
1080.	TWI: Akwapim	Ghana
1081.	TWI: Akyem (Akim)	Ghana
1082.	TWI: Asen-Twifo ("Assin")	Ghana
1083.	TWI: Ashanti (Asante)	Ghana; Swaziland
1084.	TWI: Fanti	Cameroons; Ghana; Nigeria
1085.	TWI: Kwahu	Ghana
1086.	TWI: Wasa ("Wassa", "Wassaw")	Ghana
1087.	"Twitwirega"	Ghana
1088.	"Uhami-Iyayu" (Ishua)	Nigeria
1089.	"Ukiwe"	Nigeria
1090.	"Ungwe"	South & West Africa
1091.	"Urhore"	Nigeria
1092.	"Utipahort"	Nigeria
1093.	"Uvaha"	Nigeria
1094.	"Uzekwe (Ezekwe, Ezeke)"	Nigeria
1095.	Vagala ("Vagla")	Ghana
1096.	Vai	Liberia/Guinea
1097.	Valé ("Valer", "Valet")	Central African Rep.; Chad
1098.	ba-Venda	South Africa
1099.	"Vidunda"	Tanzania
1100.	"ba-Vira"	Central & East Africa; Zaire (in Burundi)
1101.	Waka	Nigeria
1102.	Wala	Ghana
1103.	Walamo (Wolamo, Walaitza)	Ethipia
1104.	Wandya ("*Wanda*")	Tanzania
1105.	Wanji	Tanzania; Zambia
1106.	Warain ("*Guerouane*")	North Africa
1107.	"Warri" (War?)	Nigeria
1108.	Watyi ("Ouatchi")	Togo
1109.	We ("*Weh*")	Cameroons
1110.	"Weisa"	Ghana
1111.	"Windji-Windji"	Benin
1112.	Wolof (Jolof; Ouolof)	West Africa
1113.	Wum (Aghem) ("Ajem")	Cameroons
1114.	Wuri (Buli, "Wouri")	Cameroons
1115.	Wute (Bute, "*Baboute*")	Cameroons

116.	Yako ("*Ugep*")	Nigeria
117.	Yakoma	Central African Republic
118.	"Yakombo"	Cameroons
119.	"Yala" (Yale?)	Cameroons
120.	"Yamado(u)"	Chad
121.	Yambassa	Cameroons
122.	"Yamoyong"	Cameroons
123.	wa-Yao (Adjao; Adsoa, Ajawa, etc.)	Malawi; Tanzania; Zambia
124.	"Yassamane" (Yasa? Yassing?)	Cameroons
125.	"Yebekolo"	Cameroons
126.	ba-Yeke	Zaire
127.	"Yemvak" (Yemba?)	Cameroons
128.	Yergum (Yergam)	Nigeria
129.	"Yevol"	Cameroons
130.	"Yoko"	Cameroons
131.	Yoruba	West Africa
132.	YORUBA: "Holli"	Benin
133.	YORUBA: Ila	Nigeria
134.	YORUBA: Kabba	Nigeria
135.	YORUBA: "Nagot"	Benin; Niger; Togo
136.	YORUBA: Oyo	Nigeria
137.	"Yumbu"	Tanzania
138.	"Zaa" (Berber: Zaer?)	Cameroons
139.	"Zafisoro"	Madagascar
140.	"Zaliduwa"	Nigeria
141.	"Zamran"	North Africa
142.	Zanaki ("Mzanaki")	Tanzania
143.	Zaramo (wa-Saramo)	Tanzania
144.	Zerhana ("Zar'houn")	North Africa
145.	"Zia" (Sia?)	Central African Republic
146.	Zigula (wa-Segua, *Zigua*)	Tanzania
147.	Zinza (wa-Sinja)	Tanzania
148.	Znassen ("Benin Z'nassen")	North Africa
149.	"Zongendwa"	Swaziland
150.	ama-Zulu	Southern Africa
151.	ZULU: Ixopo	South Africa
152.	"Zuru" (Sura? Zumu?)	Nigeria

THE AMERICAS

	Tribe or Minority	*Country or Area of Origin*
1.	Achumawi (*Pitt River*)	United States (California)
2.	Acoma	United States (South West)
3.	Agua Caliente	United States (California)
4.	Aguaruna	Peru
5.	Ahtena	Alaska
6.	Akwa'ala (*Paipai*)	Mexico (Baja California Norte)
7.	Alacaluf	Chile
8.	Aleut	Alaska
9.	Amarakaeri	Peru

10.	Amuesha	Peru
11.	Amuzgo	Mexico
12.	APACHE, EASTERN: Jicarilla	United States (South West)
13.	APACHE, EASTERN: Mescalero	United States (South West)
14.	APACHE, WESTERN: San Carlos	United States (South West)
15.	APACHE, WESTERN: White Mountain	United States (South West)
16.	Arapaho	United States (West Central)
17.	ARAUCANIAN: Mapuche	Argentina; Chile
18.	ARAUCANIAN: Pehuenche	Chile
19.	Arecuna	Guyana
20.	Arhuaco	Colombia
21.	Arikara	United States (West Central)
22.	Ashuslay (*Chulupi*)	Paraguay
23.	Assiniboin (Stoney)	Canada; United States
24.	"Atikum" (Uaimare?)	Brazil
25.	Aymará	Bolivia; Chile; Peru
26.	Baniwa ("Baniva")	Venezuela
27.	Bannock	United States (North West)
28.	Bari ("Los Barre", *Dobokubi*)	Venezuala
29.	Baure	Bolivia
30.	Beaver	Canada
31.	Bellacoola	Canada
32.	Blackfoot	Canada; United States
33.	Blood	Canada
	BUSH NEGROES:	
34.	"Aloekoes"	French Guiana
35.	Aucaner	Suriname
36.	Djuka	French Guiana; Suriname
37.	"Matuaris" ("Matawai")	Suriname
38.	Saramacca	Guyana; French Guiana; Suriname
39.	"Cabboco" ("Cabloco")	Venezuela
40.	CAHITA: Mayo	Mexico
41.	CAHITA: Yaqui	Mexico; United States
42.	Cahuilla (Kawia)	United States (California)
43.	Callinago (Island Carib)	Dominica; St. Vincent
44.	"Cambiuá" ("Kambiwá")	Brazil
45.	Campa	Peru
46.	Canari	Ecuador
47.	Capanawa (Kapanawá)	Brazil
48.	Carib (Galibi)	French Guiana
49.	"Carib (Moreno)"	Honduras
50.	Carina (Karinya)	Suriname; Venezuela
51.	Carrier	Canada
52.	Cayapa	Ecuador
53.	Cenu	Colombia
54.	CENU: Catío (Katio)	Colombia
55.	CHAMA: Shipibo	Peru
56.	Chapacura: Moré (*Itene*)	Bolivia
57.	Chatino	Mexico (Oaxaca)
58.	Cherokee	United States (South Eastern)
59.	Chetco	United States (North West)
60.	Cheyenne	United States (West Central)

61.	Cheyenne, "Northern"	United States
62.	Chilcotin	Canada
63.	Chinantec	Mexico (Oaxaca)
64.	Chinook	United States (North West)
65.	CHINOOK, UPPER: Wasco	United States (North West)
66.	Chipaya	Bolivia
67.	Chipewyan	Canada
68.	"Chiquitano" (Chiquito?)	Bolivia
69.	Chiriguano ("Chahuanco")	Argentina; Bolivia
70.	"Chochotecos"	Mexico
71.	CHOCO: Emberá	Panama
72.	CHOCO: Noanoma (Waunaná)	Colombia; Panama
73.	Choctaw	United States (South East)
74.	Chontal (de Tabasco)	Mexico
75.	Chorotí ("Manjuy")	Paraguay
76.	"Chukchansi" (*Chook Chansee*)	United States (California)
77.	Cochimi	Mexico (Baja California Norte)
78.	"Cocal"	Brazil
79.	Cocopa ("Cucapa")	Mexico; United States
80.	Cofan[es]	Ecuador
81.	Colorado (Tatchila)	Ecuador
82.	Comanche	United States (South Central)
83.	Cree, "Plains"	Canada
84.	Cree, "Swampy"	Canada
85.	Creek	United States (South East)
86.	Creole	Nicaragua
87.	Crow	United States (West Central)
88.	"Cuicateco"	Mexico (Oaxaca)
89.	Cuna (Kuna)	Panama
90.	Curipaco ("Corripaco")	Colombia
91.	Delaware (Lenape)	Canada; United States
92.	DHEGIHA: Omaha	United States (West Central)
93.	DHEGIHA: Osage	United States (West Central)
94.	Diegueno	United States (California)
95.	DIEGUENO: Kiliwa	Mexico (Baja California Norte)
96.	D[o]ukhobors	Canada
97.	Eyak	Alaska
98.	Fulnio ("Funi-o")	Brazil (Pernambuco)
99.	Garif[una] ("Black Carib")	Belize; Honduras
100.	Gitksan	Canada
101.	Goajiro (Guajiro) Colombia	Colombia; Venezuela
102.	Gros Ventre	United States (West Central)
103.	Guajibo (Guajivo)	Colombia; Venezuela
104.	Guaná	Paraguay
105.	Guarani	Argentina; Brazil; Paraguay
106.	GUARANI: Ava-Chiripa	Paraguay
107.	GUARANI: "Izozeño-Chiriguano"	Bolivia
108.	Guarayú (Guarayo)	Bolivia
109.	"Guarijio" (Varohio?)	Mexico (Chihuahua)
110.	Guatuso	Costa Rica
111.	Guaymi	Panama
112.	Haida	Alaska; Canada

113.	Han	Alaska
114.	Havasupai	United States (South West)
115.	Hidatsa	United States (West Central)
116.	"Hispanics"	United States
117.	"Holikachuk"	Alaska
118.	Hopi	United States (South West)
119.	Huastec	Mexico
120.	Huave	Mexico (Oaxaca)
121.	Ingalik	Alaska
	INUIT (ESKIMO):	
122.	Angmagsalik ("Ammassalimiut")	Greenland
123.	"Franklin"	Canada
124.	Greenlandic, North Western	Greenland
125.	Greenlandic, "Central Western"	Greenland
126.	"Keewatin"	Canada
127.	"Northern" (Inupiaq)	Alaska
128.	"Ungav[a]" (Eastern Arctic)	Canada (Quebec)
129.	IROQUOIS: Mohawk	Canada; United States
130.	IROQUOIS: Onandaga	Canada
131.	IROQUOIS: Oneida	Canada; United States
132.	IROQUOIS: Seneca	Canada
133.	IROQUOIS: Tuscarora	Canada; United States
134.	Isleta	United States (South West)
135.	"Ixcatec" ("Izcatec")	Mexico (Oaxaca)
136.	Jemez	United States (South West)
137.	Jicaque (Xicaque)	Honduras
138.	"Kaiambés" (Cayabi?)	Brazil
139.	Kalapuya (*Wapato*)	United States (North West)
140.	Karok	United States (California)
141.	Kekchi ("Quecchi")	Belize; Guatemala
142.	KERES: Zia	United States (South West)
143.	Kickapoo	United States
144.	Kiowa	United States
145.	Kirirí	Brazil (Bahia)
146.	KIRIRÍ: Shucurús ("Xucurús")	Brazil
147.	Klamath	United States (North West)
148.	Koasati (*Alabama-Coushatta*)	United States (South East)
149.	Konkau ("*Concow*")	United States (California)
150.	Koyukon	Alaska
151.	"Ku-Miai" ("Kum-Yiy"; Kamia?)	Mexico (Baja California Norte)
152.	"Kuskokwim, Upper"	Alaska
153.	Kutchin (Loucheux)	Alaska; Canada
154.	Kutenai (Kootenay)	Canada
155.	Kwakiutl	Canada
156.	Lenca	Honduras
157.	"Lengua"	Paraguay
158.	Locono ("*Arawak*")	Guyana; Suriname
159.	Lumbee	United States (South East)
160.	Macá (Macca)	Paraguay
161.	Machiguenga	Peru
162.	"Maco" (Saliva Maco? Macu?)	Venezuela
163.	Macusi ("Macuxi")	Bolivia; Brazil; Guyana

270

64.	Malecite ("Maleseet")	Canada
65.	MALECITE: Passamaquoddy	United States (North East)
66.	Mahican ("*Mohican*", *Stockbridge*)	United States (North East)
67.	Makah	United States (North East)
68.	Mandan	United States (West Central)
69.	Maricopa	United States (South West)
70.	Maroons	Jamaica
71.	MASCOI: "Toba"	Paraguay
72.	Mataco	Argentina
73.	Maya(n)	Belize; Mexico
74.	Mazatec	Mexico (Oaxaca; Vera Cruz)
75.	Mennonites	Canada
76.	Mestizo	Colombia; Panama
77.	Metis, Red River	Canada
78.	Micmac	Canada (Nova Scotia)
79.	Miskito (Mosquito)	Honduras; Nicaragua
80.	Miwok	United States (California)
81.	Mixe	Mexico
82.	Mixtec	Mexico
83.	Mocoví	Argentina
84.	Moguex ("*Guambanó*")	Colombia
85.	Mojo ("*Moxos*")	Bolivia
86.	MOJO: Ignacio ("Ignaciano")	Bolivia
87.	MOJO: Trinitario	Bolivia
88.	Nahane ("Nahani")	Canada
89.	NAHANE: Tahltan	Canada
90.	Nahua (Nahuatl, "Aztec")	Mexico
91.	Navajo (Navaho)	United States (South West)
92.	Nevome (Pima Bajo)	Mexico
93.	Nez Perce	United States (North West)
94.	Niska	Canada
95.	Nootka	Canada
	OJIBWA (CHIPPEWA):	
96.	Woodlands, Northern (Saulteaux)	Canada, United States
97.	Woodlands, Southern (Chippewa)	Canada, United States
98.	"Mississauga"	Canada
99.	Ona	Argentina (Tierra del Fuego)
00.	Otomi	Mexico
01.	Paez	Colombia; Panama
02.	Paiute	United States
03.	Pancararú	Brazil
04.	Pame	Mexico
05.	Papago	Mexico (Sonora); United States
06.	Paraujano	Venezuela
07.	PASTO: Camsá	Colombia
08.	PASTO: Ingano ("Inga", "Ingla")	Colombia
09.	Pawnee	United States (West Central)
10.	Paya	Honduras
11.	Piapoco	Venezuela
12.	Piegan (Peigan)	Canada; United States
13.	Pilaga	Argentina
14.	Pima	United States (South West)

215.	Pomo	United States (California)
216.	"Popolaca" (Popoloca?)	Mexico (Puebla)
217.	Popoluca	Mexico (Vera Cruz)
218.	Quechua	Bolivia; Ecuador; Peru
219.	QUECHUA: Alamas	Ecuador
220.	QUECHUA: Caranquis	Ecuador
221.	QUECHUA: Cayambe	Ecuador
222.	QUECHUA: Chibuleo	Ecuador
223.	QUECHUA: Gualacatas	Ecuador
224.	QUECHUA: Imantags	Ecuador
225.	QUECHUA: Mojandas	Ecuador
226.	QUECHUA: Otavalos	Ecuador
227.	QUECHUA: Oyacachis	Ecuador
228.	QUECHUA: Pujilies	Ecuador
229.	QUECHUA: Puruaes	Ecuador
230.	QUECHUA: Salasacas	Ecuador
231.	QUECHUA: Saraguros	Ecuador
232.	QUECHUA: Tocachis	Ecuador
233.	QUECHUA: Tocagones	Ecuador
234.	Quinault	United States (North West)
235.	Rama	Nicaragua
236.	"Sabobo" (Acaxee: Saboba?)	United States
237.	"Sac & Fox"	United States
	SAHAPTIN:	
238.	Tenino (*Warmsprings* Sahaptin)	United States (North West)
239.	Umatilla	United States (North West)
240.	Wallawalla	United States (North West)
241.	Yakima	United States (North West)
	SALISH, NORTH EASTERN (INTERIOR):	
242.	Lilloet	Canada
243.	Okanagan	Canada
244.	Shuswap	Canada
245.	Thompson	Canada
	SALISH, NORTH WESTERN (COAST):	
246.	Cowichan	Canada
247.	Squamish	Canada; United States
	SALISH, PUGET SOUND:	
248.	Lummi	United States (North West)
249.	Nisqualli	United States (North West)
250.	Nootsak ("Nooksak")	United States (North West)
251.	Snoqualmi	United States (North West)
252.	Songish	Canada
	SALISH, SOUTH EASTERN (INTERIOR):	
253.	Colville	United States (North West)
254.	Saliva	Venezuela
255.	SALIVA: Piaroa	Venezuela
256.	Sarsi (Sarcee)	Canada
257.	Sekani ("Sekam")	Canada
258.	Seminole	United States (South East)
259.	Seri	Mexico (Sonora)
260.	Shoco ("Cariris Choco")	Brazil
261.	Shoshone	United States

262.	Shuara (Jivaro)	Ecuador
263.	"Sierra"	United States
264.	Sikhs	Canada
265.	"Sioux"	Canada; United States
266.	Sirionó	Bolivia; Brazil
267.	Slave	Canada
268.	SLAVE: Dogrib	Canada
269.	"Steilacoom"	United States
270.	"Stello" (Stalo?)	United States
271.	Sumo	Honduras; Nicaragua
272.	Tacana	Argentina; Bolivia
273.	TALAMANCA: Bribri	Costa Rica
274.	TALAMANCA: Cabecar	Costa Rica
275.	TALAMANCA: Terraba ("Teribe")	Costa Rica; Panama
276.	Tanacross	Alaska
277.	Tanaina	Alaska
278.	Tanana	Alaska
279.	Tanana, Upper	Alaska
280.	Taos	United States (South West)
281.	Tapiete (Guasurango)	Paraguay
282.	Tarahumara	Mexico
283.	Tehuelche ("Tewelche")	Argentina
284.	"Tejas"	United States
285.	Tequistatec ("Chontal de Oaxaca")	Mexico
286.	Tewa	United States (South West)
287.	Tlingit	Alaska; Canada; United States
288.	Toba	Argentina
289.	Totonac	Mexico
290.	Trique	Mexico
291.	Tsimshian	Alaska; Canada
292.	TUCANO: Cubeo	Colombia
293.	TUCANO: Desana ("Desanos")	Colombia
294.	TUCANO: Uanano ("Guanano")	Colombia
295.	Tucuna (*Ticuna*)	Colombia; Peru
296.	"Tulalip"	United States
297.	TUPINAMBA: Potiguara	Brazil
298.	Tzeltal	Mexico
299.	Tzotzil	Mexico
300.	Ute, Southern	United States
301.	Wailaki ("Wailake")	United States (California)
302.	Waiwai	Guyana
303.	Wapishana ("Apishana")	Brazil; Guyana
304.	Warao (Warrau, Guarao, Guarauno)	Venezuela
305.	Washo[el]	United States (South West)
306.	Wichita	United States (South Central)
307.	Winnebago	United States (East Central)
308.	Witoto ("*Huitoto*")	Colombia
309.	Yagua	Peru
310.	Yahgan	Argentina (Tierra del Fuego)
311.	"Yanaigua"	Paraguay
312.	Yariqui	Ecuador
313.	Yaruro	Venezuela

314.	Yuco (Yuko, Yukpa)	Colombia; Venezuela
315.	Yuit ("Siberian Eskimo")	Alaska
	YUPIK (ESKIMO):	
316.	Central (Yuk)	Alaska
317.	Sugpiak	Alaska
318.	ZAMUCO: Moro ("Ayoré[o]")	Bolivia; Paraguay
319.	Zapotec	Mexico
320.	Zuni	United States (South West)

ASIA

Tribe or Minority   *Country or Area of Origin*

1.	"Adiyan"	India
2.	Aeta (Agta, Eta, Ita)	Philippines
3.	Agaria (Agariya)	India
4.	"Ahumes" (Ahom?)	India
5.	Ainu	Japan
6.	Ami	Taiwan
7.	"Ammareen" ("Iwainreen")	Jordan
8.	Andamanese	India
9.	Apayao	Philippines
10.	Arabs	
11.	Armenian	Turkey; U.S.S.R.; et al
12.	Ata	Philippines
13.	Atayal (Tayal, Taroko)	Taiwan
14.	Bagobo	Philippines
15.	BAGOBO: Gianga ("Guianga(n)")	Philippines
16.	Bagris (Baghris)	Pakistan
17.	BAHAU: Kayan	Malaysia
18.	BAHAU: Kenya(h)	Malaysia
19.	BALUCHI: "Hajina"	Pakistan
20.	BALUCHI: "Surabi"	Pakistan
21.	"Bana" (Bahnar?)	Vietnam
22.	"Bani Khaled"	Jordan
23.	"Baní Túrf"	Iran
24.	Banuauon ("Banaw-on", "Panaw-on")	Philippines
25.	Batak (Tinitian)	Philippines
26.	Batak	Sumatra
27.	"Belaits"	Malaysia
28.	Bengalis	India
29.	Bhil (Bhilala)	India
30.	BHIL: Merwari	Pakistan
31.	BHIL: Sindhi	Pakistan
32.	BHIL: Thari	Pakistan
33.	"Bhutia" (Bhotia?)	Sikkim
34.	Bilaan	Philippines
35.	"Bisaya"	Malaysia
36.	Black Thai (*Taidam*)	Laos, Vietnam
37.	Bontok, (Bontoc)	Philippines
38.	Buhid ("Bukid")	Philippines

39.	"Búkhárí"	Iran
40.	Bukidnon	Philippines
41.	Burukumin	Japan
42.	Cantonese	Hong Kong
43.	"Chabacano" (Zamboangueño?)	Philippines
44.	Chakma	Bangladesh
45.	Cham	Vietnam
46.	Chin	Burma
47.	Chodhara	India
48.	Chrau (*Tamun*)	Vietnam
49.	"Dangi"	India
50.	"Danu"	Burma
51.	D'babaon (Debabaon)	Philippines
52.	"Diango' ("Jango")	Philippines
53.	"Elianon"	Philippines
54.	"Erkala" (Eruka? Erku?)	India
55.	"Fuko"	Vietnam
56.	Gaddang ("Gaddung")	Philippines
57.	"Gadi" ("Gaddi")	India
58.	Garo	Bangladesh; India
59.	Gond	India
60.	GOND: Koi (*Koya*)	India
61.	GOND: Pardha ("*Pardhi*")	India
62.	Gurkha	India
63.	"Gurgala"	Pakistan
64.	"Gurung" ("Gurang")	Nepal; Sikkim
65.	Hanunoo ("Mangyan")	Philippines
66.	Ho	Laos
67.	"Hoti"	Pakistan
68.	"Ibaloy"	Philippines
69.	Iban (Sea Dayak)	Malaysia
70.	Ibanag (Kagayan)	Philippines
71.	Ifugao	Philippines
72.	Igorot	Philippines
73.	IGOROT: Kankanai (Kankanay)	Philippines
74.	Ilongot	Philippines
75.	"Imugan"	Philippines
76.	Iraya ("Mangyan")	Philippines
77.	Irula (*Irulur*)	India
78.	Isinai ("Isinay")	Philippines
79.	Jarai (Djarai)	Vietnam
80.	Jaunsar(y)	India
81.	Javanese	
82.	"Kábulí"	Afghanistan
83.	Kachari (Bodo, "*Boro*")	India
84.	"Kadiya"	India
85.	Kaili	Indonesia
86.	"Kalbeli" ("Kalbelia")	India
87.	Kalinga ("Kalingga")	Philippines
88.	Kannikaran	India
89.	Karen	Burma
90.	"Keput"	Malaysia

91.	"Kha" (Laotheung)	Laos
92.	"Khangar" (Kanjar?)	India
93.	Kharia	India
94.	Khasi	India
95.	Khmer (Kampuchean)	Thailand, et al.
96.	KLAMANTAN: Dusun ("*Kadazan*")	Brunei; Malaysia
97.	KLAMANTAN: Milanau (Melanau)	Malaysia
98.	KLAMANTAN: Murut	Malaysia
99.	Koho	Vietnam
100.	"Koki, Nagaland" (?Kuki?)	India
101.	"Kokna" ("Koukna")	India
102.	"Kokri" (Kokni?)	Pakistan
103.	"Kolha" ("Kolloh")	India
104.	Koli	India
105.	"Koli"	Pakistan
106.	"Kombi"	India
107.	KORKU (KORWA): Majhi	India
108.	Kota	India
109.	Kubu	Sumatra
110.	Kuki	Burma
111.	"Kuku, Manipur"	India
112.	"Kulmis"	India
113.	"Kurbas" (Kherwa? Korku (Korwa)?)	India
114.	Kurds	Pakistan
	KURDISH-SPEAKING TRIBES:	
115.	Gooran Iadegari	Iran
116.	Gooran-Khamooshi	Iran
117.	Gooran Shah-Ebrahimi	Iran
118.	Kalhor	Iran
119.	Khazai(e)	Iran
120.	Mamosh-Ghaderi	Iran
121.	Zarza	Iran
122.	Lambadi (Lambani)	India
123.	LAND DAYAK (BIDAYUH): Bau Jagoi	Malaysia
124.	LAND DAYAK (BIDAYUH): Biatah	Malaysia
125.	LAND DAYAK (BIDAYUH): Biratak	Malaysia
126.	LAND DAYAK (BIDAYUH): Bukar Sadong	Malaysia
127.	LAND DAYAK (BIDAYUH): Selakau (Lara)	Malaysia
128.	Lehri	Baluchistan
129.	Lepcha ("Rong")	Sikkim
130.	Limbu ("Limboo")	Nepal; Sikkim
131.	Lu(é)	Laos
132.	Lúr	Iran
133.	LÚR: "Bahmá'í"	Iran
134.	LÚR: Bakhtiari	Iran
135.	LÚR: "Boyer Ahmad"	Iran
136.	Lushai ("Lusai")	India
137.	"Mahar" ("Mhar") (Magar?)	India
138.	Malays	
139.	Maldivian	Sri Lanka
140.	"Malhi" (Mahli?)	Pakistan
141.	Mandaya	Philippines

142.	MANDAYA: Mansaka	Philippines
143.	MANGYAN, CENTRAL: Baribi	Philippines
144.	MANGYAN, CENTRAL: Pula	Philippines
145.	Manobo	Philippines
146.	"Marathas" ("Marathi?)	India
147.	"Maroma" ("Moroma") (Marma?)	Bangladesh
148.	"Mathura" (Mathuri?)	India
149.	"Mauser"	Thailand
150.	"Meghwari"	Pakistan
151.	Meithei (Manipuri)	India
152.	"Memalo"	Malaysia
153.	"Mengal"	Pakistan
154.	Menghwal	India; Pakistan
155.	Mentaweian	Mentawei Islands
156.	Meo (Hmong, Laoseung, Miao)	Laos; Thailand; Vietnam
157.	"Molbog"	Philippines
158.	"Mong[h]" (Marma Mogh)?)	Bangladesh
159.	MONGOL: Hazara (Hizárih)	Afghanistan
160.	"Morang"	Bangladesh
161.	MORO, COASTAL: Samal	Philippines
162.	MORO, INLAND: Maguindanao	Philippines
163.	MORO, INLAND: Maranao	Philippines
164.	"Murmur"	India
165.	NAGA: Angami	India
166.	NAGA: Ao	India
167.	NAGA: Kabui	India
168.	NAGA: Khiamagar (Khemungar, Kienmunjhan)	India
169.	NAGA: Konyak ("Konyab", "Koyab")	India
170.	NAGA: Mao	India
171.	NAGA: Rengma	India
172.	NAGA: Sangtam	India
173.	NAGA: Sema	India
174.	NAGA: Tangkhul	India
175.	"Newar"	Nepal
176.	Nung ("*Nhung*")	Vietnam
177.	Oraon ("Oraun"; Kurukh)	India
178.	"Pai" (Pai-á?)	Laos
179.	Paiwan ("Paywan")	Taiwan
180.	Palaumg ("Paluang")	Burma
181.	Pampangan	Philippines
182.	Paniyan	India
183.	Panjabi	
184.	"Paoú'o" ("Paoh", "Iaoh")	Burma
185.	Pashtun (Pushtún; Afghan)	Afghanistan
186.	"Pogot (Cagayan Aeta)"	Philippines
	PROTO-MALAY (TEMUAN BULANDA):	
187.	Jakun	Malaysia
188.	Semelai	Malaysia
189.	Temuan	Malaysia
190.	Punan (Inland Melanau)	Malaysia
191.	PUNAN (INLAND MELANAU): Bukitans	Malaysia

192.	"Putai" (Puthai? Phutai?)	Laos
193.	Qashgai	Iran
194.	"Qizilbásh"	Afghanistan
195.	"Rahulan"	India
196.	Raisani	Baluchistan
197.	Rajang	Malaysia
198.	Rajput	Pakistan
199.	"Rakhain" ("Rakhine", Arakanese)	Bangladesh
200.	Ratagnon	Philippines
201.	Rawat ("Ravat")	India
202.	Rhade	Vietnam
203.	"Rodiya"	Sri Lanka
204.	"Ronghai"	India
205.	"Sa'bi'ín"	Iran
206.	Sakai	Sumatra
207.	Santal (Santhal)	Bangladesh; India
208.	"Sebuyan" (Sebuyau?)	Malaysia
209.	SEMANG (NEGRITO): Jahai	Malaysia
210.	SEMANG (NEGRITO): Kensiev	Malaysia
211.	SEMANG (NEGRITO): Lanoh	Malaysia
212.	SENOI (SAKAI): Semai	Malaysia
213.	SENOI (SAKAI): Temiar	Malaysia
214.	Shan	Burma
215.	"Shetkai Varg"	India
216.	"Shikari"	Pakistan
217.	"Sholagar" ("Soligas"; Solaga?)	India
218.	"Sibri"	India
219.	Singhalese	Sri Lanka
220.	"Sino-Kadazan"	Malaysia
221.	"Skepan"	Malaysia
222.	Stieng ("Steng")	Vietnam
223.	"Sugalis"	India
224.	Tadzhik (Tadjik)	Afghanistan
225.	Tagabili	Philippines
226.	Tagbanua	Philippines
227.	TAGBANUA: Palawan[on]	Philippines
228.	"Talaingod"	Philippines
229.	"Tamang"	Nepal
230.	"Tanjong"	Malaysia
231.	"Thakur"	India
232.	Tharu	Nepal
233.	Tibetans	Bhutan; Sikkim
234.	Timorese	Timor
235.	Tinggian (Tinguian)	Philippines
236.	Tippera ("*Tipura*")	Bangladesh
237.	Tiruray	Philippines
238.	Toda	India
239.	Toradja	Celebes
240.	Turcoman (Turkmen)	Iran
	TURKI-SPEAKING TRIBES	
241.	Afshar	Iran
242.	Atesh Baig	Iran

243.	Chahar Dooli (Chardooli)	Iran
244.	Gharah-Choor-Loo	Azerbaijan
245.	Gharah-Papagh	Iran
246.	Soor Chi	Iran
247.	Tarom	Iran
248.	Tavaleshi	Iran
249.	"Turia" (Turi?)	Bangladesh
250.	"Tutong"	Malaysia
251.	"Vania"	Pakistan
252.	Vedda(s)	Sri Lanka
253.	Warli (Varli, "Worli")	India
254.	"Yadav"	Nepal
255.	Yami	Taiwan
256.	"Yang"	Thailand
257.	Yao	Laos; Thailand

AUSTRALASIA AND THE PACIFIC ISLANDS

	Tribe or Minority	*Country or Area of Origin*
1.	Abelam (Tshwosh)	Papua New Guinea (E. Sepik Dist.)
2.	ABORIGINES:	Australia
3.	Bunanditj (Drual gp)	(South Australia)
4.	Jirkla Minning	(Western Australia)
5.	Minen (Nyunga? Minang?)	(Western Australia)
6.	Narrogin	(South Australia)
7.	Ambrym, S.E.	Vanuatu (Ambrym Island)
8.	"Andilyaugwa"	Australia (Groote Island)
9.	Aneityum	Vanuatu (Aneityum Island)
10.	Angal (Mendi)	Papua New Guinea (S. Highlands)
11.	Anir [Feni Islanders]	Papua New Guinea
12.	Aniwa	Vanuatu (Aniwa Island)
13.	Aoba, North East	Vanuatu (Aoba Island)
14.	Aomie	Papua New Guinea (Northern Prov.)
15.	Arapesh, Mountain	Papua New Guinea (E. Sepik Dist.)
16.	"Arawe"	Papua New Guinea
17.	Asaro, Lower	Papua New Guinea (E. Highlands)
18.	Ata (Wasi)	Papua New Guinea (W. New Britain)
19.	Awin	Papua New Guinea (Western Dist.)
20.	Baimuru	Papua New Guinea (Gulf Dist.)
21.	Bakovi (Kove, Kombe)	Papua New Guinea (W. New Britain)
22.	Banaban	Fiji Islands (Ocean Island)
	BANKS ISLANDERS:	
23.	Mota Lava	Vanuatu (Banks Island)
24.	Vanua Lava	Vanuatu (Banks Island)
25.	Barai	Papua New Guinea (Central Dist.)
26.	Barok	Papua New Guinea (New Ireland)
27.	Bela	Papua New Guinea (W. New Britain)
28.	Belan Bilbil	Papua New Guinea (Madang Dist.)
29.	Belep Islander	New Caledonia
30.	Bellonese	Solomon Islands (Bellona Is.)

31.	Bena Bena	Papua New Guinea (E. Highlands)
32.	Bohutu	Papua New Guinea (Milne Bay Prov.)
33.	Buang	Papua New Guinea (Morobe Dist)
34.	Buin	Papua New Guinea (Bougainville I.)
35.	Buka	Papua New Guinea (N. Bougainville)
36.	Bukaua (Bukawa)	Papua New Guinea (Morobe Dist.)
37.	"Bush Pagan"	Solomon Islands
38.	Caledonian	New Caledonia
39.	Carteret Islanders	Papua New Guinea (Bougainville)
40.	Chamorro	Mariana Islands (Guam)
41.	Chimbu	Papua New Guinea
42.	Daga	Papua New Guinea (Milne Bay Prov.)
43.	Doromu	Papua New Guinea (Central Dist.)
44.	"Duke of Yorks"	Papua New Guinea (E. New Britain)
45.	Easter Islanders	Easter Islands
	EFATESE:	
46.	Erakor	Vanuatu (Efate)
47.	Fila	Vanuatu (Efate)
48.	Moso	Vanuatu (Efate)
49.	Nguna	Vanuatu (Efate)
50.	Pele	Vanuatu (Efate)
51.	Pango	Vanuatu (Efate)
52.	Elimbari	Papua New Guinea (Chimbu Pr.)
53.	Emae	Vanuatu (Emae Island)
54.	Enga	Papua New Guinea
55.	ENGA: Kyaka	Papua New Guinea
56.	Eromanga ("Erromango")	Vanuatu (Eromanga Island)
	ESPIRITU SANTO:	
57.	"Big Bay"	Vanuatu (Espiritu Santo)
58.	"Port Olry"	Vanuatu (Espiritu Santo)
59.	"Roria"	Vanuatu (Espiritu Santo)
60.	"Euronesians"	Fiji
61.	Fijian	Fiji
62.	Fore	Papua New Guinea (E. Highlands)
63.	Futuna (Erroman)	Vanuatu (Futuna)
64.	Futunian	New Caledonian (Futuna [Horn] Is.)
65.	Gadsup	Papua New Guinea (E. Highlands)
66.	Gahuka	Papua New Guinea (E. Highlands)
67.	"Gela" (Nggela?)	(Solomon Is.) (Florida Island?)
68.	Gidpa	Papua New Guinea (Western Dist.)
69.	Gilbertese	Kiribati (formerly Gilbert Is.)
70.	GOLIN: Gumine	Papua New Guinea (Chimbu)
71.	Guamanian	Mariana Is. (Guam)
	GUADALCANALIAN:	
72.	"Lambi Bay"	Solomon Islands (Guadalcanal)
73.	Tasimboko	Solomon Islands (Guadalcanal)
74.	Haura (Orokolo)	Papua New Guinea (Gulf Dist.)
75.	Hawaiian	Hawaii
76.	Iai	Papua New Guinea
77.	"Ibogu"	Papua New Guinea (S. Highlands)
78.	Ile des Pins	New Caledonia
79.	Junjan	Papua New Guinea

80.	Kairi	Papua New Guinea
81.	Kamare	Papua New Guinea (Gulf Dist.)
82.	Kamatai	Papua New Guinea
83.	Kamono-Kafe	Papua New Guinea (E. Highlands)
84.	Kapingamarangian	Eastern Caroline Islands
85.	Kara ("Karu")	Papua New Guinea (New Ireland)
86.	Keapara (Hula)	Papua New Guinea (Central Dist.)
87.	Kiari-Nomane	Papua New Guinea (Chimbu Dist.)
88.	Kikori (Kerewo)	Papua New Guinea (Gulf Dist.)
89.	Kilavila (Kiriwina)	Papua New Guinea (Milne Bay)
90.	Kilenge	Papua New Guinea
91.	Koiari, "Grass"	Papua New Guinea (Central Dist.)
92.	Koiari, "Mountain"	Papua New Guinea (Central Dist.)
93.	Koita	Papua New Guinea (Central Dist.)
94.	Kolombangara ("Gizo")	Solomon Islands (nr. New Georgia)
95.	Kora	Papua New Guinea
96.	Koriki	Papua New Guinea (Gulf Dist.)
97.	Kosraean (Kusiaean)	Eastern Caroline Islands
98.	Kouerga ("Kergoua")	New Caledonia
99.	"Kowai" (Kiwai?)	Papua New Guinea
100.	Kuman	Papua New Guinea (Chimbu Dist.)
101.	Kuot (Panaras)	Papua New Guinea (New Ireland)
102.	Kwale	Papua New Guinea (Central Dist.)
103.	Lau-Baluan-Pam	Papua New Guinea (Manus Is.)
	LIFUAN (LIFOUAN):	
104.	Mou-Xodré	Loyalty Islands (Lifu)
105.	Thouhaitch	Loyalty Islands (Lifu)
106.	Tingating	Loyalty Islands (Lifu)
107.	Wé	Loyalty Islands (Lifu)
	MALAITANS (MWALA):	
108.	AreAre	Solomon Islands (Malaita)
109.	Kwaio (Koio)	Solomon Islands (Malaita)
110.	Langalanga	Solomon Islands (Malaita)
111.	Lau	Solomon Islands (Malaita)
112.	Toqabaita (To'ambaita, etc.)	Solomon Islands (Malaita)
	MALEKULA (MALLICOLO):	
113.	Atchin	Vanuatu (Malekula)
114.	"Big Nambas"	Vanuatu (Malekula)
115.	Unua	Vanuatu (Malekula)
116.	Vao	Vanuatu (Malekula)
117.	Wala-Rano	Vanuatu (Malekula)
118.	Malo	Vanuatu (Malo Island)
119.	Managalas[i]	Papua New Guinea (Northern Prov.)
120.	Mandak	Papua New Guinea (New Ireland)
121.	Mangap	Papua New Guinea
	MAORI, New Zealand	
122.	Atihau (Whanganui)	New Zealand
123.	Ngati Awa	New Zealand
124.	Ngati Kahungunu	New Zealand
125.	Ngati Pikiao: Arawa	New Zealand
126.	Ngati Porou	New Zealand
127.	Ngati Raukawa	New Zealand

128.	Ngati Ruanui	New Zealand
129.	Ngati Toa	New Zealand
130.	Ngati Tuwharetoa	New Zealand
131.	Ngati Whatua	New Zealand
132.	Rongoehakaata	New Zealand
133.	Taipokerau: Nga Phui	New Zealand
134.	Tuhoe	New Zealand
135.	Maori, Rarotongan	Cook Islands
	MAREEN:	
136.	Hnawayetch	Loyalty Islands (Maré)
137.	La Roche	Loyalty Islands (Maré)
138.	Nakety	Loyalty Islands (Maré)
139.	Netché	Loyalty Islands (Maré)
140.	Roh	Loyalty Islands (Maré)
141.	Tadine	Loyalty Islands (Maré)
142.	Wakuari	Loyalty Islands (Maré)
143.	Maria	Papua New Guinea (Central Dist.)
144.	Marshallese	Marshall Islands
145.	Maskelyne Islander	Vanuatu (Maskelyne Island)
146.	Medlpa	Papua New Guinea (W. Highlands)
147.	Mekeo	Papua New Guinea (Central Dist.)
148.	Menyama	Papua New Guinea
149.	Midwahgi	Papua New Guinea (W. Highlands)
150.	Métis (French/Vietnamese)	New Caledonia
151.	Mikoruan	Papua New Guinea (Gulf Dist.)
152.	Mokilese	Eastern Caroline Islands
153.	Mortlockese (Marqueen, Marken)	Solomon Islands
154.	Mortlockese (Nomoi)	Eastern Caroline Islands
155.	Motu	Papua New Guinea (Central Dist.)
156.	MOTU: Toaripi	Papua New Guinea (Gulf Dist.)
157.	Move	Papua New Guinea (E. Highlands)
158.	Mumeng	Papua New Guinea (Morobe Prov.)
159.	Nalik	Papua New Guinea (New Ireland)
160.	Naroki	Papua New Guinea (W. Highlands)
161.	Nauruan	Kiribati; Nauru; Samoa
	NEW GEORGIAN:	
162.	Maravovo	Solomon Islands (New Georgia)
163.	Rendova	Solomon Islands (New Georgia)
164.	Viru Harbor	Solomon Islands (New Georgia)
165.	Ngatikese	Eastern Caroline Islands
166.	Niuean	Niue; New Zealand
167.	Notsi	Papua New Guinea (New Ireland)
168.	Nukuroan	Eastern Caroline Islands
169.	Ontong Java	Solomon Islands (Lord Howe Is.)
170.	Orokaiva	Papua New Guinea
171.	Paama	Vanuatu (Paama Island)
172.	Pak-Tong	Papua New Guinea (Manus Island)
173.	Palauan	Western Caroline Islands
174.	Pawaia[n]	Papua New Guinea (Chimbu, Gulf Prs.)

PENTECOSTANS:

175.	Central	Vanuatu (Pentecost Island)
176.	North	Vanuatu (Pentecost Island)
177.	South (Homo Bay)	Vanuatu (Pentecost Island)
178.	Petats	Papua New Guinea (Bougainville)
179.	Pingelapese	Eastern Caroline Islands
180.	Ponapean	Eastern Caroline Islands
181.	Port Olry	Vanuatu
182.	Pulawatese	Eastern Caroline Islands
183.	Rennellese	Solomon Islands
184.	Roro	Papua New Guinea (Central Dist.)
185.	Rotanese	Mariana Islands (Rota)
186.	Rotuman	Fiji Islands (Rotuma)
187.	Russell Islanders	Solomon Islands
188.	Samoans	Samoa
189.	"San Cristobal"	Solomon Islands
190.	Satawalese	Western Caroline Islands
191.	Savoese	Solomon Islands
192.	Siane ("Siyani")	Papua New Guinea (E. Highlands)
193.	Sikaianan	Solomon Is. (Sikiana=Stewart I.)
194.	Sinagoro	Papua New Guinea (Central Dist.)
195.	Sinasina	Papua New Guinea (Chimbu Prov.)
196.	Siuai ("*Siwai*")	Papua New Guinea (Bougainvialle)
197.	Sonsorolese	Western Caroline Islands
198.	Suau	Papua New Guinea (Milne Bay)
199.	Suki (Wiram)	Papua New Guinea (Western Dist.)
200.	Tabar	Papua New Guinea (New Ireland)
201.	Tahitian	Society Islands (Tahiti)

TANNA ISLANDERS:

202.	Imlao (Nvhal!)	Vanuatu (Tanna Island)
203.	Lenakel	Vanuatu (Tanna Island)
204.	Middle Bush	Vanuatu (Tanna Island)
205.	"North Tanna Islander"	Vanuatu (Tanna Island)
206.	"North West Tanna Islander"	Vanuatu (Tanna Island)
207.	Port Resolution (Kwamera?)	Vanuatu (Tanna Island)
208.	Siwi	Vanuatu (Tanna Island)
209.	"South West Tanna Islander"	Vanuatu (Tanna Island)
210.	Whitesands	Vanuatu (Tanna Island)
211.	Tauu (Mortlock Is.)	Papua New Guinea
212.	Tavio	Vanuatu (Epi Island)
213.	Tawara (Tavara)	Papua New Guinea (Milne Bay)
214.	Tebera	Papua New Guinea
215.	Thio	New Caledonia
216.	Tigak	Papua New Guinea (New Ireland)
217.	Tikopian	Tikopia
218.	Titan	Papua New Guinea (Manus Island)
219.	Tobian	Western Caroline Is. (Tobi)
220.	Tokelauans	Tokelau Islands
221.	Tolai (Kuanua)	Papua New Guinea (E. New Britain)
222.	Tongans	Tonga

223.	Tongoa, South-eastern	Vanuatu (Tongoa Island)
224.	Touho	New Caledonia
225.	Trukese	Caroline Islands; Mariana Islands
226.	Tumoan	Fiji
227.	Tuvaluan (formerly "Ellicean")	Tuvalu (formerly Ellice Islands)
228.	Ulithian	Western Caroline Islands
229.	Unama	Papua New Guinea (Gulf Dist.)
	UVEAN (OUVÉAN)	
230.	Banout	Loyalty Islands (Uvéa)
231.	Fayaoue	Loyalty Islands (Uvéa)
232.	Velerupu	Papua New Guinea
233.	Vella Lavella	Solomon Islands
234.	Wallisian	New Caledonia (Wallis Is.)
235.	Wampar	Papua New Guinea (Morobe Dist.)
236.	Wedau	Papua New Guinea (Milne Bay)
237.	Woleanian	Western Caroline Islands
238.	Yabim (Jabim)	Papua New Guinea (Morobe Dist.)
239.	Yabuyufa	Papua New Guinea (E. Highlands)
240.	Yagaria	Papua New Guinea (E. Highlands)
241.	Yapese	Western Caroline Islands
242.	Yare	Papua New Guinea (Gulf Dist.)
243.	Yaté (Iaté)	New Caledonia
244.	Yareba	Papua New Guinea (Northern Prov.)
245.	"Ysabel"	Solomon Islands (Santa Isabel)
246.	Yungum	Papua New Guinea

APPENDIX III

LANGUAGES AND DIALECTS INTO WHICH BAHÁ'Í WORKS HAVE BEEN TRANSLATED

AFRICA

Language/Dialect	*Where Spoken*
1. Adangme	Ghana
2. Afrikaans	South Africa
3. Akan: Asante dialect	Ghana
4. Akan: Fante dialect	Ghana
5. Akan: Twi (Akwapem) dialect	Ghana
6. Akoli (Acholi)	Sudan; Uganda
7. Alur	Uganda
8. Amharic (Amarigna)	Ethiopia
9. Amharic: Braille text	Ethiopia
10. Anyi: Baule dialect	Ivory Coast
11. Anyi: "Yaouré" ("Yahore") dialect	Ivory Coast
12. Arabic: Chadian dialect	Chad
13. Asu (Pare; Kipare)	Tanzania
14. Awing	Cameroons
15. "Bakuba"	Zaire
16. Bambara	Mali; Sénégal; Upper Volta
17. Bamoun	Cameroons
18. Bargu (Bariba)	Benin; Nigeria; Togo
19. "Basoundi"	Congo
20. Bassa (Gbasa)	Liberia
21. Bassa (Koko; Mvele)	Cameroons
22. e-Beembe (Kibembe)	Zaire; Zambia
23. ici-Bemba (Wemba)	Zaire; Zambia
24. Berba	Benin
25. Bete	Ivory Coast
26. Bini (Edo)	Nigeria
27. Bobo (Bwamou)	Upper Volta
28. Bulu (Boulou)	Cameroons
29. Chagga: ki-Mashami dialect	Tanzania
30. Chagga: Vunjo dialect	Tanzania
31. Chiripon-Lete-Anum (Cherepong)	Ghana
32. Ciokwe (Chokwe)	Angola; Zaire
33. Creole, Indian Ocean	Mauritius; Réunion; Seychelles
34. Dagbani (Dagbane)	Ghana; Togo
35. Dan (Gio; Yacouba)	Ivory Coast; Liberia
36. Dan: Ngere (Guéré) dialect	Ivory Coast
37. "Dinka (Jieng)"	Sudan
38. Diola (Jola): Fogny dialect (Jóola Fóoni)	The Gambia; Guinea; Sénégal
39. Diola (Jola): Kasa dialect	The Gambia
40. Duala (Douala)	Cameroons
41. Dyula (Jula)	Upper Volta
42. Efik	Cameroons; Nigeria
43. Ekoi: Ejagham dialect	Cameroons; Nigeria

44.	Ewe: Adja dialect	Benin
45.	Ewe: Ge (Mina) dialect	Benin; Niger; Togo
46.	Ewe: Watyi (Ouatchi, Waci) dialect	Benin; Togo
47.	Ewondo ("Yaounde")	Cameroons
48.	"Fadambo"	Anabon Island
49.	Fo (Fon; Dahoméen)	Benin
50.	Frafra	Ghana
51.	Ful (Fula; Fulani; Peulh)	West & Upper West Africa
52.	Ful: Adamawa dialect	Cameroons; Nigeria
53.	Ful: West African dialect	Mali; Guinea; etc.
54.	Ful: Torado dialect	Sénégal
55.	Ga: Accra dialect	Ghana
56.	Gambai (Sara-Ngambaye)	Chad
57.	olu-Ganda (Luganda)	Uganda
58.	Gbaya (Baya)	Central African Rep.; Cameroons; Congo
59.	"Goun"	Benin
60.	Grebo	Liberia
61.	Guan	Ghana
62.	Gurma (Gourmantche)	Togo; Upper Volta
63.	eke-Gusii (Kisii)	Kenya
64.	lu-Gwere (Lugwere)	Uganda
65.	G//wi(khwe) (!Kwi)	Botswana
66.	Hausa: Arabic script	West Central Africa
67.	Hausa: Eastern (Kano) dialect	West Central Africa
68.	Hausa: Western (Sokoto) dialect	West Central Africa
69.	Hausa: "Zazzau (Zaria)" dialect	West Central Africa
70.	Herero (Otjiherero)	South West Africa/Namibia
71.	Hoa	Botswana
72.	Hua (!xo)	Botswana
73.	Igbo (Ibo; Igho)	Nigeria
74.	Ijo (Ijaw)	Nigeria
75.	Kaba (Sara Kaba)	Central African Rep.; Chad
76.	Kabre (*Kabye*)	Togo
77.	Kabyle	Algeria
78.	ke-Kamba (Kikamba)	Kenya
79.	Kanuri	Chad; Niger; Nigeria
80.	Karamojong	Uganda
81.	Kasem (Kasseme; Kasena)	Ghana; Upper Volta
82.	Kefa (Kaffa; Kaffigna)	Ethiopia
83.	e-Kele (Lokele)	Zaire
84.	di-Kele: Ngom ("Bungom") dialect	Gabon
85.	Kenga	Chad
86.	"Keponnon"	Congo
87.	Kikuyu	Kenya
88.	Kim	Central African Rep.; Chad
89.	"Kimpin/Kipindi"	Zaire
90.	Kombe	Equatorial Guinea
91.	Komoro (Comorian)	Comoro Islands
92.	Kongo (Kikongo)	Angola; Congo; Zaire
93.	Kongo: Kimanianga dialect	Zaire
94.	Kongo: Laadi (Balari, Kilari) dial.	Congo; Gabon
95.	Kongo: ki-Ntaandu (Kintandu) dial.	Zaire

96.	Kongo: ki-Zombo dialect	Angola; Zaire
97.	olu-Konzo (Lukonjo)	Uganda; Zaire
98.	ra-Kpa (Bafia)	Cameroons
99.	Kpelle	Guinea; Liberia
100.	Krio	West Africa
101.	"Kru"	Liberia
102.	Kumam	Uganda
103.	Kunama	Ethiopia; Sudan
104.	Kusal (Kusaal)	Ghana; Upper Volta
105.	Kawkum (Bakoum)	Cameroons
106.	oci-Kwanyama (Kuanjama; Ovambo)	Angola; South West Africa/Namibia
107.	Kweni (Gouro)	Ivory Coast
108.	Lamba	Togo
109.	Lendu	Uganda, Zaire
110.	Logo (Logoti)	Sudan; Zaire
111.	Logooli (Luragoli; Maragoli)	Kenya
112.	Losengo: Mangala (Lingala) dialect	Zaire
113.	si-Lozi	Zambia
114.	ki-Luba-Katanga (Shaba)	Zaire
115.	Luba-Lulua (Tshiluba; Ciluba)	Zaire
116.	Luba-Lulua: Luba-Kasai dialect (Tshiluba of Kasai)	Zaire
117.	Lugbara	Uganda; Zaire
118.	Luhya: "Kabras" dialect	Kenya
119.	Luhya: lu-Maraci (Olumarachi) dialect	Kenya
120.	Luhya: lu-Tiriki dialect	Kenya
121.	ci-Lunda	Angola; Zaire; Zambia
122.	ci-Lunda: Ndembo dialect	Zaire
123.	Luo (DhoLuo)	Kenya; Tanzania
124.	ki-Luuwa (Kiluwa)	Zaire
125.	Lwo	Sudan/Uganda
126.	Lyele (Lele; L'élé)	Upper Volta
127.	Il-Maasai	Kenya; Tanzania
128.	Madi	Sudan; Uganda
129.	Maka (Makaa)	Cameroons
130.	ci-Makonde ("Shimakonde")	Mozambique; Tanzania
131.	i-Makua (Makhuwa)	Malawi; Mozambique
132.	Malagasy	Madagascar
133.	Mandankwe	Cameroons
134.	Mandinka: Arabic script	West & Upper West Africa
135.	Mandinka: Latin script	West & Upper West Africa
136.	Mano	Guinea; Liberia
137.	Masa (Massa)	Chad; Cameroons
138.	Masaba (Lumasaba): ulu-Bukusu dialect	Kenya; Uganda
139.	Masaba (Lumasaba): lu-Gisu dialect	Uganda
140.	Mashi	Zaire; Zambia
141.	Mbai (Mbaye)	Chad
142.	"M'Baka"	Central African Rep.
143.	Mbosi (Mboshi)	Congo
144.	Mbundu (Kimbundu)	Angola
145.	i-Mbuti: Batua (Lutua-Bambote) dialect	Zaire
146.	Mbuun ("Embun"; Mbunda)	Zaire

147.	Mende: Kpa dialect	Sierra Leone
148.	ke-Mero (Kimeru; Meru)	Kenya
149.	Moba	Ghana; Togo; Upper Volta
150.	Mongo-Nkundo: Ekondo Mongo (Lomongo) dial.	Zaire
151.	More (Mossi)	Ghana; Togo; Upper Volta
152.	Nama: Damara dialect	South West Africa/Namibia
153.	Nandi	Kenya; Tanzania; Uganda
154.	Nandi: Kipsigis dialect	Kenya
155.	Nandi: Sapiny (Sebei) dialect	
156.	Nankanse (Nankani)	Ghana; Upper Volta
157.	isi-Ndebele (Sindebele)	Zimbabwe
158.	ci-Ndonde ("Kimawanda")	Tanzania
159.	oci-Ndonga (Ambo; Ochindonga)	South West Africa/Namibia
160.	Ngombe (li-Ngombe)	Zaire
161.	Nguni: isi-Swati (Siswati; Swazi) dialect	Swaziland; South Africa
162.	Nguni: isi-Xhosa (!Xhosa; Kaffir)	Botswana; Transkei; South Africa
163.	Nguni: Zulu dialect	South Africa
164.	Nika: Giryama (Giriama) dialect	Kenya; Tanzania
165.	"Nubian"	Sudan
166.	ki-Nyakyusa	Tanzania
167.	ki-Nyakyusa: Ngonde (Konde) dialect	Malawi; Tanzania
168.	ki-Nyamwesi	Tanzania
169.	Nyang (Kenyang)	Cameroons
170.	ci-Nyanja	Malawi; Zambia
171.	ci-Nyanja: ci-Cewa (Chichewa) dialect	Malawi; Zambia
172.	olu-Nyole (Lunyore)	Kenya
173.	oru-Nyoro (Runyoro-Rutoro)	Uganda
174.	Oromigna (Galla; Galligna)	Ethiopia; Kenya
175.	Pokot (Suk)	Kenya; Uganda
176.	Riff (Tarifit)	Algeria; Morocco
177.	shi-Ronga (Shironga)	Mozambique; South Africa
178.	Ruanda (Kinyarwanda)	Rwanda
179.	iki-Rundi	Burundi
180.	"Runyankole-Rukiga"	Uganda
181.	olu-Saamia (Lusamia)	Uganda
182.	Sango	Central African Rep.; Chad; Congo
183.	Sara: Sara-Majingai dialect	Central African Rep.; Chad
184.	Sara: Sara Ngama dialect	Central African Rep.; Chad
185.	Serer (Serere)	The Gambia; Sénégal
186.	Shilha ("Shluh")	Algeria; Morocco
187.	Shilluk (Sholuk)	Ethiopia; Sudan
188.	Shona	Mozambique; Zimbabwe
189.	Shona: Kalaka ("Kalanga") dialect	Botswana
190.	Shua (Shuakhwe)	Botswana
191.	Sidamo (Sidamigna)	Ethiopia
192.	Somali	Somalia
193.	Somba: Niende ("Gniandé") dialect	Benin; Togo
194.	lu-Songe (Kisonge)	Zaire
195.	Songhai: Dendi dialect	Upper West Africa
196.	Songhai: Songhai dialect	Upper West Africa
197.	Songhai: Zarma (Djerma) dialect	Niger; Nigeria

198.	Sotho, Northern (se-Pedi)	South Africa
199.	Sotho, Southern (se-Sotho)	Lesotho; South Africa
200.	ki-Sukuma	Tanzania
201.	Susu	Guinea; Sierra Leone
202.	Swahili	East & Central Africa
203.	Swahili: "Mashingoli" dialect	Somalia
204.	Swahili: ci-Miini ("Bravanese") dialect	Somalia
205.	Taita	Kenya
206.	Tamazight	Algeria; Libya; Mali; Morocco; Nigeria
207.	Teke, Central ("Batéké"): Nziku dialect	Congo
208.	Temen (Temne)	Sierra Leone
209.	Teso (Ateso)	Kenya; Uganda
210.	Tigrinya	Ethiopia
211.	Tiv	Nigeria
212.	Tobote (Busari, Bassar)	Ghana; Togo
213.	ci-Tonga, Malawian (Kitonga; Siska)	Malawi
214.	ci-Tonga, Zambian (Plateau Tonga)	Zambia
215.	ki-Tuba: Monokutuba dialect	Zaire
216.	shi-Tsonga (Shangaan)	Mozambique; South Africa
217.	shi-Tsonga: "Phikhani" dialect	Mozambique
218.	se-Tswana	Botswana; South Africa; Zimbabwe
219.	Tumbuka (ci-Tumbuka)	Malawi; Tanzania; Zambia
220.	Tumbuka; Kamanga (Henga) dialect	Zambia
221.	Tupuri	Cameroons; Chad
222.	Wescos (Cameroonian Pidgin)	West Africa
223.	Wolof (Jolof; Oulof): Classical	Gambia; Mauritania; Sénégal
224.	Wolof: "popular Sénégalese" dialect	Sénégal
225.	ci-Yao	Malawi; Mozambique; Tanzania
226.	Yoruba	Benin; Nigeria; Togo
227.	Zande	Central African Rep.; Congo; Sudan; Zaire
228.	ki-Zaramo	Tanzania
229.	olu-Ziba (olu-Haya)	Tanzania

THE AMERICAS

	Language/Dialect	*Where Spoken*
1.	Aguacateco	Guatemala
2.	Alacaluf	Chile
3.	Aleut: Eastern dialect	Alaska
4.	Amuesha	Peru
5.	Apache: Mescalero dialect	United States
6.	Amuzgo	Mexico
7.	"Araucan"	Colombia
8.	"Arhuaco"	Colombia
9.	Ashushlay (Chulupi)	Paraguay
10.	Aymará	Bolivia; Peru
11.	Bauré	Bolivia
12.	Blackfoot	Canada; United States
13.	Bribri	Costa Rica; Panama

14.	Cakchiquel	Guatemala
15.	Campa	Peru
16.	Carib: Galibi (Carina, Karinja) dial.	Guyana; Venezuela
17.	"Carib: Moreno"	Honduras
18.	Carib, Island ("Caribe")	Honduras
19.	Catio	Colombia; Venezuela
20.	Cayapa	Ecuador
21.	Cherokee	United States
22.	Chinantec: dialect of Ayotzintepec	Mexico
23.	Chinantec: dialect of Mano Marquez	Mexico
24.	Chinantec: dialect of Usila	Mexico
25.	Chinantec: dialect of Valle Nacional	Mexico
26.	Chipaya (Pukina)	Bolivia
27.	Chipewyan: Slave (Slavey) dialect	Canada
28.	"Chiquitano"	Bolivia
29.	"Choco: Colombian"	Colombia
30.	"Choco: Panamanian"	Panama
31.	Chortí	Guatemala
32.	Chujean	Guatemala
33.	Cocopa	United States
34.	Conibo: Shipibo dialect	Peru
35.	Cree	Canada
36.	Creole, Haitian (Criole)	Haiti
37.	Creole, Lesser Antilles: Guadelupéen dial.	Guadeloupe
38.	Creole, Lesser Antilles: Martiniquais dial.	Martinique
39.	Cubeo	Brazil; Colombia
40.	Cuicatec	Mexico
41.	Cuna (Kuna)	Panama (San Blas Islands)
42.	Dakota (Sioux): Lakota dialect	United States
43.	Diegueno ("Kum-Yíy")	Mexico; United States
44.	Garifuna	Belize
45.	Guajibo	Colombia; Venezuela
46.	Guajiro	Colombia; Venezuela
47.	Guaymí	Panama
48.	Haida	Alaska; Canada
49.	Huave	Mexico
50.	Inuit (Inupiaq): Barren Grounds dialect (Latin script)	Canada
51.	Inuit (Inupiaq): Barren Grounds dialect (Eastern Arctic Syllabics script)	Canada
52.	Inuit (Inupiaq): Barrow ("North Slope") d.	Alaska
53.	Inuit (Inupiaq): Keewatin dialect	Canada
54.	Inuit (Inupiaq): Kobuk (Kotzebue) dialect	Alaska
55.	Inuit (Inupiaq): Seward Peninsula (Diomed)	Alaska
56.	Inuit (Inupiaq): Southern Baffin dialect (Eastern Arctic Syllabics script)	Canada
57.	Jicaque (Xicaque)	Honduras
58.	Kalispel (Salish): Flathead dialect	United States
59.	Kanjobal	Guatemala
60.	Kekchí	Belize; Guatemala
61.	Koyukon	Alaska
62.	Kuchin (Kutchin)	Alaska

63.	Kuchin (Kutchin): Fort Yukon dialect	Alaska
64.	Kuchin (Kutchin): Loucheux dialect	Canada
65.	Lokono (Continental Arawak)	French Guiana; Guyana; Suriname
66.	Machiguenga	Peru
67.	Macu (Maco)	Venezuela
68.	Mam	Guatemala; Mexico
69.	Mapuche	Argentina; Chile
70.	Mapuche: "Chilean dialect"	Chile
71.	Masco: Huachipairi (Amaracaeri) dialect	Peru
72.	Mascoy: Lengua dialect	Paraguay
73.	Mataco	Argentina; Bolivia; Paraguay
74.	Maya	Belize; Guatemala; Mexico
75.	Maya: Mopan dialect	Belize; Guatemala
76.	Mazatec: dial. of San Antonio Eloxochitlan	Mexico
77.	Mbaya-Guiacurú: Payaguá (Lengua) dial. ("Toba Lengua")	Paraguay
78.	Menomini	United States
79.	Micmac	Canada
80.	Miskito: Honduran dialect	Honduras
81.	Miskito: Nicaraguan dialect	Nicaragua
82.	Mixe: dialect of Zacatal	Mexico
83.	Mixe: dialect of Zacatepec	Mexico
84.	Mixtec: dialect of San Antonio Huitepec, Zaachila	Mexico
85.	Mixtec: dialect of San Miguel Piedras, Nochistlan	Mexico
86.	Mixtec: "de la Canada"	Mexico
87.	Mixtec: "de la Costa" (Pinotepa Nacional)	Mexico
88.	Mixtec: "de la Mixteca Alta" (Tlaxiaco Dist.)	Mexico
89.	Mixtec: "de la Mixteca Baja" (Nochistlan D.)	Mexico
90.	Mocoví	Argentina
91.	Mohawk	Canada; United States
92.	Mono (Monachi)	United States
93.	"Motilon"	Colombia; Venezuela
94.	Moxo: Trinitarios dialect	Bolivia; Brazil; Paraguay
95.	Nahua (Nahuatl; "Aztec")	Mexico
96.	Navajo	United States
97.	Ojibwa (Chippewa): Mississagi dialect	Canada
98.	Ojibwa (Chippewa): Salteaux dialect	Canada; United States
99.	Ojibwa (Chippewa): Woodlands dialect	Canada; United States
00.	Oneida	United States
01.	Otomi	Mexico
02.	Otomi: dialect of Amealco	Mexico
03.	Paez	Colombia
04.	Paiute, Southern: Ute dialect	United States
05.	Papiamento	Aruba; Bonaire; Curacao
06.	Patois	Windward Islands
07.	Paya	Honduras
08.	Piaroa	Venezuela
09.	Pima: Papago dialect	United States
10.	Piro	Peru
11.	Pokonchi (Pocomchi)	Guatemala

112.	Quechua: unspecified Bolivian dialect	Bolivia
113.	Quechua: Cuzqueno dialect	Peru
114.	Quechua: unspecified Ecuadorian dialect	Ecuador
115.	Quiché	Guatemala; Mexico
116.	Rama	Nicaragua
117.	Salish, Puget Sound	United States
118.	Saramaccan	Suriname
119.	Shoshoni (Shoshone)	United States
120.	Shuara (Jivaro)	Ecuador; Peru
121.	Shuara (Jivaro): Aguaruna dialect	Ecuador; Peru
122.	Sirionó	Bolivia
123.	Sranan (Sranan Tongo; Surinamese; Taki-Taki)	Suriname
124.	Sumo: Musawas dialect	Honduras; Nicaragua
125.	Sumo: Twahka dialect	Nicaragua
126.	"Tacana"	Bolivia
127.	Tanaina: Kenai dialect	Alaska
128.	Tanana	Alaska
129.	Tanana: Tanacross dialect	Alaska
130.	Tarascan	Mexico
131.	Tewa: Santa Clara Pueblo dialect	United States
132.	Tlingit	Alaska; Canada
133.	Toba	Argentina
134.	Tucuna (Ticuna)	Brazil; Colombia; Peru
135.	Tupi: Chiriguano (Chahuanco) dialect	Argentina; Bolivia
136.	Tupi: Guarani dialect	Argentina; Brazil; Paraguay
137.	Tupi: "Classical Guarani"	
138.	Tupi: Guarayú ("Guarayo") dialect	Bolivia
139.	Tzeltal	Mexico
140.	Uapichana (Wapishanna)	Brazil; Guyana
141.	Uspanteca	Guatemala
142.	Yagua	Brazil; Colombia; Peru
143.	Yaqui	Mexico; United States
144.	Yaruro	Venezuela
145.	"Yukpa"	Colombia; Venezuela
146.	Yupik, Central Alaskan: Kuskokwim dialect	Alaska
147.	Yupik, Central Alaskan: Yuk dialect	Alaska
148.	Yupik, St. Lawrence Island	Alaska
149.	Zamucoan; Northern (Ayoré, Ayoréo)	Bolivia; Paraguay
150.	Zapotec: dialect of Betaza, Villa Alta	Mexico
151.	Zapotec: "del Istmo" (Tehuantepec, Juchitlan)	Mexico
152.	Zapotec: dialect of Lachigolóo	Mexico
153.	Zapotec: dialect of Mitla, Tlocolula Dist.	Mexico
154.	Zapotec: d. of San Juan Tagui, Villa Alta	Mexico
155.	Zapotec: "de la Sierra" (Ixtlan District)	Mexico
156.	Zapotec: "de la Sierra" (Villa Hidalgo)	Mexico
157.	Zapotec: "del Sur" (Pochutla District)	Mexico
158.	Zapotec: "del Sur" (San Pedro Mixtepec)	Mexico
159.	Zapotec: "del Sur" (San Vicente Cuatlan)	Mexico
160.	Zapotec: dialect of Tlalixtac	Mexico
161.	Zapotec: "del Valle" (San Baltazar Chichicapan)	Mexico
162.	Zapotec: dialect of Zoquiapan	Mexico
163.	Zoque	Mexico

APPENDIX III–Continued

ASIA

	Language/Dialect	*Where Spoken*
1.	Adi (Abor Miri)	India
2.	"Aeta"	Philippines
3.	Agusan Manobo	Philippines
4.	Aklanon	Philippines
5.	Alangan	Philippines
6.	Arabic	
7.	Aramaic, East: "Assyrian" dialect	Iraq; Syria; et al.
8.	Armenian	Turkey; U.S.S.R.; et al.
9.	Azerbaijani (Azeri): Persian script	Iran; Soviet Azerbaijan
10.	Bagobo: Gianga dialect	Philippines
11.	Bahnar	Vietnam
12.	Bajau	Celebes; Sulu Arch.; Borneo
13.	Balinese	Bali
14.	Balochi (Baluchi)	Baluchistan
15.	"Batak"	Sumatra
16.	Bengali	Bangladesh; India
17.	Bengali: Assamese dialect	N.E. India
18.	"Benguet"	Philippines
19.	Bihari: Bhojpuri dialect	India
20.	Bihari: Maithili dialect	India
21.	Bihari: Tharu dialect	Nepal
22.	Bikol (Bicol; Bikolano)	Philippines
23.	Bilaan	Philippines
24.	Bisaya	Borneo; Brunei; Sarawak
25.	Bontok ("Bonyoc")	Philippines
26.	Brahui	Baluchistan
27.	Buginese	Celebes
28.	Bukidnon	Philippines
29.	Burmese	Burma; Bangladesh
30.	Buru (Masarete)	Indonesia
31.	Car	Nicobar Islands
32.	"Cham"	Kampuchea; Vietnam
33.	"Chin"	Burma
34.	Chinese, Classical	
35.	Chinese, Modern	
36.	Cuyunon	Philippines
37.	Dayak, Land ("Bidayuh"): Bukar Sadong d.	Borneo; Sarawak
38.	Dayak, Land ("Bidayuh"): Jagoi (Biratak) d.	Borneo; Sarawak
39.	Dayak, Sea (Iban)	Borneo: Sarawak
40.	Dusun (Kadazan): Penampang dialect	Sabah
41.	Gaddang	Philippines
42.	Garhwali	India
43.	Georgian	Soviet Georgia; et al.
44.	Gondi: Bethul dialect	India

45.	Gujarati	India
46.	Hantik (Antiqueno)	Philippines
47.	Hanunóo	Philippines
48.	Hebrew	
49.	Hindi, Eastern: Bagheli (Baghelkandi) d.	India
50.	Hindi, Eastern: Chhatishgarhi dialect	India; Nepal
51.	Hindi, Western (Hindi; "Hindustani")	India; Africa; Americas; Fiji
52.	Ibanag	Philippines
53.	Ilocano	Philippines
54.	Ilonggo (Hiligaynon)	Philippines
55.	Jahai	Malaysia; Thailand
56.	Jakun	Malaysia
57.	Japanese	
58.	Japanese: Braille text	
59.	Japanese: Katakana script	Caroline Islands
60.	Javanese	Indonesia
61.	Kalinga	Philippines
62.	"Kalingga-Apayao"	Philippines
63.	Kankanay	Philippines
64.	Kannada (Kanarese)	India
65.	Kannada (Kanarese): Badaga dialect	India
66.	"Karen"	Burma; Thailand
67.	Kashmiri	India; Pakistan
68.	Kazakh: Cyrillic script	Kazakhstan; et al.
69.	Kazakh: Latin script	Kazakhstan et al.
70.	Kayan	Borneo; Sarawak
71.	Kenyah	Borneo; Sarwak
72.	Khalka (Mongolian): Cyrillic script	Mongolia
73.	Khalka (Mongolian): local script	Mongolia
74.	Khandesi: Dangi dialect	India
75.	Khasi	India
76.	Khmer (Cambodian)	Kampuchea; Thailand; Vietnam; et al.
77.	Kinaraya	Philippines
78.	Korean	Korea; China; Japan
79.	Kui (Khondi)	India
80.	Kumauni	India; Nepal
81.	Kurdish	Kurdistan; et al.
82.	Lao (Laotian)	Laos; Thailand; et al.
83.	Lepcha	Bhutan; India; Nepal
84.	Madurese	Indonesia
85.	Malay ("Bahasa Malaysia")	Malaysia
86.	Malay: Arabic script (Djawi)	Malaysia
87.	Malay: "Bahasa Indonesia" dialect	Indonesia
88.	Malayalam	India; incl. Laccadive Is.
89.	Maldivian (Divehi Bas): Divehi script	Maldives; Minicoy Island
90.	Maldivian (Divehi Bas): Latin scrip	Maldives; Minicoy Island
91.	"Manchurian"	Manchuria
92.	"Manobo"	Philippines
93.	Marathi (Maharatti)	India
94.	Marathi: Konkani dialect	India
95.	Meithei (Manipuri)	India
96.	Melanau: Mukah dialect	Sarawak

97.	Melanau: Oya/Dalat dialect	Sarawak
98.	Mentawei	Mentawei Islands
99.	Meo	China; Laos. Thailand; Vietnam; et al.
100.	Murut, Sarawak ("Lun Dayah")	Borneo; Sarawak
101.	Nepali (Nepalese)	Nepal
102.	Newari	Nepal
103.	Nias	Nias & Batu Islands
104.	Oriya	India
105.	Oriya: Halbi dialect	India
106.	Ossetic	U.S.S.R.
107.	Pahari, Western: Jaunsari dialect	India
108.	Palawanon	Philippines
109.	Pali (Buddhist scriptural language)	
110.	Palu (Kaili)	Celebes
111.	Pampangan	Philippines
112.	Pangasinan	Philippines
113.	Panjabi (Punjabi): Gurmukhi script	India; Pakistan
114.	Panjabi (Punjabi): Persian script	India; Pakistan
115.	Pashto (Pushtu)	Afghanistan; Pakistan
116.	Persian (Farsi)	Iran; et al.
117.	Persian: Hebrew script (Judeo-Persian)	
118.	Portuguese, Malacca Creole (Papia Kristang)	Malaysia
119.	Pula	Philippines
120.	Rade (Rhade)	Kampuchea; Vietnam
121.	Rajasthani	India; Pakistan
122.	Rajasthani: Gujuri dialect	India; Pakistan
123.	Rajasthani: Lambadi (Lambani) dialect	India
124.	Rajasthani: Malvi dialect	India
125.	Rajasthani: Marwari dialect	India; Pakistan
126.	Samal	Philippines
127.	Sambali: "Botolan (Aeta)" dialect	Philippines
128.	Sanskrit	India
129.	Santali: Bengali script	India
130.	Santali: Oriya script	India
131.	Sebuano (Cebuano)	Philippines
132.	Semai	Malaysia
133.	Semelai	Malaysia
134.	Sindhi	India; Pakistan
135.	Sinhalese	Sri Lanka
136.	Sundanese	Java
137.	Tagalog (Filipino)	Philippines
138.	Tagbanua	Philippines
139.	Tai Noir (Black Tai; Taidam)	Laos; Vietnam
140.	Talaud	Talaud Islands
141.	Tamil	India; Sri Lanka; et al.
142.	Tatar	U.S.S.R.
143.	Taw Sug (Joalano Sulu)	Borneo; Philippines
144.	Telugu	India
145.	Temiar	Malaysia
146.	Temuan	Malaysia
147.	Tettum (Tetum)	Timor Island
148.	Thai	Thailand

149.	Thô	Vietnam
150.	Tibetan, Central: Lhasa (Dbus) dialect	India; Tibet
151.	Tibetan, West: Balti dialect	Baltistan
152.	Tibetan, West: Ladakhi dialect	India; Tibet
153.	Tiruray	Philippines
154.	Toradja	Celebes
155.	Tripuri ("Kok-Borok")	India
156.	Tulu	India
157.	Turkish	Cyprus; Turkey; et al.
158.	Turkish: Arabic script ("Ottoman Turkish")	
159.	Turkmen (Turkoman)	Turkmenistan
160.	Urdu	India; Pakistan
161.	Vietnamese	Vietnam; et al.
162.	Waray (Samar-Leyte; Samareno)	Philippines

AUSTRALASIA AND THE PACIFIC

	Language/Dialect	*Where Spoken*
1.	Akei (Navaka; Tasmalum)	Santo Island; Vanuatu
2.	Aneityum	Vanuatu
3.	Areare	Malaita; Solomon Islands
4.	Baining	New Britain Island
5.	Bakovi (Kombe; Kove)	New Britain Island
6.	Binandere	Papua New Guinea
7.	Bogutu	Santa Isabel; Solomon Is.
8.	Carolinian	Caroline Islands; Saipan
9.	Chamorro	Guam; Mariana Islands
10.	Chimbu (Kuman)	Papua New Guinea
11.	Easter Island (Pascuense)	Easter Island
12.	Efate (Efatese): Erakor dialect	Vanuatu
13.	Enga: Laiap dialect	Papua New Guinea
14.	Enga: Mae dialect ("Maenga")	Papua New Guinea
15.	Fijian	Fiji Islands
16.	"Fiji Hindi"	Fiji Islands
17.	Futuna (East Futuna)	Futuna (Hoorn) Islands
18.	Gao	Santa Isabel; Solomon Is.
19.	Gilbertese	Kiribati; et al.
20.	Gnivo	Reef Islands: Solomon Is.
21.	Hawaiian	Hawaiian Islands
22.	Houailou (Wailu)	New Caledonia
23.	"Ifira"	Vanuatu
24.	Kara	Papua New Guinea
25.	Kosrean (Kusaiean)	Caroline Islands
26.	Kwara?ae	Malaita; Solomon Islands
27.	Langalanga	Malaita; Solomon Islands
28.	Lau	Malaita; Solomon Islands
29.	Lengo ("Tasiboko")	Solomon Islands
30.	Lifu (Lifouan)	Loyalty Islands
31.	Makura ("Namakuran")	Vanuatu
32.	"Mandar"	New Ireland

33.	"Manus Island"	Admiralty Islands
34.	Maori, Cook Islands (Rarotongan)	Cook Islands
35.	Maori, New Zealand	New Zealand
36.	Marina (Big Bay)	Vanuatu
37.	Marquesan	Marquesas Islands
38.	Marshallese	Marshall Islands
39.	Mele: Fila dialect	Fila & Efate Is., Vanuatu
40.	Motu, Hiri (Police Motu)	Papua New Guinea
41.	Mussau	Bismarck Archipelago
42.	Nalik	New Ireland
43.	Nengone (Maréen)	Loyalty Islans
44.	Niuean	Niue Island
45.	Omo (Tigak)	New Ireland
46.	Paici (Ponerihouien)	New Caledonia
47.	Palauan (Palau)	Caroline Islands; Guam
48.	Panaras (Kuot)	New Ireland
49.	Petats	Bougainville Island
50.	Pidgin, Fijian	Fiji Islands
51.	Pidgin, New Hebrides (Bislama)	Vanuatu
52.	Pidgin, Papuan (Neo-Melanaesian)	Papua New Guinea
53.	Pidgin, Solomon Islands	Solomon Islands
54.	Ponapean	Eastern Caroline Islands
55.	Rabaul Creole German ("Unserdeutsch")	Papua New Guinea
56.	"Raga (Pentecost)"	Vanuatu
57.	Rennellese (Munggava)	Solomon Islands
58.	Rennellese (Munggava): Bellona dialect	Solomon Islands
59.	Rotuman	Rotuma Island
60.	Roviana	New Georgia; Solomon Is.
61.	Samoan	Samoa; et al.
62.	Sengan: Babatana dialect	Choiseul Is., Solomon Is.
63.	"Sepik"	Papua New Guinea
64.	Siane: Arango dialect	Papua New Guinea
65.	Tahitian	Society Islands, et al.
66.	"Tanglamet"	New Ireland
67.	Tanna: Lenakel dialect	Vanuatu
68.	Tanna: Nupuanmen (Weasisi; Whitesands) dial.	Vanuatu
69.	Tongan	Tonga Islands; et al.
70.	"Tongoa"	Vanuatu
71.	Toqabaita (To'ambaita)	Malaita; Solomon Islands
72.	Torau	Solomon Islands
73.	Trukese	Caroline Islands
74.	Tuvaluan (Ellicean)	Tuvalu; Nauru; et al.
75.	Tuvaluan: Tokelauan dialect	Tokelau Islands; et al.
76.	Uripiv	Vanuatu
77.	Uvean, West (Ouvéan)	Loyalty Islands
78.	"Vaho"	Vanuatu
79.	Yabim	Papua New Guinea
80.	Yapese	Caroline Islands

APPENDIX III –Continued

EUROPE

	Language/Dialect	*Where Spoken*
1.	Albanian	Albania; et al.
2.	Arabic: Maltese dialect	Malta
3.	Basque: Labourdin dialect	France
4.	Basque: unspecified Spanish dial. ("Vasco")	Spain
5.	Bielorussian (White Russian)	Bielorussian SSR; et al.
6.	Breton	North Western France
7.	Bulgarian	Bulgaria; et al.
8.	Catalan	Andorra; Spain; et al.
9.	Croatian (Serbo-Croatian: Latin script)	Yugoslavia; et al.
10.	Czech	Czechoslovakia; et al
11.	Danish	Denmark; et al.
12.	Dutch	Netherlands; et al.
13.	English	
14.	English: Braille text	
15.	English: Moon text (also for the blind)	
16.	Estonian	Estonia; et al.
17.	Faroese	Faroe Islands
18.	Finnish	Finland; et al.
19.	Flemish	Belgium; et al.
20.	French	
21.	French: Braille text	
22.	Frisian	Frisian Islands; et al.
23.	Gaelic, Irish (Erse; Irish)	Ireland; United Kingdom
24.	Gaelic, Scottish	Scotland
25.	German	Austria; Germany; Switzerland; et al.
26.	German: Braille text	
27.	German: Alsatian dialect	France
28.	German: Luxemburgian (Letzeburgische) dial.	Luxembourg
29.	German: Yiddish dialect	
30.	Greek, Modern	Cyprus; Greece; et al.
31.	Hungarian	Hungary; et al.
32.	Icelandic	Iceland; et al.
33.	Inuit: Greenlandic	Greenland
34.	Inuit: Greenlandic, "West Central" dial.	Greenland
35.	Italian	Italy; Switzerland; et al.
36.	Italian: Corsican dialect	Corsica; Italy
37.	Italian: Logodurese dialect	Sardinia
38.	Italian: Piedmontese dialect	North Western Italy
39.	Italian: Sardinian dialect	Sardinia
40.	Ladin	Italian & Swiss Tyrol
41.	Latin	
42.	Lettish (Latvian)	Latvia; et al.
43.	Lithuanian	Lithuania; et al.
44.	Mordvin ("Mordoff"; Mordva): Erzja dial.	U.S.S.R.
45.	Norwegian: Nynorsk (Landsmal)	Norway
46.	Norwegian: Riksmal (Bokmal)	Norway
47.	Polish	Poland; et al.
48.	Portuguese	

49.	Romansch: Upper Engadine ("Puter") dialect	Switzerland
50.	Romansch: Sursilvan dialect	Switzerland
51.	Romany: Anglo-Romani dialect	British Isles
52.	Romany: Vlax dialect	
53.	Romany: Sinto dialect	Northern Italy; et al.
54.	Rumanian	Rumania; et al.
55.	Rumanian: Moldavian dialect	Moldavia
56.	Russian	
57.	Same: Lulesamiska (Lule Lapp)	Swedish Arctic
58.	Same: Nordsamiska (Northern Lapp)	Scandinavian Arctic
59.	Same: Sydsamiska (Southern Lapp)	Norway; Sweden
60.	Serbian (Serbo-Croatian: Cyrillic script)	Yugoslavia; et al.
61.	Slovak	Czechoslovakia; Hungary; Yugoslavia; et al.
62.	Slovene	Yugoslavia; et al.
63.	Spanish	
64.	Spanish: Braille text	
65.	Swedish	Sweden; Finland; et al.
66.	Ukrainian	Ukrainian S.S.R.; et al.
67.	Welsh (Cymraeg)	Wales; et al.
68.	Zyrian (Komi; Perm) (Cyrillic script)	U.S.S.R.

INVENTED LANGUAGES

1.	Esperanto
2.	Esperanto: Braille text
3.	Glosa
4.	Interlingua

APPENDIX IV

A SELECT LIST OF BAHÁ'Í PUBLICATIONS

Writings of Bahá'u'lláh

Book of Certitude, The (Kitáb-i-Íqán)
　　Reveals the continuity and progressive nature of religion as it has evolved through the lives and teachings of successive Prophets of God.

Epistle to the Son of the Wolf
　　Bahá'u'lláh's last major work, addressed to a Muslim clergyman who was a ruthless persecutor of Bahá'ís in Iran. Contains Bahá'u'lláh's own selection of major passages from His Writings.

Gleanings From the Writings of Bahá'u'lláh
　　Selected passages from many of Bahá'u'lláh's Tablets, dealing with important themes of His Revelation — the spiritual nature of man, oneness of the Prophets, life after death, the establishment of peace and transformation of human society.

Hidden Words of Bahá'u'lláh, The
　　The essential message of God's love for man at the heart of all religions, expressed in brief and moving epigrams.

Seven Valleys and The Four Valleys, The
　　Two Tablets concerning the stages of spiritual development through which the human soul must pass in its journey to God.

Tablets of Bahá'u'lláh Revealed After the Kitáb-i-Aqdas
　　Significant works from the later years of Bahá'u'lláh's Revelation. Major themes include the establishment of peace, the preservation of the unity of the Bahá'ís and their influence on future world affairs, as well as matters of individual spiritual importance.

Writings of the Báb

Selections From the Writings of the Báb
　　The most comprehensive collection of the Báb's Writings in English: selections from His major works, as well as prayers and meditations.

Writings and talks of 'Abdu'l-Bahá

'Abdu'l-Bahá in London
　　Talks and notes of conversations during 'Abdu'l-Bahá's visit to London in 1911. Includes record of His very first appearance before a Western audience.

300

Foundations of World Unity
>   Collection of important talks given by 'Abdu'l-Bahá to audiences in North America, dwelling on various aspects of unity — of races, nations and religions.

Paris Talks
>   Short talks given in Paris, 1912, setting out the basic principles of the Bahá'í Faith in simple terms.

Promulgation of Universal Peace, The
>   A compendium of 139 public talks given in the United States and Canada, 1912.

Secret of Divine Civilization, The
>   Written anonymously to the government and people of Persia in 1875, outlining the requirements of true statecraft and the measures necessary to transform that land to a modern nation-state.

Selections From the Writings of 'Abdu'l-Bahá
>   Widest available collections of 'Abdu'l-Bahá's Writings. 236 selections from Tablets to the East and West, covering a vast range of subjects — education, equality of the sexes, interpretation of prophecies from the Bible and the Qur'án, and copious guidance for the establishment and growth of the early Bahá'í communities.

Some Answered Questions
>   "Table talks" of 'Abdu'l-Bahá recorded in 'Akká by an early American pilgrim over the years 1904-06. Covers a wide range of spiritual, philosophical and political issues such as the nature of man, the mission of the Prophets, prison reform and strikes. Comprehensive section on Christian subjects.

Tablets of the Divine Plan
>   Fourteen letters written by 'Abdu'l-Bahá to the Bahá'ís of North America during the First World War, giving detailed instructions for the spread of the Bahá'í message. Still the basis of the expansion and consolidation plans pursued by the Bahá'í world community.

Writings of Shoghi Effendi and compilations of his letters

Advent of Divine Justice, The
>   Clarifies the moral, intellectual and social requirements of Bahá'í life . Closing section on the spiritual destiny of North America.

God Passes By
>   The history of the first one hundred years of the Bahá'í religion. Draws on a wealth of first-hand accounts not published elsewhere in English.

Principles of Bahá'í Administration
  A compilation of Shoghi Effendi's instructions for the workaday
  functioning of Bahá'í Assemblies, Committees and Conventions.
  Includes useful material on aspects of Bahá'í personal and
  community life.

Promised Day is Come, The
  An analysis of the social and moral breakdown of society in the light
  of Bahá'u'lláh's proclamations and prophecies to the kings and
  rulers of the earth.

World Order of Bahá'u'lláh, The
  A collection of seven letters to the Bahá'ís of North America. Of
  seminal influence in understanding the process of evolution
  operating within the Bahá'í community across the globe. Contains
  the clearest statement of Bahá'í theology in the section *The
  Dispensation of Bahá'u'lláh.*

Letters and statements of the Universal House of Justice

Constitution of the Universal House of Justice

Messages From the Universal House of Justice
  Covering the years 1968-73.

Promise of World Peace, The
  The basis of the worldwide Bahá'í Peace Initiative, issued in the
  United Nations International Year of Peace.

Letter on Social & Economic Development, 23 October 1983
  The inspiration for the burgeoning number of social and economic
  development projects in which Bahá'ís are involved throughout the
  world.

Wellspring of Guidance
  Letters from the Universal House of Justice during the first five
  years of its existence, from 1963-68.

Compilations made by the Research Department of the Universal House of Justice

Bahá'í Education

Bahá'í Writings on Music

Heaven of Divine Wisdom, The (Bahá'í consultation)

Inspiring the Heart
  A selection of devotional writings by Bahá'u'lláh, the Báb and
  'Abdu'l-Bahá.

Lifeblood of the Cause (Bahá'í Funds)

Living the Life
> Quidance from Shoghi Effendi on the moral and ethical aspects of individual and social Bahá'í life.

Local Spiritual Assemblies
National Spiritual Assembly, The
Women

Other Compilations

Bahá'í Electoral Process, The
Bahá'í Law
Divine Art of Living, The
Dynamic Force of Example, The
Fortress For Wellbeing, A
> The Bahá'í approach to marriage.

Guidelines for Local Spiritual Assemblies
Pattern of Bahá'í Life
Political Non-Involvement and Obedience to Government
Power of the Covenant (3 volumes)
> A study series on the means by which the unity of the Bahá'ís is maintained.

Biographies of Central Figures

'Abdu'l-Bahá (H.M. Balyuzi)
Báb, The (H.M. Balyuzi)
Bahá'u'lláh: The King of Glory (H.M. Balyuzi)
Priceless Pearl, The (Rúḥíyyih Rabbaní)
> A life of Shoghi Effendi, written by his widow.

History

Bábí and Bahá'í Religions, 1844-1944, The: Some Contemporary Western Accounts (edited by Moojan Momen)
> Reports of the new religion to reach the West during its first hundred years. Includes critical analyses and biographical information on the authors.

Dawnbreakers, The (Nabíl)
> First-hand account of the dramatic events surrounding the life of the Báb and the endeavours of His followers to spread His religion in Iran and Iraq.

Edward Granville Browne and the Bahá'í Faith (H.M. Balyuzi)
> Examines the encounter of Professor Browne from Cambridge University with the early Bahá'ís and Bábís of the Middle East and the importance of his writings for academic study of the Bahá'í Faith.

Persecution of the Bahá'ís in Iran, 1844-1984 (Douglas Martin)
> How three regimes have dealt with the Bahá'í community.

Portals to Freedom (Howard Colby Ives)
> Recollection of 'Abdu'l-Bahá's visit to America, written by a former Unitarian Minister.

Revelation of Bahá'u'lláh (Adíb Taherzadeh)
> *Vol. 1 Baghdad 1853-63*
> *Vol. 2 Adrianople 1863-8*
> *Vol. 3 'Akká, The Early Years: 1868-77*
> *Vol. 4 Mazráih and Bahjí: 1877-92*
> Fills out much of the historical and biographical context of Bahá'u'lláh's Writings.

Studies in Bábí and Bahá'í History, Vols. 1-3
> A continuing series of original academic studies on various aspects of Bahá'í history.

Other useful titles

Bahá'í Focus on Human Rights (Philip Hainsworth)
> Pursues the argument that human rights are God-given and not the prerogative of governments and rulers.

Becoming Your True Self (Daniel Jórdan)
> How the Bahá'í Faith releases human potential.

Christ and Bahá'u'lláh (George Townshend)
> An appreciation of the relationship between the two Manifestations of God, written by a former Archdeacon in the Church of Ireland.

Christianity of Jesus, The (Richard Backwell)
> A new look at the message of the Gospels.

God of Buddha, The (Jamshed Fozdar)
> Buddhism seen through the eyes of a Bahá'í.

Heavens are Cleft Asunder, The (Huschmand Sabet)
> Essays on the theme "Is there a need for religion?"

Light Shineth in Darkness, The (Udo Schaeffer)
> Responses to arguments against the Bahá'í Faith raised by Protestant theologians.

Promise of All Ages, The (George Townshend)
> The spiritual history of mankind, culminating in the appearance of Bahá'u'lláh.

Proposals for Charter Revision Submitted to the United Nations. (Bahá'í International Community)

APPENDIX IV–Continued

Purpose of Physical Reality, The (John S. Hatcher)
> Justification for the belief in a just and loving God in a world full of suffering and hardship. The Bahá'í view is compared with those voiced in great works of literature and philosophy.

Thief in the Night (William Sears)
> An examination of religious prophecies which foretell the coming of the Báb and Bahá'u'lláh.

Violence-Free Society, The (Hossian Danesh)
> How the Bahá'í teachings on family life and human worth break the cycle of unhappiness and fear which breed violence.

World Peace and World Government (Jay Tyson)
> Their interplay examined from a Bahá'í viewpoint.

INDEX

INDEX